'Plowright's excellent book c  Macron's life.'

'Eye-catching detail.'

The Financial Times

'For real insight into the remarkable rise – and character – of the new French president, Plowright's is the book to read.'
The Sunday Telegraph

'A highly readable and well-judged portrait of a fascinating character.'

The Times

'Most political biographies are perfunctorily written, not this one. Adam Plowright is fascinated by his subject.'
The Sydney Morning Herald

'Expertly researched ... a fine addition to the bookshelf of anyone interested in France, Europe and international geopolitics.'

The Hindu

THE FRENCH
EXCEPTION

THE FRENCH EXCEPTION

EMMANUEL MACRON

THE EXTRAORDINARY RISE AND RISK

Adam Plowright

ICON

This edition published in the UK and USA in 2018
by Icon Books Ltd, Omnibus Business Centre,
39–41 North Road, London N7 9DP
email: info@iconbooks.com
www.iconbooks.com

First published in the UK in 2017 by Icon Books Ltd

Sold in the UK, Europe and Asia
by Faber & Faber Ltd, Bloomsbury House,
74–77 Great Russell Street,
London WC1B 3DA or their agents

Distributed in the UK, Europe and Asia
by Grantham Book Services,
Trent Road, Grantham NG31 7XQ

Distributed in the USA
by Publishers Group West,
1700 Fourth Street, Berkeley, CA 94710

Distributed in Australia and New Zealand
by Allen & Unwin Pty Ltd,
PO Box 8500, 83 Alexander Street,
Crows Nest, NSW 2065

Distributed in South Africa
by Jonathan Ball, Office B4, The District,
41 Sir Lowry Road, Woodstock 7925

Distributed in India by Penguin Books India,
7th Floor, Infinity Tower – C, DLF Cyber City,
Gurgaon 122002, Haryana

Distributed in Canada by Publishers Group Canada,
76 Stafford Street, Unit 300
Toronto, Ontario M6J 2S1

ISBN: 978-178578-362-3

Typeset in Adobe Garamond by Marie Doherty

Printed and bound in the UK
by Clays Ltd, St Ives plc

For Natacha, Arlette and Marlow

Contents

CHAPTER 1

Lost Glory

'I BET HE'S TURNING IN HIS GRAVE SEEING THE LOT WE have governing us nowadays,' sighed Sylvie Gautier, a 52-year-old former policewoman standing in spring sunshine in the small French village of Colombey-les-Deux-Églises at the end of March 2017.

She and her partner Didier Consigny had come to pay their respects at the final resting place of Charles de Gaulle, France's most illustrious 20th-century leader, who died here in his family home in 1970.

The small and peaceful village, with its stone cottages surrounded by gently rolling hills, is a French pilgrimage site with a symbolic value every bit as important as the great royal or revolutionary landmarks of Paris.

The Louvre and the Palace of Versailles, the Place de la Concorde, Place de la République or the Bastille column around the capital are monuments to the great clashes of the last two centuries that saw the French Republic ultimately triumph over royal autocracy.

Each of them bears witness to France's epic history, to its role as a cradle of democracy and its people's fight for human rights and the freedom of speech. This battle, which shaped the modern state, helps explain why the French seem so assured of their own exceptionalism and convinced that their experience carries a universal message to the world.

Colombey-les-Deux-Églises, a three-hour drive into the countryside east of Paris, is a place to reflect not on France's role as a beacon for democracy, but rather on its own salvation from chaos and defeat, as well as the fraught relationship between the French people and their leaders.

In 1934, Charles de Gaulle, then a lieutenant-colonel in the French army, bought a large home here, La Boisserie, at a bargain price from an elderly local woman, in order to provide a stable base for his wife and young children as Europe was again lurching towards war.

This pretty but unexceptional village set around a church dating back to the 12th century would become the place he would write, brood and plot, as well as the backdrop to some of the great political theatre of his extraordinary life.

'Whenever it is possible, we go to La Boisserie,' he wrote, reflecting on his life a few months before his death at the age of 80. 'It's there that I go to think. There that I write the speeches which are a painful and perpetual effort. There that I read the books which are sent to me. There, watching the horizon of the land and the immensity of the sky, that I restore my serenity.'

Today, politicians as well as thousands of visitors like Gautier and Consigny come every year to visit his grave in the church cemetery where he was buried in 'France's good and blessed land' next to fellow villagers.

Beside his tomb, marked by a simple cross in white stone and the inscription 'Charles de Gaulle 1890–1970', lie his beloved wife Yvonne and his handicapped daughter Anne, whom the devoted general once credited as an inspiration for his achievements.

The manor house of La Boisserie, where de Gaulle would work in his downstairs office admiring the view of the morning fog, or the forested hills beyond, has been turned into a visitors' centre.

The handsome building with its ivy-covered facade is now a museum containing his belongings, including his books and the dining table where he would eat his favourite meal, roasted pig's ears, after attending mass with Yvonne on Sundays. It also contains the table where the famously straight-backed 1.95-metre lover of cards slumped over during a game of patience after suffering a massive heart attack on the evening of 9 November 1970, less than a fortnight before his 80th birthday.

As a statesman, de Gaulle continues to tower over French public life. He set a precedent so high that none of his successors ever seem to match up. As a general, as the leader of French resistance to Nazi occupation and then as father of the modern Republic, he is the epitome of how extraordinary individuals are able to shape history through their own personality and will.

His incredible life is told at a second museum in Colombey-les-Deux-Églises, the Charles de Gaulle Memorial, an angular, white building of modernist design which opened in 2008 on a site set slightly above the roofs of the village below. Behind the memorial, at the top of the hill and visible above the trees, stands a giant Cross of Lorraine in granite and bronze – a cross with two bars that de Gaulle adopted as a symbol of French resistance during the Second World War. Its construction was one of the few things he expressly wished for after his death: 'It will inspire rabbits around there to stand and resist,' he joked.

Unfolding from the museum's entrance is a panoramic view of the fields and woodland below, which was eulogised by de Gaulle in his memoirs: 'Vast, uncultivated and sad horizons; wood, meadow, crops and melancholic fallows; the outlines of former mountains worn down and resigned; quiet villages of little wealth of which millennia have changed neither the soul nor location.'

The serenity he found in the landscapes can be appreciated when set against the photographs, videos and recordings on show in the museum that place him at the centre of the disintegration and rebuilding of 20th-century France.

They provide an insight into de Gaulle's enormous personal courage as a soldier in the First World War, during which he was injured on three occasions, the last time in 1916 when he was captured and presumed dead before being imprisoned in Germany. As a tank commander in 1940, he demonstrated similar bravery when the vastly superior and more organised German forces, backed by air power, left the French outgunned and out-manoeuvred on the eastern front.

Faced with the defeatism of his superiors, his moral clarity shone through as he continued to urge the government to regroup their forces and continue fighting the Germans, first as an outspoken general in the French army, and then when he was promoted to deputy war minister. Throughout the 1930s de Gaulle had urged the government to modernise the army and invest in tank technology – in vain.

As his government capitulated to the Nazis in 1940, de Gaulle fled to London on a British plane, watching from the window as smoke billowed up from destroyed ships and burning munitions dumps below in his shattered country. After stopping off on the island of Jersey in the English Channel to refuel the plane and buy a case of whisky for British Prime Minister Winston Churchill, de Gaulle headed for London to present himself to the British government as the leader of Free French Forces.

'Whatever happens, the flame of the French resistance must not be extinguished and will not be extinguished!' he said in his famous first address to the French people on 18 June 1940, which was broadcast across the channel by the BBC.

After the entry of American forces decisively swung the war in favour of the Allies, de Gaulle's triumphant return home in 1944 for the liberation of France provided the French people with a new narrative for their war-time experience, which had hitherto been one of military humiliation and capitulation. But like the great war leader Churchill, de Gaulle later found himself surplus to requirements in peacetime. He disagreed with the new constitution that had been proclaimed in 1946, which created the Fourth Republic* based on a parliamentary system which he felt gave too little power to the government. De Gaulle headed his own party, the Rassemblement du Peuple Français (RPF, the Rally of the French People) but after his failure in general elections in 1953, he abandoned politics. So began his 'wilderness years' at La Boisserie in Colombey-les-Deux-Églises (which had been

---

* France's 'First Republic' was proclaimed in 1792 after the Revolution against the monarchy. It was short lived, but a seminal moment in European and world history, kicking off more than 200 years of instability and constitutional changes in France. There have been five Republics in total (including the current one), interspersed with periods of empire following coups by Napoleon I and his nephew Napoleon III, as well as constitutional monarchy.

occupied by German forces during the war), where he devoted himself to writing his memoirs and spending time with his family.

But after he had helped save France once, the natural authority of the man nicknamed 'the constable' was required a second time in 1958, when political deadlock and the possibility of a coup by the rebellious generals fighting France's brutal war in Algeria threatened a civil war in mainland France. Answering the request from President René Coty for 'the most illustrious of Frenchmen' to take charge, de Gaulle put an end to his political exile and stepped forward to take control of the government as prime minister and steer France away from another precipice.

The new Republic he ushered in, the Fifth, endures to this day: it scrapped the parliamentary system, which had been blamed for unstable coalition governments and political squabbling, in favour of an executive presidency to be headed by a towering and unifying national leader who was given powers that far exceed equivalents in other democracies. The presidency was built in de Gaulle's image: the spirit of the French presidential election was to be 'the meeting of a man and his people,' he famously declared (no woman has ever held the position). Long viewed as an authoritarian regime by critics, this system was decried as a 'permanent *coup d'état*' by the Socialist François Mitterrand, who would become the first left-wing leader of the Republic in 1981 and then use – and abuse – the immense power of the position.

De Gaulle, as the architect of this system and the first holder of the office, in which he served for eleven years, left a personal stamp and an idealised memory of the role of a president that few, if any, have been able to live up to since. He defined France's role in the world and demonstrated remarkable strategic vision, helping to launch the country's nuclear programme and a host of state-backed industrial projects. His 'Gaullist' foreign policy doctrine of keeping France independent and positioned between the super powers – the United States and the Soviet Union, in his day – has been diluted over time, but it still endures as an idea and influences policy. In his personal life, he was a model of integrity and public service. He refused a state funeral for his death and was so parsimonious that he and Yvonne insisted on paying their own bills at the presidential palace while in office.

The genius – and flaw – of the Fifth Republic was the way that it elevated the head of state into a position that was effectively that of an elected monarch: an alloy forged from France's struggle between royalist and republican forces. The president was a democrat, but one who lived beneath the tall gilded ceilings of the Élysée Palace – built for a French nobleman in the 18th century – with its more than 300 rooms and 800 staff. The transfer of power from one head of state to another takes place at a ceremony whose pomp and splendour would make many kingdoms blush.

But in 2017, 47 years after de Gaulle's death, France and the Republic he had bequeathed to the nation were sick.

The country was still a world power: it boasted the sixth-biggest economy, a seat on the UN Security Council and a world-class military that was carrying out combat operations against Islamic extremists in Africa and the Middle East. Average income per person was around $40,000 – three times the global average – while it had a public health system, transport networks and multinationals that were the envy of the world. More tourists visited France every year than any other country, marvelling at the slow pace of life in its villages, the elegance and grandeur of its cities or the variety of its landscapes from the Alps to the Atlantic.

The famed French lifestyle of long holidays, fine dining and family time seemed to be resisting the march of modernity. Though its dominance had declined, relative to other countries, France was still a world-leading cultural force in film, food, fashion and literature, as well as a sporting powerhouse at the Olympics and football World Cup.

But on this sunny spring day in Colombey-les-Deux Églises at the end of March, seven weeks before France headed for fresh presidential elections, the people arriving in a steady trickle at the de Gaulle Memorial revealed a mix of nostalgia for the past, anger at the present and a dark foreboding about the future.

Gautier, the former policewoman, stood in the sunshine outside the museum and summed up her view of the outgoing president, François Hollande, as 'that guy who's a big nothing, who hired his hairdresser for €13,000 a month.'

The hairdresser's salary – actually €9,895 pre-tax as revealed in a press report in June 2016 – was far from the worst of the personal embarrassments for the balding Hollande, who had also been caught having croissants delivered by moped to his mistress at public expense.

At least – so Hollande's supporters pointed out – he departed the office without leaving behind a string of legal cases to answer: unlike his right-wing predecessor Nicolas Sarkozy, who is still surrounded by a cloud of suspicion. Sarkozy, the hyperactive president who married a supermodel, left office in 2012 as the most unpopular president in France's history – only to see his unenviable record immediately beaten by Hollande.

French people are 'sick of it all', explained Gautier, who hailed from the local Champagne region. Her partner Consigny nodded along in agreement; he didn't understand 'why we've let in all these people, immigrants, when we don't have enough work already and there's mass unemployment.'

France and Europe were in the grip of the biggest migrant crisis since the Second World War – caused by instability and poverty in the Middle East, Africa and South Asia – that had led to more than a million people crossing the Mediterranean Sea into Europe in 2015.

Consigny, who worked for a local waste management company, thought Muslims in particular were a problem. 'It's always the same profile you see on the telly,' he explained, referring to the mostly young men of North African descent who had carried out a series of terror attacks in France that had killed more than 200 people since 2015.

Both the ex-policewoman and her partner repeated the words that were ringing out at far-right rallies across the country at the time, which crystallised a widespread feeling of resentment in France about immigrants and insecurity: '*On est chez nous*', they said. 'This is *our* country'.

Faith in French politics had plummeted across the board, while the vicious election campaign that was already underway in spring 2017 had seen other cornerstones of the Republic – notably the justice system and the independent media – attacked and further undermined. Less than a third of French people at the time thought that democracy was working well. Less than half had faith in the justice system and only a quarter trusted the media.[1]

François Hollande, who had promised to be a 'normal' president who was close to the people, was coming to the end of a presidency that many saw as having debased the institution beyond repair, with the 62 year old showing an approval rating of just 4 per cent at the end of 2016.

The sense of disenchantment in France created by Hollande's major policy U-turns, his lack of personal authority and the fact that his presidency had seen record unemployment of 3.5 million people, had been made worse by the series of appalling terror attacks. 'He was never up to the job,' François Guillot, a grey-haired retired doctor, said bitterly as he stood with his wife outside the memorial museum. 'We need a father of the nation.'

Each interview in Colombey brought fresh complaints or grievances, all underpinned by the feeling that France had somehow lost its way and lacked the leadership to correct its course. All chimed with the sour national mood in a country that had spawned a new category of social scientists, the so-called '*declinologues*', experts in diagnosing France's decline.

In a major survey of public opinion by polling group IPSOS Mori in 25 countries at the end of 2016, France came off as the most pessimistic by far, with nearly nine in ten people saying they believed the country was on the wrong track.

Walking into the non-fiction section of a book shop at the time was a spirit-sapping experience. *Two Presidents for Nothing* was the title of a book by a leading political commentator. *Understanding the French Tragedy*, read another by a famed historian. *Jihad: It's Arrived in Your Neighbourhood* was on sale next to *Don't Know What To Do, Don't Give a Shit?*, a book by a respected pollster about how many French people were now so despondent that they had tuned out of politics altogether.

France's leading economic indicators gave scant reason for cheer. No French government had managed to balance the national budget since the early 1970s. The national debt, swollen by huge bailouts after the global financial crisis of 2008, had shot up to nearly the equivalent of a whole year's economic output at more than €2 trillion. The unemployment rate was around 10 per cent of the working population and was double that for the under 25s. There was growing inter-generational tension between the wealthy, consumerist post-war 'babyboomers' and young people who will inherit the crushing national debt and a polluted planet showing signs of climate change.

Gael Chocteau, a carpenter from northern France a few years from retirement, was hurrying back to the car park away from the museum when he stopped for a chat about the election. 'We thought we'd have a look as we were driving through, but it's not free. Sixteen euros each to get in. It's too much, isn't it?', he said, squinting into the sunshine under a blooming cherry tree.

'There's really not enough work in this country,' he explained, adding that he was anxious about his pension. The problems were down to too much immigration – 'We've sort of let anyone in' – and the global financial crisis, which had hurt his business in the construction industry particularly badly.

He hadn't made his mind up yet who to vote for, but one thing was certain. 'It won't be for one of the traditional parties. Definitely not,' he said.

Rosa Sion, a 66-year-old retired secretary visiting from the Vosges area of eastern France, stopped to talk in front of exhibits recounting de Gaulle's wilderness years on the periphery of national politics from 1953 to 1958. 'It would do our politicians good to come here and learn about humility,' she said. The spectacle of parliament she saw on television seemed completely out of touch with reality. 'They don't know about real problems, they're completely out of it. They don't even know how much a baguette costs,' she said. The cost of everyday baked goods had tripped up a leading conservative only a few months earlier. The presidential candidate and former head of the right-wing UMP party, Jean-François Copé, had underestimated the price of a pain au chocolat by a factor of ten.

Sion's husband Jacques, who had spent much of his working life running funeral parlours, thought that many politicians were simply in it for the perks nowadays. 'They've got no idea what real work is,' he said.

But it wasn't just France's political system that was showing signs of strain. On the same day, 400 kilometres to the north in the Belgian capital, the British ambassador to the EU handed over a letter to the European Commission formalising Britain's decision to quit the 28-member European Union, the cornerstone of post-war peace and stability in Europe, after the UK's in-out referendum.

Colombey-les-Deux-Églises had played its part in healing the wounds of the continent and spurring the integration of conflict-scarred Europe. Despite his experience of two world wars and his having been a prisoner-of-war in German camps, de Gaulle invited the German Chancellor Konrad Adenauer to La Boisserie shortly after taking power in 1958. The two men strolled in the garden and ate dinner together, which had been prepared by Yvonne. Adenauer became the only head of state to spend the night there, in a powerful personal and public gesture of reconciliation. Five years later, the two men would go on to sign a historic treaty of friendship between France and Germany.

Nonetheless, de Gaulle, a proud nationalist opposed to any attempt to limit French sovereignty, would have been appalled by the modern European Union. He would have been even more horrified by the way France had been surpassed by Germany as the organisation's dominant force and was now yoked into an unloved and half-completed federation that looked as if it were only one election away from catastrophe.

The French far-right leader and 2017 presidential candidate Marine Le Pen, running on an anti-EU, anti-immigration platform, had promised to withdraw from the European common currency area, at the risk of triggering a financial crisis. She had also promised a referendum to end what she called France's 'submission' to the European Union.

Civil servant Thierry, 44, was visiting Colombey with his friend Jean-Pierre, 53, and they too were a picture of disenchantment. Neither planned to vote in the upcoming election.

'Everything is dictated by the European Union nowadays, so from that point of view what's the use in voting?', said Jean-Pierre. He'd love to see France follow Britain and leave 'but then it's chaos,' he said.

Thierry laughed at a question about whether France was in good health. 'It doesn't matter where you go, everyone thinks the same thing. Of course not. Actually maybe in some parts of Paris they think everything's fine,' he said. 'I think Le Pen's probably got the best ideas, but then it's a civil war.' They headed into the museum shortly after a coach had dropped off a group of noisy teenage German school children.

The in-out referendum on Britain's membership of the EU on 23 June 2016 was the first of two political earthquakes that year which many had forecast would start a domino effect of members exiting the bloc. It was followed four and a half months later by the election of Donald Trump as US president, something which looked like a potential tipping point for Western democracies.

De Gaulle had written to a friend in the 1930s that 'The world is moving and devouring itself ... our generation will have the privilege of being present at events of such a scale that no other, except perhaps at the Great Flood, will have seen so many great things in so little time.' Watching the spread of newly virulent nationalism in Russia, India and Turkey and now at the heart of the West in Britain and in the US, many historians began to discuss the parallels between the current age and the morbid 1930s.

But a different, competing historical reference point was also gaining traction in France. In an interview to the *Valeurs Actuelles* magazine which was on news-stands as the visitors wandered around the de Gaulle Memorial, the right-wing presidential candidate François Fillon said that he saw a parallel between the country in 2017 and the end of the Fourth Republic.

'With every sense of proportion, we are in 1958, at the moment of the return of de Gaulle,' the 62 year old said of his hero. Fillon was far from being alone when he warned during campaigning that France was 'on the verge of a civil war'. It was perhaps a typically French rhetorical flourish, yet the idea of a violent confrontation between citizens, or an uprising against the government, was on the lips of politicians and voters with alarming regularity as the country went to the polls.

De Gaulle's return to government in 1958 had put an end to the rebellion by French officers in Algeria and the risk of a *coup d'état*. In addition, he had neutered the flourishing far-right party, the *Poujadistes*, an alliance of shopkeepers that was the forerunner to Le Pen's National Front.

Yet though Fillon now dreamed of becoming the country's saviour after his nearly 40 years in politics, he was out of touch with the popular mood. In ordinary circumstances, the French tended to look for his blend of experience, age and solidity in their presidents. However, in spring 2017, they were driven by a desire to wreak revenge on their political class.

Instead, the man of moment was Emmanuel Macron, a 39 year old running in his first ever election who would go on to engineer the most sensational victory in modern history. The one-time economy minister, investment banker and philosopher's assistant from the provincial city of Amiens had been laughed at when he started his own political party less than twelve months earlier. He was a complete unknown to the French public until August 2014, and even in spring 2017 had barely registered internationally outside of media and political circles. Depending on who you listened to, he was either a Mozart-style genius or a shallow opportunist.

His surge in popularity defied the usual rules and had observers scrambling for an explanation. Experts like Jean Garrigues, who specialises in political history, had a theory: it was the revival of a dormant phenomenon that had repeatedly influenced French political life. Although the country prides itself on its history of battles by the people for power, it has a historic tendency to deliver itself up to charming, authoritarian figures in moments of crisis. It is both a weakness and contradiction at the heart of the national psyche. These figures are known collectively as 'providential men'.

'It's both a reality and a myth,' Garrigues said, as he commented on the emergence of Macron-mania in 2017. 'Each time French society finds itself at a dead end or in crisis it has a tendency to look for an exceptional individual: someone to offer a personal solution to our collective problems.' Famous examples included Napoleon Bonaparte, the brilliant military commander who grabbed power in the chaos of post-Revolution France, but all great French leaders of the past, including the First World War hero Georges Clemenceau and particularly de Gaulle, have been propelled in part by the perception of them as redeemers of lost national prestige. 'It's a sort of nostalgia for the unifying figure of the monarch,' added Garrigues, who wrote a book on the subject of providential men in 2012.[2] Over the past centuries, these figures have tended to emerge from outside the political system and are seen as heroes able to reverse the failures of the elites in power, or offer a balm to the nation's conscience.

France's first so-called 'providential man' was actually a woman: the national heroine Jeanne d'Arc, a peasant girl who believed she was acting with divine guidance when she led the French army into victorious battles with the English in 1429.

The concept is the French equivalent of the popular 19th-century 'Great Man Theory', espoused by the Scottish philosopher Thomas Carlyle and others, which posited that history was forged by the actions of exceptional individuals whose time had come.

This concept also dovetails with the secular idea of the 'cunning of reason' put forward by the German philosopher Hegel, who Macron has studied. Hegel stated that humankind, in its quest for freedom, was served by 'world historical' figures who advanced the cause, driven by their own self-interest.

'There's also a form of charisma, an ability to create a sort of collective enthusiasm, which Bonaparte and de Gaulle clearly had,' Garrigues continued. 'And a Christ-like dimension, a sort of mysticism.'

'The comparison with Macron is undeniable,' Garrigues said. 'We've arrived at a sort of impasse in the Fifth Republic. The failures of Sarkozy and Hollande are obvious with the rejection of them as two symbols of the political system. We're in a period of a total breakdown in confidence between the French people and their political leaders. And those moments create the ideal conditions for the emergence of a providential man.'

On 7 May 2017, Macron triumphed in the second round of the presidential election, becoming the country's youngest ever president in a victory that exploded the traditional parties who had run France for nearly 60 years. He inherited a deeply demoralised and divided country, in which at least half of voters saw him as a dose of plague, rather than a providential man of yore.

'The confidence that the French people have shown in me fills me with immense energy,' Macron said in his inaugural address at the Élysée Palace, where one of his earliest political backers, the 70-year-old mayor of the city of Lyon, Gérard Collomb, shed tears at the sight of the new leader who was nearly half his age.

'The intimate belief that together we can write one of the most beautiful pages in our history will guide my action,' Macron concluded. 'At these tipping points, the French people have always known how to find the energy, the discernment and the spirit of togetherness to bring about profound change. We're at one of those moments. It's in the pursuit of this goal that I will humbly serve the country.'

Like his predecessors, he headed out of the Élysée Palace for the ceremonial trip up the Champs-Élysées to visit the tomb of the unknown soldier below the Arc de Triomphe, which lies at the top of the gently sloping avenue. Macron chose a military command car for his first journey as president, standing ram-rod straight at the back in a deliberate nod to the legacy and image of General de Gaulle. In his official photo, which now hangs in government buildings across the country, a volume of de Gaulle's wartime memoirs lies open on the table behind him.

In an interview two years before he took power Macron had been asked for his view on what the French people looked for in their leaders. There was always a sense of something missing in French democracy, he said. 'This absence is the figure of the king, whom I don't think fundamentally the French people wanted to kill,' Macron added, referring to the guillotining of Louis XVI, the last king before the Revolution.

Macron perhaps pondered this fact as he wandered alone around the graves of Louis XVI and his wife Marie Antoinette only hours after announcing his run for the presidency in November 2016. After firing the starting gun on his campaign, he asked to be dropped off at the Basilica of St Denis north of Paris, the final resting place for more than 70 French kings and queens.[3]

The problem of the Fifth Republic, according to Macron, was that since de Gaulle's departure 'the normalisation of the presidential figure has created an empty seat at the heart of our political life. Except that what people expect from the president is that he takes this position. This is the source of our misunderstanding.'[4]

As he sat on the throne of the Republic in the summer of 2017, Macron had every intention of filling that space, and of aping the regal style de Gaulle had pioneered that had fused France's monarchical and democratic traditions. The new young president held his election night victory party amid the splendour of the Louvre, home to successive monarchs since the early 16th century including Louis XVI; two months later he called a joint meeting of parliament in the Palace of Versailles, the first time that both houses of the legislature were united there, other than at a time of a national emergency. Restoring French pride and faith in their leader would be one of the priorities of the reign of Emmanuel I.

CHAPTER 2

The Small-town Boy

THE MAYOR OF AMIENS, A JOLLY WOMAN CALLED BRIGITTE Fouré who is sometimes referred to as the 'mother' of the city by her supporters, shuffles on the edge of her seat and sucks her teeth as she ponders the local inhabitants in her corner of northeast France.

After a moment's reflection from an armchair in her office in the city hall, the former university lecturer hits on some of the characteristics of Amiens, which is situated around half way between Paris and the Belgian border: 'Firstly, in terms of temperament, we're a workers' town, so that tells you about the sociology,' she says of the city, which is split in two by the placid waters of the river Somme.

But its once important textile industry, famed for its velour and a blue vegetable dye which helped finance the city's dazzling gothic cathedral, has all but disappeared. Its more modern car parts companies and factories are also heading the same way, part of a broad trend of industrial decline across the surrounding Picardy region.

This is reflected in local politics, where Communist and Socialist mayors held sway for decades until the end of the 1980s, before being replaced by Fouré and her fellow centrists as the city's economy shifted towards retail, science and higher education. Unemployment remains high here, at around 12 per cent, two points above the national average, and far higher in the poorest neighbourhoods. Worse-off areas in north-east France have shifted gradually towards the far-right National Front.

'And I'd say the *Amiénois* don't open up spontaneously,' Fouré continues, warming to the task of analysing her electorate. 'You need to get to know them. They won't let you in easily. That's probably linked to our history of war and invasions,' she says.

Amiens is a story both of tragedy and a form of uncelebrated glory, the scene of military victories won at devastating cost. The centre of the town had to be rebuilt twice: first after a desperate and unsuccessful last-ditch German offensive in 1918 at the end of the First World War and again after its bombing and occupation in the Second World War.

The UNESCO-listed 13th-century cathedral, the largest of the gothic period in France, is visible from miles away in the flat fertile fields of the Somme floodplain, where hundreds of thousands of soldiers were slaughtered in the rain-soaked trenches of the First World War. Miraculously, the cathedral escaped major damage during the 20th-century fighting and today it is the main tourist attraction in the tastefully restored heart of the city. Trams, bicycles and pedestrians have gradually pushed out cars and trucks from its cobbled streets.

'On the negative side, there's also a real lack of pride and ambition here: you don't have confidence in yourself if you're *Amiénois*,' Fouré adds of the city's 200,000 residents. 'It's often people from the outside who come and say "your town is beauti-ful" and we're tempted to reply "do you really think so?" I'm always fighting against this.'

Like much of France, its streets are often picturesque, mixing old-fashioned shops, bakeries and cafés alongside more modern retailers. A charming central area of canals and landscaped river-banks draws foreign visitors who stop off here during their tours of the surrounding battlefields.

But the city's fortunes and self-image were further under-mined by the loss of Amiens' status as regional capital in 2016, while mass layoffs announced for a factory owned by the American appliance maker Whirlpool were another blow to its brittle self-confidence. In 2014, another US multinational, tyre maker Goodyear, shut its factory here, leading trade union lead-ers to lock up an HR executive and a production manager at the plant for 30 hours in protest. Eight of them received jail terms afterwards for illegal confinement.

'We sometimes have the impression that we're only there to maintain the cemeteries and provide cannon fodder,' Fouré adds sadly, alluding to the hundreds of neatly-tended graves through-out the Picardy region filled with servicemen, French and foreign.

Gloomy old Amiens. Even the weather, which is often over-cast and rainy, seems appropriate for the place. One of its biggest claims to fame is being the one-time home of French novelist Jules Verne, the author of *Twenty Thousand Leagues Under the Sea* (among other prescient works of science fiction), whose name has been given to the bustling modern university. Even then, most French people associate Verne with Nantes, the city of his birth.

In 2017, Amiens, a place with no recent history of producing national leaders, suddenly had a famous new son to put it on the map: Emmanuel Macron was France's biggest political celebrity at the time of the interview with Fouré in early spring. But was the young presidential candidate, with his outsized ambition and unshakeable self-assurance, a typical local?

'Not at all,' Fouré said, her eyes twinkling.

Emmanuel Jean-Michel Frédéric Macron was born on 21 December 1977 at 10:40 am in the city, and spent all of his childhood here.

As he took his first breaths, the centrist president Valéry Giscard d'Estaing, a man remembered now not for his ambitious plans to modernise the economy but for the social changes he pushed through in France, was mid-way through his one and only term in power.

Less than two years later, Margaret Thatcher became prime minister in Britain, and the following year Ronald Reagan was elected president in the United States, unleashing a wave of deregulation, global trade and free-market economics that would eventually hit the heavy industry of France's north-east.

Contrarian France would take a different path from '*les anglosaxons*', electing as its president a Communist-backed Socialist in 1981, François Mitterrand, who nationalised the country's banks at the same time as the Chicago school of liberal economics was finding favour in the White House and in Westminster.

The Macron family home is a short ten-minute drive to the south from the town hall, in the wealthy area of Henriville, which prospered from the 19th-century textile trade and escaped the worst of the 20th-century war damage.

Henriville boasts street after street of elegant two or three-storey homes built in terraces of red brick, which gives Amiens and the surrounding towns of north-east France their distinctive look – attractive for visitors, less so for locals, or so it seems.

It's an image of gentle, provincial bourgeois France, a haven of middle-class comfort that is distinct from the commercial centre, the scruffier student areas of the city, or the rough neighbourhoods of north Amiens. The view at the end of the Macrons' street offers a glimpse of the poorer side of the city. The descending lines of homes frame a distant picture of high-rise tower blocks, home to some of the city's African-origin immigrants.

In Henriville, the terraced homes are made from the same brick as the rows of workers' cottages that were built at the same time in other parts of the city. But the facades of the buildings here are embellished with intricate stonework, small mosaics or wrought-iron balconies. It's not flashy and neither are the cars parked in the street, but comfortable lives are being led here by doctors, lawyers, academics or small business owners. Most homes have gardens, often behind neatly trimmed hedges.

The local café is still a simple '*Bar Tabac*', of the sort found all over France serving coffee, beer, cigarettes and lottery cards. The décor – assorted photographs and pictures on the walls, plastic-topped tables and wooden chairs – remains predictably stuck in time. Only the cigarette packets have changed: they're now mostly foreign and covered in a ghastly array of tumours and infections designed to put off smokers.

The owner, known as Fifi to his clients, confirms that Macron's father, a professor at the medical university in Amiens and a neurologist who is divorced from Macron's mother, still lives in the family home a short walk up the street. He doesn't come to the bar though, and in any case Fifi initially says he doesn't want to talk politics.

He leans over the local paper, the *Courrier Picard*, which he reads from the metal counter of the bar. 'We, the French people, have gone completely mad, we really have,' he says, his face lined with fatigue.

Its front page carries the horrifying story of a local three-year-old girl who was set on fire by a disturbed neighbour, while playing in front of her home in a village near the city.

Having read the report to the end, Fifi opened up a bit more about his views on France. He wouldn't be voting in the coming election and had completely given up on the country's politicians. 'One bad leader you could understand, but look what's happened to the country! It's not getting better, it's getting worse. Wouldn't you think we'd have learned?', he says. 'It's been 30 years, 35 years, of the same shitty policies and crisis after crisis.

'France's problem is work. They've let all the employers leave here. It's all gone. And it's not just the big names; before there were small companies in the local villages,' he says.

Fifi lay much of the blame for this with the European Union, headquartered in Brussels, 200 kilometres to the north-east. 'This "Europe" of ours: it's great if you've got capital to move around – the companies love it, don't they? It's not meant for us, though.'

He suggested a wander up to look at the Macron home and the nearby private Catholic school, the Lycée La Providence, which Emmanuel joined at eleven, after his early years in the local state-run primary.

A client, one of only two who stopped for coffee in the otherwise empty bar, said it was the most prestigious school in the city: for the sons and daughters of anyone with money and ambition, as well as the wayward offspring of wealthy parents based in the capital. 'Some parents send their kids there to keep them out of trouble back in Paris,' he says.

Unlike most of the buildings in Henriville, the two-storey Macron home is detached and slightly set back from the road. Its two downstairs windows and main door open out onto a small front garden separated from the street by a black metal fence. Jean-Michel and Françoise Macron moved here when Emmanuel was a toddler, anticipating their need for more space and the arrival of his other siblings.

The couple had met in medical school in the early 1970s, falling in love after a class on neurology and marrying a year later – in church despite their lack of faith – while Françoise was four months pregnant.

After the joy and euphoria of the ceremony, their life together got off to the worst possible start. Their first baby was stillborn, a trauma felt particularly acutely by Françoise, who had specialised in paediatrics. The daughter was never named and, in the wretchedness and grief that followed, Françoise herself nearly died after contracting septicaemia.

Both in their twenties, they would only start to recover from this ordeal with the arrival of their eldest son. Macron's father says there was no intended symbolism in their choice of name for him (Emmanuel is the messiah foreseen by the prophet Isaiah in the Old Testament), but as a baby, Emmanuel Macron was also keenly awaited, and his arrival was experienced as a mixture of happiness and deliverance from his parents' past suffering.

'Emmanuel's birth was a huge joy for me after this painful period,' Françoise acknowledged in an interview with French journalist Anne Fulda.[1]

He was followed by two other children. A brother, Laurent,

was born two years later: sporty with brown hair and glasses, he would remain slightly in the shadow of his academically brilliant older sibling. But Laurent was a popular boy with a large group of friends. The brothers later lived together in Paris but despite this are not close. 'I've never heard Emmanuel talk about him, not once,' a friend of Macron's in Paris, who has known him for nearly a decade, said on condition of anonymity.

Laurent, now married with three children, has never spoken to the media and barely features in Macron's own account of his childhood. His only public appearance in support of his brother was for his inauguration. He followed his parents into medicine, becoming a cardiovascular radiologist and researcher who currently practises in a northern suburb of Paris.

Their sister Estelle, five years younger than Emmanuel, is similarly low-profile and keen to avoid the limelight. She, too, embraced the family profession and became a kidney specialist, working in the south-west city of Toulouse.

Medical careers had been a means of social ascent for both of Macron's parents, with the previous generation of his family comprising a railway employee and road engineer as well as a teacher and social worker.

'I'm the only one not to have taken this path,' Macron explained in his book *Révolution*, a mix of autobiographical information and his political manifesto, which was published in French five months before the presidential election. 'In no way because of an aversion to medicine, because I've always had a liking for the sciences. But at the time when one chooses one's life, I wanted a world, an adventure of my own.'

In Macron's telling, his home was a place of hard work and highbrow culture, where both of his parents had a keen appreciation of the value of education. Conversations with his parents were about literature or philosophy, but he was also subjected to 'medical discussions for hours too, during which life in the hospital, changes in practices or research, were the subject of constant debate.'

'Some years later, my brother Laurent … and sister Estelle … would take over,' he writes of these discussions with what sounds like relief.[2]

His father was a clever, well-read but also austere presence who gave his son Greek lessons. He kept an office that was out-of-bounds for the children, in which he worked on dozens of research papers that he has published over his four-decade career. One of his specialisms is the brain, and muscular processes that control sneezing in cats. He was pictured at Macron's inauguration wearing a bow tie.

Few of Emmanuel's friends came to visit the family home, and he spent hours reading in his bedroom with its Peter Rabbit wallpaper. His tastes were anything but childish however, and included French classics by Molière, Camus and Jean Racine, as well as books by Guy de Maupassant and André Gide, all of which he devoured in his teens or before. Many of them were chosen for him by his maternal grandmother who made him read passages out loud at her home, including from other lesser-known authors such as the First World War surgeon Georges Duhamel, who brought to life the slaughter and suffering that had taken place in the fields around his home.

This habit of reading, picked up early in childhood, continues today, even though the demands of the presidency have compressed his free time. 'There's not a day when I don't read a book,' Macron said in early 2017.[3] He reads and re-reads, naming *The*

Red and the Black by Stendhal as his favourite book. This 19th-century novel tells the tale of Julien Sorel, an ambitious dreamer from the French provinces, and invites obvious comparisons with Macron's own personal story. 'I admit a certain weakness for romantic heroes whose lives lead them into the unknown, into danger and big open spaces,' he has said.[4] Another of his favourites is the Stendhal character Fabrice del Dongo from the 1839 novel *The Charterhouse of Parma*, which is considered a masterpiece of French literature. Del Dongo is an Italian aristocrat who makes a life for himself first as a soldier in Napoleon's army, and then as a priest, in a tale of intrigue and sexual frustration.

'Literature enlightens us in every situation we find ourselves in. It names our experience. It gives substance to our lives,' Macron explained in a newspaper interview.[5]

He credits the source of this passion for fiction to his mother's mother, who lived a few streets away in Henriville and treated him as her favourite grandchild. Her home is described romantically in *Révolution* as a loving cocoon, a place of homework and hot chocolates, where afternoons were spent listening to Chopin's piano concerti.

Germaine Noguès, known affectionately as Manette, had a profound and lasting influence on him during her life, with a relationship which went far beyond what most people experience of their elderly relatives. The death of this former teacher and retired headmistress from the Pyrenees mountains would lead Macron to reassess his career choices in 2013, when he briefly left politics.

'As a child, every day I would take up the discussion that had been interrupted [the day before] and I travelled through her life as if returning to a novel,' he wrote. Most school days he ate at her home at lunch-time instead of at the canteen, and he would return there after the end of classes for homework and reading. There were frequent overnight stays, and she would join the family for holidays together in the Pyrenees.

These summer road trips to the village of Bagnères-de-Bigorre in the shadow of snow-capped mountains were the first opportunities for the young Emmanuel to discover his country. 'These thousands of French odysseys create the invisible map of a France that is united yet diverse, mysterious and transparent, loyal and refractory,' he wrote in *Révolution*, in a breathless description of the traffic-clogged French motorways during the mass migration for the August holidays.

Among other evocative memories of Manette which feature in his book is 'the smell of coffee that she would make sometimes in the middle of the night. And the door of my room opened at seven o'clock in the morning if I hadn't already come to see her.'[6]

This bond caused jealousies between Macron's grandmother and his parents during his childhood, particularly when the five-year-old Macron asked his parents if he could move in with Manette. This painful family dynamic was revived by the tone of Macron's book with its distant and cool description of his immediate family, who are thanked for providing stability and safety; Manette, by contrast, is credited with firing his imagination and making him dream.

This apparently ungrateful treatment of his parents was perhaps another of Macron's acts of quiet but forceful rebellion against them. Throughout his life he has asserted his right to personal freedom and autonomy, and as a child he appears to have selected his own guardian, emancipating himself even from his own immediate genealogy.

'My flaw? Maybe that I'm claustrophobic,' he said in late 2017. 'Not in the physical sense: I don't have any listed phobias but I'm claustrophobic about life. I can't stand being shut in, I have to get out.'[7]

As well as in his relationship with Manette, he further defied his father by asking to be baptised at the age of twelve. Macron described this moment as 'the start of a mystical period that lasted for several years' in an interview with the magazine *L'Obs* (he is no longer religious). When he was sixteen, he again held out against his father's wishes, to pursue a scandalous relationship with his teacher. And after spurning the medical path taken by everyone else in the family, he then seemed to relegate his parents to being peripheral figures in the public's imagination.

Some observers have suggested that Macron exaggerated the personal narrative around his grandmother for political reasons, to push a story that helped in creating his unusual public identity. Manette, the literature-loving and left-wing headmistress who had an illiterate mother from the mountains, is a vivid illustration of the social mobility made possible by France's state education system. As an obsessive student of power, Macron was acutely aware of the influence of personal storytelling on voters, both as a means for a politician to stand out from his opponents and to lend authenticity to his project. No one had done this better in recent times than US President Barack Obama, particularly in 2008, whose successful campaign Macron had followed closely. Obama's personal story – of a black kid raised by a single mum who had been a one-time community organiser on the South Side of Chicago – echoed his core message to the American people of 'Yes We Can!'

Macron had nothing this powerful himself, but Manette was a working-class success story, a symbol of hard work and a way for him to stress both his link to older generations and his grounding in France's rich and sophisticated culture. His admiration appears entirely sincere. But the emphasis placed on her in his writing and his speeches was also political.

Macron's description of his family life was clearly hurtful for Jean-Michel and Françoise, however, leading both of them to make attempts to correct perceptions encouraged by their own son. 'No, we were not austere parents who abandoned their child to his grandmother!' Françoise said in an interview in February 2017. 'No, it was never a question of her adopting him.'[8]

'According to some articles, Emmanuel had no family!' she lamented in a separate interview, adding that she had always made her children a priority. 'It's something that I find very difficult to deal with.'[9]

The more reserved Jean-Michel, now divorced from Françoise and suspicious of the media and of politics in general, also spoke out in a bid to give a more rounded view of his son's child-hood. 'He wasn't a zombie always shut in his room!' he told the authors Caroline Derrien and Candice Nedelec for their book *Les Macron*.

Emmanuel enjoyed fishing and football and played tennis at the local club over the road from his home, where paunchy businessmen and local notables can still be found today meeting for food and drinks in the clubhouse.

As well as the summer road trips to the Pyrenees, there were other holidays in exclusive Alpine ski resorts like Courchevel, or in Greece or on the dreamy Mediterranean island of Corsica, none of which are mentioned in his book.

It was an upbringing in comfort and privilege, between a private school, a home in an upmarket neighbourhood of the city and decent family holidays. He was a first child, who never wanted for support, care or attention.

Underneath the florid prose of his book and the selective air-brushing of parts of his middle-class life, there is no doubt about the depth of his feelings for his grandmother Manette. Nor about her influence on his education and politics, with her left-wing views credited by Macron as having had more influence on him than those of his more conservative father.

'Ever since she's gone, there isn't a day when I don't think about her or seek her gaze,' Macron told the authors Bernard Pascuito and Olivier Biscaye in their book *Les Politiques Aussi Ont une Mère* (Politicians Also Have Mothers).[10] Above all, she established a pattern that runs throughout his life: his attraction and fascination for people one, or sometimes several generations older than him.

'He always told me that he was brought up by his grandmother,' said Catherine Goldenstein, a 69-year-old friend who has stayed in contact with him since his time as a student in Paris. 'As for the relationship between him and his father, I don't think they are particularly close.' The long-time friend from Paris said that 'there are some people he never talks about, like his father ... He's a bit secretive.'

His embrace of Manette in his private life and political career, despite the tension caused with his parents, perhaps illustrates another characteristic. 'I don't think he's ever felt indebted to anyone,' one of his closest school friends from Amiens, Renaud Dartevelle, explained.

Dartevelle came to know Macron at the local private Catholic school La Providence – referred to as '*la Pro*' locally – which was built during the post-war reconstruction of Amiens, less than five minutes' walk from the Macron family home.

Its main four-storey building and accompanying annexes spread over twelve hectares stand grandly behind a three-metre metal fence, its entrance manned by security guards. Multiple playing fields, a swimming pool and auditorium offer opportunities for pupils to 'Be, Act, Succeed and Grow', the school's motto. The state secondary school just next door looks tatty in comparison.

After a subscription fee, annual costs are modest compared to prestigious private schools in Britain or America – it costs a few thousand euros a year – and are adjusted depending on a family's ability to pay.

'There was some degree of social diversity,' remembers Dartevelle over a glass of wine at his home in a southern suburb of Paris. 'But were there kids from the economically less-developed areas of northern Amiens? No. And there was no racial diversity.'

Arnaud de Bretagne, a retired teacher who taught for nearly twenty years at La Providence, puts it more succinctly: 'It's a school whose intake comes from the local bourgeoisie.'

The religious education was limited to a few hours a week, but the school's Jesuit philosophy encouraged pupils to take part in charitable causes like sponsored walks, to raise money for local associations.

Macron was enrolled for the high school, joining the 'sixième' year for pupils aged eleven to twelve. Thanks to his reading habits and a maturity beyond his years, he instantly stood out. According to his contemporaries there, he was brilliant, yet modest. Charming, yet slightly distant. Teachers fawned over him. Fellow pupils were jealous, but they found him difficult to dislike.

'He had incredible results in everything. It was always between eighteen and twenty [out of twenty] in every subject,' remembers Dartevelle. 'If you got a better score than Emmanuel it was the event of the year. It was always like that.'

De Bretagne, who taught him geography and history in his final year at the school, recalls a pupil of 'enormous ability, but nice and well-liked by his contemporaries.'

Another teacher, Léonard Ternoy, who taught Latin and French to Macron, said his praise for the cultured and naturally curious pupil caused tensions at home. Macron would often come to chat to him in private after class. 'My daughter was in the school too and she got tired of hearing about him,' he said. 'There was some jealousy I think.' For Macron, managing his evident difference and superiority over his classmates was a social challenge. From a young age he appears to have adopted a strategy: conceal and joke. Only share the parts of his life that were necessary or relevant, while deploying humour and his toothy smile for self-effacement. He would take the same approach throughout his life, charming many people in the process but leaving others with a sense that they do not fully know or understand him.

As president, he continued to be light-hearted behind closed doors, occasionally making jokes at his own expense in front of aides and visitors. He uses humour constantly as a way to charm and avoid tension, mixing self-mockery with quirky old-fashioned phrases or quotes from humorists or plays. 'His vocabulary and humour is often more like someone's from two or three generations ago,' an old friend from his student days and presidential aide Aurélien Lechevallier said in an interview.

'He was always quite clever at avoiding being pretentious while at the same time making you aware of his obvious intellectual abilities,' explained Dartevelle, whose comment chimes with some of Macron's own words in early 2017 which offered a glimpse into his thinking. They were made in the context of the presidential campaign at the time, but they are just as easily applied to the way he has built relationships with colleagues, political allies or journalists. 'You need to oscillate between humility and arrogance,' he told the *Journal du Dimanche* newspaper, 'If you fall on one of the two sides, you become either inefficient or dangerous.'[11] There's something cold and calculating, unmistakeably Machiavellian, in the statement.

Back at La Providence, he and Dartevelle shared a love of books, classical music and an early interest in politics. Both were more comfortable one-to-one than in large groups and neither was interested in chasing girls, according to Dartevelle. That said, Macron had a girlfriend for a few months in his early teens, a classmate called Anne-Cécile.

'Going out partying, going to nightclubs? Not at all. I never set foot in a club and neither did he,' Dartevelle said, adding that he 'would be surprised if anyone knew him better than I did at the time.' They talked about books and listened to music, with Dartevelle remembering first discovering the *Goldberg Variations* by Bach at his friend's home. They also listened to the complete repertoire of the Belgian singer Jacques Brel, which Macron had received as a Christmas present in his mid-teens. 'High culture might seem boring to some people. It didn't to us,' Dartevelle added.

Yet looking back, and in spite of his belief that no one knew Emmanuel better than him, Dartevelle realises there were also things he was unaware of. Macron's skill on the piano, for example: he took lessons for ten years (winning a prize, naturally) at the Amiens music conservatory in the centre of the city. Or even the role of his grandmother in bringing him up.

Dartevelle's first visit to the Macron family home was not until several years into their friendship; other friends from later stages of Macron's life recount similar experiences – of being jolted by the discovery of a separate interest or hidden talent. 'It was always easy being in his company. There were lots of acquaintances, but not many friends, and even with friends there was a certain distance,' Dartevelle says. Macron is both a skilled compartmentaliser with a diverse range of interests, but also instinctively private, keeping his inner emotional life to himself.

Their other shared passion was theatre. Both helped set up a school drama club, performing *Jakub and his Master*, a philosophical work by Czech writer Milan Kundera, which conveniently features two lead male roles that were claimed by the boys.

The following year the club was taken over by a free-spirited teacher called Brigitte Auzière, a 39-year-old mother of three children, one of whom was in Macron's year. Madame Auzière, who also taught French and Latin, was adored and respected in equal measure. She had a form of *Willy Wonka* star-power as the daughter of a famed local chocolate maker, but she also won over pupils with her commitment, and enthusiasm for the profession she had stumbled into.

The youngest of six children, Brigitte was born into a family of wealth and political influence in Amiens, and admits to being spoiled, although her childhood was also marked by tragedy. Brigitte has a pronounced fear of death that lasts to this day: when she was eight, her pregnant older sister died along with her husband in a car crash. Her late father Jean Trogneux was a local businessman who ran numerous companies and local associations, including, at one point, the tennis club opposite the Macrons' home.

'They're a very well-known family, very involved,' says the mayor, Brigitte Fouré.

The family still owns a flagship chocolate shop on the city's main shopping street, along with six other sales points across northern France. The dated storefront in beige-and-brown reads simply 'Jean Trogneux, for five generations.' Family legend has it that Brigitte's mother once refused to serve the Nazi general Erwin Rommel during the occupation.[12] Inside nowadays is a chocolate wonderland of delicately packed boxes, sugar-coated eggs and cocoa-based sculptures of animals, instruments and even a Princess Leia. Many people come for the house speciality: macaroons, dense sugary concoctions wrapped in red-and-gold foil which taste like marzipan.

At the age of twenty, while studying literature in the nearby city of Lille, Brigitte married André-Louis Auzière, the Africa-born son of a French diplomat from Amiens.

She first aimed for a career in human resources and had a brief stint as a press officer for the regional council. But the extroverted fan of short skirts and rock 'n' roll eventually found her vocation at the age of 30 while living in Strasbourg, where her husband was posted for an international bank.

After returning to Amiens, she was taken on at La Providence. 'I remember Madame Auzière as the best teacher I ever had,' beamed Antoine Joannes, one of her former pupils in Amiens, now living in Paris where he works for the TF1 television channel. 'She was someone who lifted us all with her generosity, her energy, her force.'

The Trogneux clan – connected, wealthy, visible – moved in different circles to the discreet, cerebral Macrons. But the two families came together, with life-changing consequences, thanks to the theatre troupe.

'We all had a passion for theatre, but we were driven on by Brigitte who was even more passionate than us. She helped us develop a desire to communicate,' remembered Joannes. 'And it was very informal. We called her Brigitte, not "Madame".'

Pupils were authorised to use the informal '*tu*' when addressing her instead of the '*vous*' which is a mark of respect in French culture. There were rehearsals at her home, a spacious house a few streets from where the Macrons lived in Henriville. Visits confirmed what pupils already sensed from her choice of clothes and car: that she was not from the same background as many of her colleagues in the staff room.

Emmanuel, who never had Brigitte as a class teacher at La Providence, repeatedly made the short walk from school to her home, as did other children, some of whom would call by to do extra homework or to visit her children. It was not uncommon for pupils to telephone Brigitte at home in the evening. Some sent her letters.

Using '*tu*' to address her, and the porous barrier between the school and Brigitte's private life, had upset the strict hierarchy normally respected in French schools. 'I remember wondering what was the right distance to keep,' Dartevelle said of his relationship to the outgoing and breezy teacher, who was around the same age as both his mother and Emmanuel's.

Even before meeting Macron for the first time, Brigitte had already heard of him via her daughter Laurence, who was in the same year as him. Although only in his early teens, his reputation had preceded him in a school of several thousands. 'There's a mad kid in my class who knows everything about everything' was Laurence's verdict.[13]

In 1993, the school drama club performed an adaptation of

La Comédie du Langage ('The Comedy of Language'), a piece by the absurdist French playwright Jean Tardieu whose other work includes *La Serrure*, a contemplation of voyeurism in which a man watches a woman undress through the keyhole of a brothel.

Emmanuel played a scarecrow in the play. A video of the performance broadcast in a French documentary shows the already handsome fifteen-year-old in a straw hat and patchwork jacket, making long pauses for effect and delivering his lines confidently in a baritone voice. 'What makes people most scared? The barking of a dog, or the shadow of a man?', he asks during a monologue, alone on stage in the spotlight.

'In all the plays we performed, I never saw Emmanuel interested in anything except the lead roles,' commented Dartevelle.

Brigitte was spellbound by Emmanuel's acting skills. He needed little instruction and already had his own ideas about choreography. 'I thought he was incredible on the stage. What a presence!' she told a documentary broadcast in 2016.[14]

The next year, as the school returned in September, they discussed the next production. Emmanuel proposed *The Art of Comedy*, a play by Italy's Eduardo De Filippo that recounts a theatre director's struggle with local authorities to save his troupe.

Naturally, Emmanuel would play the theatre director. But there was a problem: the play had too few roles and not enough female characters for a club that included many girls. For whatever reason, Emmanuel, headstrong and highly opinionated, would not be deterred from staging it.

Over months, he and Brigitte rewrote parts of the play, creating characters and adding scenes, including one in which seven girls dressed in wedding dresses discussed their ideal man. It was a daring addition by a teenage pupil and his teacher.[15] Once finished, they decided they would direct it together, organising for it to be staged in a real theatre in central Amiens instead of the school auditorium.

'There was a real understanding between them, a sort of symbiosis,' remembered Joannes. 'They had a relationship that was very complicit and close, something completely natural.'

Even accounting for Emmanuel's precocious talent and his highly developed intellect, there was and should have been a gulf between them. Emmanuel was sixteen; Brigitte 39. The legal age of consent in France for a student in a relationship with a teacher is eighteen.

A relationship between them would have been scandalous anywhere, but it risked being particularly so in a small town like Amiens. On top of this, she was from a conservative family and taught in a well-to-do private Catholic school; she had a husband, who had welcomed the boy at the family home; her son was three years older than Emmanuel, one of her daughters was in the same year as him and she was the teacher of his younger brother and sister. There were many entanglements, not to mention the social and potentially legal conventions being breached.

In addition, the tragic personal tale of Gabrielle Russier was seared into the minds of teachers of Brigitte's generation in France. Russier, a divorced mother-of-two working in a school in the southern port of Marseille, had gassed herself in 1969 after receiving a one-year jail term for having a relationship with a seventeen-year-old pupil. Russier's love story, set against the backdrop of student revolts in protest at the tradition-bound French society of the late 60s, had been turned into a popular film (*Mourir d'Aimer* – To Die of Love) which Brigitte had seen. 'It wasn't passion at all,' Russier's real-life lover, Christian

Rossi, told the *Nouvel Observateur* magazine in an interview in
1971 before he faded into obscurity. Amid public outrage and
incomprehension, he had been briefly interned in a psychiatric
home by his parents. 'It was love,' he explained. 'Passion isn't
lucid. This was lucid.'

In discussing her own experience, Brigitte implies that she
didn't see the relationship with Emmanuel developing until it
was too late: 'I thought that we were going to write a bit and
then grow tired of it. I didn't have the measure of him,' she told
a television documentary team.[16] 'We wrote together and then
little by little I was taken in by his intelligence. And I still haven't
grasped the full depth of it.'

Sounding like a mixture of teacher, proud mother and
wife, she compared her time adapting the play to 'working with
Mozart.' But she also addressed the biggest question of all, which
continues to fascinate and baffle: how could she consider a relationship with a child?

'He wasn't like the others,' she said. He was 'always with the
teachers, always with lots of books. He wasn't an adolescent, he
had a relationship as an equal with adults.'[17]

Macron has echoed this version of events in his own words,
speaking of a coming together of two minds. It was 'surrepti-
tiously that things happened and I fell in love,' he wrote. 'An
intellectual complicity which day by day became a conscious
proximity. Then, without anyone fighting it, [it became] a passion which endures to this day.'[18]

The play was a hit. To celebrate, the entire troupe – including
Brigitte – had dinner together in high spirits in a restaurant in
central Amiens. Dartevelle remembers seeing her and Emmanuel
together around this time and realising that something was

happening. He pretended not to notice, finding the thought 'uncomfortable'.

Brigitte's colleague Léonard Ternoy said teachers in the staff room had also begun to speculate about their relationship, knowing how much time they were spending together and how they had often stayed on after rehearsals in the evenings. 'Some people began to wonder,' he said.

Had Brigitte found the 'lucidity' experienced by the tragic Russier and Rossi back in 1968? 'I understood that it was changing imperceptibly from an intellectual relationship to a more emotional one. It was tacitly understood,' she said.[19] 'I knew that he was the man for me, but it wasn't possible.'

He was coming to the close of middle-school at La Providence. So far, no one had any proof of the still-hidden relationship – until Emmanuel was busted by his parents for pretending to be away at a school friend's house revising for his exams when he was, in fact, with Brigitte.

Jean-Michel and Françoise were shocked, then angry. They initially thought that Emmanuel was dating Brigitte's pretty and similarly blonde daughter Laurence, according to the account they gave to the French journalist Anne Fulda. The boy's parents summoned Brigitte to a meeting.

'I forbid you from seeing him until he's eighteen,' Jean Michel told her face-to-face. They could, legally, have pressed charges for statutory rape, but decided against it.

'I can't promise you anything,' replied Brigitte, in tears.

'You don't understand, you've already got your life,' said Françoise. Then, prophetically: 'He'll never have children.' In retrospect, this was a remarkable display of mother's intuition, perhaps borne of an awareness that her son was different, more single-minded and resistant to pressure than his peers or siblings.

Having never become a father, Macron was asked by a group of schoolchildren whether he felt he had missed out, during a TV programme broadcast in March 2017.[20] 'It's a choice I made. Brigitte had three children when I met her, older and younger ones,' he replied. 'We did wonder about it [having our own], but I thought the most important thing was bringing up the children well, loving them, and you know, I've got seven grandchildren now.'

He went on to ask the children, sitting at their desks in a classroom, how many of them had divorced parents and half-brothers or sisters, leading many to raise their hands. 'There are lots of different families nowadays,' he said, adding: 'The idea that you're from the same family for your whole life isn't true.'

After the teary meeting between Brigitte and Macron's parents, plans to send him to Paris to finish his school education took on an added urgency, though both parents deny suggestions made in the French media that they banished him to the capital. Brigitte, her domestic life in crisis, also encouraged Emmanuel to leave.

Aged sixteen, he boarded the train for Paris, his head full of literature and ambitions of becoming an actor or a writer. He was destined not just for any French school: he had a place at Henri IV, one of the city's most prestigious establishments. Celebrated former pupils include the philosopher Jean-Paul Sartre, novelist André Gide and the recent Nobel Prize winning author Patrick Modiano. Nestled in the heart of the Latin Quarter on a grand street opposite the Pantheon, the honorary burial ground for national heroes, the school was Macron's first leg up into the gilded world of the French elite.

Christian Monjou, who taught Macron at Henri IV and remained in contact with him for years afterwards, suspects that his father 'very likely intervened' to have him accepted by the school's management. It was 'very rare' to have pupils arrive to study just for the final years of school, he said.

Undeterred by the physical distance now between them, Macron made his intentions clear to Brigitte. 'He promised me that he'd come back,' she confided to *Paris Match*.[21] 'It was a wrench. But we didn't break it off. On the contrary, it became passionate and at seventeen Emmanuel told me "whatever happens to you, I'll marry you".'

What followed in Amiens is one of many perplexing and curious features of their relationship. Brigitte would be fired, surely? Other Macron and Auzière siblings were still enrolled in the school. How could colleagues or parents trust her? If the local media got hold of the story, private gossiping would turn into public humiliation.

'There started to be some chatter in the staff room, the year after he left for Paris,' another one of Brigitte's fellow teachers, Arnaud de Bretagne remembered. 'It was said that he'd gone to Paris after falling in love with Brigitte, that his parents had sent him there to avoid rumours spreading in Amiens.'

While out for a stroll one Sunday along the banks of the Somme after Emmanuel had left for Paris, de Bretagne stumbled upon the couple on the footpath, despite their best efforts to avoid being seen together around Amiens. Macron's parents and Brigitte's siblings were still deeply opposed to their relationship. 'I said hello. We were a bit surprised to see each other,' de Bretagne chuckled. 'I didn't talk to anyone about it but when I learned they were together, it didn't surprise me.'

Brigitte remained discreet in front of her mute but silently sympathetic colleagues. Their impulse was to quietly ignore her chaotic personal life. 'It wasn't a scandal, it would be exaggerating to call it that,' de Bretagne added.

Fellow teacher Léonard Ternoy said that some teachers and parents disapproved privately but there was never any discussion about disciplining Brigitte to his knowledge. 'She wasn't sanctioned. Maybe the headteacher called her in and gave her a warning, I don't know, but there was nothing that I recall.'

It appears that old-fashioned provincial prudishness saved the day for the couple. Brigitte was also well liked as a colleague and no one seemed to have an interest in making a fuss. 'Everyone approved of him leaving. We knew there was this relationship, but I think in the culture and philosophy of the school, there was a desire to respect their rights as individuals, their rights to a private life,' Ternoy continued.

Macron's former school colleague and friend Dartevelle carried on to finish his studies at La Providence until he was eighteen. Brigitte stayed on too, putting on a brave face in class as her marriage fell apart.

Was it awkward having your best friend's lover as a French teacher? 'It was something compartmentalised in a corner of my mind,' Dartevelle said at the end of a long chat at his home. He refused to confirm anything to curious schoolmates at the time, and he barely even broached the subject with Emmanuel, who in turn never spoke about it. Brigitte carried on teaching in Amiens until 2007 when she left for a new job at a similarly prestigious religious school in Paris.

Once he had left for the capital, Amiens would never again be a permanent home for Emmanuel Macron. It was the start of his straddling two places geographically, as well as living across two generations through his relationship with Brigitte. This pattern, seeming to be in several places at the same time but in none of them in particular, would be repeated throughout his life. It is part of what makes him such an elusive, unusual and slippery character who defies easy classification. He would later become the literary free-spirit who went into public service, the philosopher at a bank, then the banker who became a politician. Finally he would win over the French with a proposal that was 'neither of the left, nor the right'.

His relationship to Amiens is like so much else in his life. He's from there, but not obviously, and he shares few of the characteristics common to the *Amiénois*. He did absorb its history, particularly its wartime experiences, which partly explains his deeply rooted objection to nationalism. Yet his roots there are shallow.

'He's from Amiens, that's something you can't deny,' concludes mayor Fouré. 'But I'm not sure that the *Amiénois* consider him one of us.' The city would become a useful foil, however, later in his presidential campaign as part of his political image-making, and it would be the scene of a decisive moment in the latter stages of his campaign when the local Whirlpool factory would become the focus of workers' anger about the downsides of globalisation.

CHAPTER 3

Lonely and Lovestruck

LEAVING FOR PARIS 'WAS FOR ME THE MOST BEAUTIFUL of adventures. I was coming to live in places that only existed in novels, I walked the streets of the characters of Flaubert and Hugo. I was pushed onwards by the voracious ambition of the Young Turks of Balzac,' Macron wrote of his departure.[1]

The reference to Balzac, conjuring up the fictional character of Eugène de Rastignac, is an interesting choice for Macron to have made. Rastignac was a handsome social climber from the provinces who arrived in the capital to study before being sucked in by the wealth, glamour and moral corruption of 19th-century high society. Being described as a '*Rastignac*' is not complimentary. It also recalls Macron's fascination for the Stendhal character Julien Sorel, the bookish anti-hero in *The Red and the Black* who is blessed with good looks and a ferocious memory, and who flees to Paris to escape an abusive father.

In Balzac's narration, de Rastignac was one of many young men who 'lay the ground for success in life in advance, by calculating the benefit of their studies and moulding them to the future course of events in order to be the first to shape them.'

To succeed, advised Rastignac's cousin Madame de Beauséant, 'see men and women as no more than post horses which you ride and then leave to die at each coaching inn. In this way you will succeed in fulfilling your desires.'

Despite his description of leaving for Paris as a 'beautiful adventure', living away from his family aged only sixteen and, perhaps more importantly, being physically separated from Brigitte, Macron found himself disoriented for the first time. At Henri IV there were other brilliant pupils. Competition was fierce. His parents rented a pokey room on the top floor of an apartment block near the school – a former servant's quarters – with a shared bathroom and toilet on the corridor. Whilst he trudged home to an empty flat with his mother's home-cooked dinners in the fridge, his classmates returned to their families in the city's most exclusive addresses in central Paris.

In the often snobbish, conservative world of Henri IV, Macron stood out physically as being both good-looking and somewhat flamboyant. One teacher remembers him as looking like a 'tousled sheep'. A school photo at the time shows him with a heap of shaggy brown-blondish hair standing in the middle of four lines of studious and neat-looking contemporaries wearing sensible shirts or sweaters. 'He had presence, the air of a German Romantic,' remembered his classmate Yannick Papaix.[2]

The academic expectations were also higher than he had been used to in Amiens and his ability to dazzle with his vocabulary was less effective than it had been at La Providence. He objected privately to the verdict of one teacher who returned an essay on politics with the word 'waffle' written on it. A submission during his philosophy class was described as 'close to hopeless and unworthy of you.'

The French public education system is famously tough, unsentimental and focused on grades. From day one, teachers at Henri IV made it clear that pupils were expected to work hard in the airy classrooms of the former monastery and to graduate from it for the Republic's best universities.

But Emmanuel's thoughts were elsewhere. He seemed to have little time for his classmates, arriving for lessons and then leaving immediately after they ended. Few of his current friends or political fellow travellers date back to this era. His most enduring relationships – note the age difference – have been with his teachers such as Christian Monjou, who is a professor and now a specialist in leadership and innovation.

'One day he told me that other young people bored him,' one of his friends from the time told the *Libération* newspaper.[3]

As well as Brigitte, there were other distractions. While his peers were toiling with homework, he found time to write a book, *Babylone, Babylone*, a hugely ambitious caper set in Latin America in the 17th century at the time of the Spanish conquistadors. It was inspired by his parents' trip to Mexico, which they had taken without the children. Living alone and with plenty of spare time on his hands, Macron spent hours researching Spanish colonialism in Latin America. Despite his efforts to interest publishers, however, the manuscript was rejected for publication. Undeterred, he started on a second literary project, a detective novel.

He also auditioned for a part in a film alongside the veteran French actor Jean-Pierre Marielle (best-known internationally for playing Jacques Saunière in *The Da Vinci Code*). Despite having excelled as a school scarecrow, Macron failed to convince the casting director.

One can imagine his disappointment: he, and almost everyone who knew him at the time, had assumed he would enjoy a brilliant future in the arts as a writer, poet, playwright or intellectual perhaps. He had discussed the idea of becoming an actor whilst still at La Providence. 'It was a difficult time,' acknowledges one of his closest friends from Paris, Marc Ferracci, over a fruit cocktail near the Montparnasse station in southern Paris.

Macron spent hours talking on the phone to Brigitte in the evenings, despite the efforts of his parents to separate them. She was having a hard time with her five older siblings who were mortified by her relationship with her former pupil, particularly her oldest brother, who was twenty years her senior. 'My brothers and sisters tried to play the role of my parents who were no longer there,' she explained.[4]

Emmanuel headed home most weekends, taking the hour-long train trip from the Gare du Nord in Paris to Amiens. Every Sunday night he would make the return journey, carrying food for the week cooked by his mother. 'There was a period of a few years of tension with his family,' Ferracci says. 'And above all in Brigitte's family, which did not see the relationship in a favourable light.'

Under immense pressure, Brigitte was now separated and doing her best to protect her three children from the collapse of her marriage. She understandably questioned the folly of upending her comfortable, stable life for the sake of a schoolboy. But Emmanuel would not let go.

'We spoke all the time ... And little by little, he overcame my resistance in an incredible way, and with patience,' Brigitte explained, sitting on the terrace of her family holiday home in the upmarket resort of Le Touquet on France's northern coast.[5]

'Love carried everything in its wake and drove me to divorce,' she added in a separate interview. She, like many of the businessmen, politicians and senior civil servants who would play a role in his rise, was seduced by his maturity, humour and intelligence. He in turn demonstrated a single-mindedness and disregard for the views of others which would be characteristic of his rise. 'It was impossible to resist him,' Brigitte said.[6]

Neither of them will pinpoint the exact start of their physical relationship, or say whether it took place before he left for Paris or during his time at Henri IV. Brigitte considers it their secret, for understandable reasons.

'What reinforced the relationship is the difficulty of cutting your ties with your family, Brigitte with her family and him to a certain extent with his. And along with all that, he gained his independence faster than he would have liked,' explained Ferracci. 'All that creates bonds, which grew stronger over time.'

At eighteen, Macron told his parents he was still with Brigitte and that, even if they didn't accept them together, he would carry on anyway. 'It required the force of conviction,' Macron explained.[7] 'They thought at several points that it would stop. And they did everything to make sure that this happened, understandably in some ways. I don't know how I would have reacted.'

Having this tension as a backdrop to his studies was far from ideal. Away from home, he was consumed by desire. On top of that, there were the acting auditions and his first attempts to write novels. He was struggling with mathematics at school.

At least his lodgings had improved slightly. Rather than the rented former servant's quarters, he had moved into a ground floor apartment his parents had acquired in southern Paris, several kilometres from the school in the 14th district of the city near the *La Santé* prison. It was small and gloomy, but at least it had its own bathroom. He lived there throughout his school and student years, later sharing it with his brother Laurent when he too moved to Paris, to study medicine.

'I admit that these first years in Paris were ones during which I chose to live and to love, rather than take part in the competition between students,' he wrote in *Révolution*.[8]

Nevertheless, in 1995 he passed his *baccalauréat*, the main high-school exams, with marks between sixteen and eighteen out of twenty. But this attitude took its toll when he began literature studies afterwards to enter the prestigious École Normale Supérieure in Paris, known as 'Normale Sup'. In one of only a handful of failures in the life of the boy always at or near the top of the class, twice he sat and failed the entrance exams.

Dating back to the Revolutionary period, École Normale Supérieure remains the most prestigious university for French academics and intellectuals, numerous Nobel prizewinners having passed through its lecture halls on the Rue d'Ulm, a few streets from Henri IV.

'The truth is that I wasn't playing the game. I was too in love to prepare for the exams properly,' he claimed afterwards.[9] 'The heart and logic are incompatible.'

The failure was a 'moment of vertigo'. Without enthusiasm, he took and passed the entrance exams for the Paris Institute of Political Studies, known as 'Sciences Po', and signed up for a philosophy course at the Université Paris Nanterre in a western suburb of the capital. While Sciences Po is one of France's best-known universities, the knock-back by Normale Sup, whose degrees are a life-long marker of superiority in French society, stung painfully.

'If he had succeeded [in getting into the Normale Sup] his political destiny might have been different,' believes Christian Monjou, Macron's teacher from Henri IV.

Though he didn't know it at the time, Sciences Po would be the incubator for his future career. By now in his late teens and more settled in his relationship with Brigitte, he began to create a lasting network of friends, academics and politicians that would be crucial for his rise.

Courses on the role of the French state, the social security system, public finance or political history soon saw him in his element, and he could indulge his interests and willingly expose his ideas in class. It also brought him face-to-face with foreign students for the first time, broadening his horizons, given that he had inhabited an overwhelmingly white and middle-class French world until then. 'I loved this experience,' he said.[10]

The feedback from lecturers from this time is familiar. 'A brilliant student,' read one assessment. 'Blessed with an original mind', said another. Several essays were returned with the comment 'too long', however, and one lecturer found him to have a 'tendency to be a bit too sure of himself' which was nonetheless balanced by 'a very convivial attitude'.[11]

His group of friends at this time included Marc Ferracci, who is now a renowned labour market economist, Aurélien Lechevallier, a now senior diplomatic aide, as well as the future senior civil servants Frédéric Mauget and Aymeric Ducrocq.

'We'd go for drinks together, mostly beers, without going over the top,' Ferracci remembers of evenings spent in *Le Basile* café near Sciences Po or the *Tourn'bride* on the cobbled and charming

Rue Mouffetard. There was 'excess' on a couple of occasions, but this was not raucous student life as lived on many American or British campuses. The area around Sciences Po in central Paris – known as the Left Bank – retains little of the rebellious reputation it earned during the 1968 student protests, being a mix of art galleries, fashion boutiques and high-end restaurants nowadays. Ferracci and Macron liked to talk philosophy and poetry.

Lechevallier said that what brought the friends together was their shared views on current affairs and politics. 'We were all very pro-European,' he remembers. 'This was a time when Europe was on the front foot. It was after the euro had been created but before the failed referendum,' he said, referring to France's stunning rejection of a proposed EU constitution in a vote in 2005.

As well as Europe, Macron's student life was later marked by terrorism after the attacks of September 11, 2001 and the US-led invasions of Afghanistan and Iraq, whose consequences are still being felt. There was also the domestic political earthquake of France's presidential elections in 2002 when the anti-Semitic and xenophobic far-right leader Jean-Marie Le Pen, father of Marine Le Pen, made it through to the second round of the vote. These themes – Europe, terrorism and right-wing nationalism – would still be playing out in France in the 2017 campaign.

At Sciences Po, Macron and his friends all identified as left-wing, 'except Ducrocq who was from a more traditional family and was more conservative,' Lechevallier remembered. Football, theatre trips and afternoons spent lolling in the perfectly-manicured Luxembourg Gardens near the university provided relief from the intensive study and, apparently, intense conversation.

All this time, Macron continued to have one foot in Paris among his student friends and another in his life with Brigitte. His friends met her and were aware of their relationship, but she was part of a separate sphere. 'We'd see Emmanuel from Monday to Friday and then he'd leave for the weekends,' Lechevallier remembers.

At Université Paris Nanterre, Macron was working on his masters in philosophy. Having already read Kant, Aristotle and Descartes in his spare time, he chose to study the German thinker Hegel and the 13th-century Italian writer and schemer Machiavelli.

But a far richer philosophical education came via a contact at Sciences Po, another admiring professor, the historian François Dosse. Macron took one of his courses on the writing of history.

'He had no background in historiography, but from one lecture to another he was able to assimilate the knowledge and then talk about it almost as a specialist. I was dazzled,' Dosse remembers. 'He also had an ability to make the links. Of course, most people can do that if they've got the notes in front of them or if they've revised. He didn't need to. He could just do it. He had the "unbearable lightness of being" as Kundera would say.'

At the time, Dosse was finishing writing a biography of the French philosopher Paul Ricœur, then in his late eighties. Ricœur was working on what would be his last book, *La Mémoire, l'Histoire, l'Oubli* ('Memory, History and Oblivion') and was getting too frail to do all the research himself.

'He asked me if I knew anyone who could help him,' Dosse remembers. 'And I said to him, yes, I've got just the person for you. He's an absolutely brilliant student.'

Orphaned young after his widower father was killed in the First World War, Paul Ricœur was a protestant from eastern France who grew up immersed in a world of literature before becoming a teacher in the 1930s.

His career was interrupted when he was drafted for the Second World War, whereupon he was soon taken prisoner and interned in Germany for four years. He later described this period as 'extraordinarily fruitful', as it had allowed him to study German masters Kant and Hegel, as well as Husserl and Jaspers.

In the late 1960s, he gained notoriety far greater than he ever sought with his writing when his philosophy faculty at Université Paris Nanterre was convulsed by the student protests of the era. He was repeatedly insulted by hardliners and had the top of a rubbish bin put over his head. When further rioting led furniture to be thrown from upper-floor windows, the police were called in. As the protests and violence escalated, Ricœur resigned in 1970 and suspended his teaching in France for two years.

When Macron met him, the pacifist Christian was hugely respected as the last surviving member of France's great pre-war generation of thinkers that had included Jean-Paul Sartre. But he was also a gentle, humble man with an extraordinary life story shaped by the cataclysms of the last century. The result after the meeting between him and the ever-curious Macron – the boy who loved travelling through his grandmother's memories – was predictable.

'I remember this young man – he was in his early twenties, the age of my children – smiley, brilliant, full of simplicity and kindness, and sitting opposite, there was Paul who seemed just as happy,' said Catherine Goldenstein, 69, who cared for Ricœur in his final years.

Initially Macron was taken on for basic editorial tasks like checking footnotes, fetching books from libraries or looking up quotations from the hundreds of works on Ricœur's bookshelves in his elegant apartment, located in a community of left-wing intellectuals south of Paris.

But he showed an early grasp of what professional career coaches call 'job shaping': adapting the role and not being constrained by the original description. Soon he was making suggestions: a young undergraduate pitching ideas to an 87-year-old icon.

In a letter to Ricœur of 15 July 1999, Macron excuses himself for sending handwritten notes due to a computer problem but goes on to elaborate his thoughts on how the philosopher's 'argumentation is based from the beginning on the idea of disassociating memory and imagination.'

The letter concludes with trademark self-effacement: 'Don't see in these reflections any sense of presumption: I am like the fascinated child who after leaving a concert or a great symphony bashes out a few notes on his piano. From reading your work and following your analysis, I had the desire, the enthusiasm to have a go.

'I don't know how to thank you for the faith that you have shown in accepting me as your first reader. And I don't know how to tell you of the happiness, the pleasure and the enthusiasm that our meetings inspire in me.'[12] The writing style – a mix of flattery, modesty and eagerness to play the young apprentice – gives a clue as to why so many older, influential or wealthy men have fallen for Macron, appearing to see in him a sort of ideal son.

The Socialist politician Julien Dray put it acidly when he called Macron '*un drageur des vieux*' – a seducer of old people.

Macron's period of philosophical musings at the feet of Paul Ricœur emerged as a subject of controversy during the election in 2017. Critics accused him of exaggerating his background as a way of giving himself an intellectual heft he had not merited.

Some of this he brought upon himself by name-checking the Marxist thinker Étienne Balibar, whose courses he followed for his philosophy masters, during an interview with the intellectual periodical *Le 1*. He also claimed to have started a thesis under Balibar's guidance.

Balibar, ideologically opposed to Macron's politics, responded by saying he had 'no memory of his work' and found 'this manipulation of his philosophy training which is organised by him or his associates to be absolutely obscene.'[13]

Others in France's self-regarding left-wing intellectual circles, still heavily influenced by Marxism, slapped down the presumptuous young upstart, taking particular issue with the way the media often described him as an 'assistant' to Ricœur rather than an 'editorial assistant'.

'Macron only performed documentation services or some archiving for him, but he's extracting a symbolic value for this which is completely exaggerated,' sniffed the left-wing philosopher Myriam Revault d'Allonnes.

He was 'neither an intellectual, nor a statesman, but a technocrat,' she said. The putdown was leavened only slightly by the acknowledgement that he was 'an intelligent and cultivated one.'

Macron is not a philosopher. Whether he is a 'philosopher-politician' as he was dubbed by *Le 1* is still the subject of a sterile debate that rages in French academic circles. What is undoubtedly true is that he was deeply influenced by his time with Ricœur, who broadened his horizons with ideas that, as we will see, have fresh and obvious resonance today.

'Paul Ricœur completely re-educated me in philosophy,' Macron told *Le 1* in one of several interviews given to the periodical, which was financed by one of Macron's friends, Henry Hermand. 'I either read or re-read the ancient philosophy. He had an exceptional vision of it due to the fact that he had studied and taught it for half a century.'

In his own book, Macron describes Ricœur as 'seeing his work as the constant reading of the major texts, he who compared himself so often to a dwarf on the shoulders of giants.'

This idea of Ricœur riding on the shoulders of previous generations chimed with how Macron saw himself: he had constantly sought relationships with his teachers from his early teens, he idolised his grandmother, and his girlfriend was 24 years older than him.

In Ferracci's explanation, Macron believes 'you go faster in life by relying on the experience of previous generations rather than trying to do yourself what has already been said or written before.' This comment by a close friend hints at the idea of him being a sponge, a great absorber of other people's ideas, able to repeat them back sometimes more convincingly than the originator.

The relationship with Ricœur was one of enduring mutual affection: Macron attended Ricœur's 90th birthday party at Goldenstein's house in the southern Parisian suburb of Sceaux, and paid visits to him at his holiday home in the western region of Brittany with Brigitte.

'It was a relationship that went beyond the generations,' says Goldenstein, an elegant, gentle woman with greying blonde hair and piercing blue eyes who speaks of the two men almost maternally. 'For Paul it was a real pleasure and for Emmanuel it was a moment of encouragement to be what he was.'

Ricœur's dense works are accessible to only the trained or highly determined reader, but there are identifiable themes running through his thinking – about man's ability to shape his own destiny, about politics, the search for compromise – that are fundamental to Macron's later approach to gaining power.

Ricœur would begin his analysis of any problem with an examination of the language he needed to use, to check for inconsistencies or misunderstandings. This belief in the 'power of the well-chosen word' is a recurrent concept found over and again in Macron's interviews and speeches.

The philosopher was also constantly in search of common ground between competing and sometimes contradictory schools of thought. Macron would later be mocked for his use of the phrase '*en même temps*' (at the same time), a verbal tic that his opponents initially seized on to attack him for his apparent incoherence or confused political positioning. It has since become a signature Macronism and the expression can no longer be used innocently, such is its association with the President. 'I refuse simplifications,' Macron said in an attempt to explain himself during an interview in March 2017. 'Our lives are always "at the same time", it's complex. I think that political action nowadays depends on your ability to appreciate the complexity of the world and not fall into a form of reductionism.'[14]

As a pacifist and witness to totalitarianism, Ricœur also venerated the power of individuals to shape the world around them. One of his books is titled *From Words to Action*. In the interpretation of his close friend Catherine Goldenstein, it is about 'this essential call to conviction: that the only solution to scepticism and to crisis is conviction. It's very striking in Emmanuel's case,' she says.

There are other echoes of Ricœur's words in Macron's actions, such as the importance of finding the 'right distance' in personal or power relationships – for example between a politician and his voters, or with the media; the importance of 'dissensus' in democracy: meaning that the airing of conflicting viewpoints is needed to find a shared direction; or the vital role politicians must play as educators as well as decision makers.

At the risk of vulgarising Ricœur's thought and in a comparison that would perhaps outrage his students and contemporaries, there's something in his protestant thinking that has echoes of American self-help books. In one of the most famous and best-selling of this prolific industry, *The Seven Habits of Highly Effective People*, author Stephen R. Covey recommends, among other things, that one should 'Be Proactive', 'Think win-win' and 'Seek first to understand, then to be understood.' It's possible to read Ricœur as a sort of life coach and political scientist as well as a philosopher.

One of the mysteries of Macron is the source of his seemingly bulletproof self-assurance and audacity, qualities that can tip into arrogance or narcissism. Did it form during his two years of being 're-educated' by the late French thinker?

Ricœur died in 2005 at the age of 92. At a ceremony to mark the centenary of his birth in 2013, Macron came to read a message on behalf of President Hollande at a Left-Bank amphitheatre in Paris packed with hundreds of admirers and family members.

'I remember that day. He [Macron] said to me "you know, it was Paul that gave me this confidence. I'll be grateful to him for my whole life",' said Goldenstein, who now guards Ricœur's archives and works for his foundation. 'It gave him an essential sense of personal recognition.'

In the small cast of characters who played an important role in Macron's first few decades, each had a specific role: his parents had passed on their work ethic; his grandmother her love of literature and classical music; Brigitte had taught him that anything was possible with sufficient willpower. While he had been lauded by teachers and professors since La Providence, it was Paul Ricœur who tested and validated his undoubted intelligence. In the process, the philosopher encouraged Macron to think more deeply about how politicians should act and exercise power.

CHAPTER 4

ENA –
Elite Networks Appear

MACRON'S EXPERIENCE WITH RICŒUR ALSO OPENED AN essential door into a new network of people, a separate sphere of contacts away from his friends at Sciences Po. Only Brigitte travelled between the two groups. By this stage, his contact with his old classmates from Amiens, like Renaud Dartevelle, was starting to fade.

Ricœur lived in Les Murs Blancs, a community of intellectuals housed in grand buildings set among parkland and trees in the suburb of Châtenay-Malabry, south of Paris. The homes were first acquired before the Second World War by Emmanuel Mounier, founder in 1932 of the intellectual periodical *Esprit*, in whose pages writers warned of the coming 'crisis of civilisation'. It was dedicated to exploring a 'third way' between liberalism and Marxism.

Having been occupied by the Nazis during the war, the buildings were restored by Mounier following France's liberation and the periodical moved its headquarters there. In the 1950s, Ricœur was invited by Mounier to move in, taking a large apartment with floor-to-ceiling windows which opened on to a terrace and the parkland outside.

Esprit continues to be published to this day and has a monthly circulation of around 8,000 copies, with articles on international affairs and politics as well as more weighty abstract fare.

From the 1950s, thinkers, politicians and financiers from the '*deuxième gauche*' (the so-called 'Second Left') started gravitating around it, sharing a belief that France needed to reduce the role of its all-powerful state while still tackling social injustice. Among them was Henry Hermand, a businessman and philanthropist who would make a fortune in supermarkets and commercial property. Another was Michel Rocard, who served as a reformist centre-left prime minister of France from 1988 to 1991.

Esprit's 'third way' mission statement naturally recalls the brand of centre-left politics – also known as social democracy – that was embraced by US President Bill Clinton, British Prime Minister Tony Blair and German Chancellor Gerhard Schröder in the 1990s.

But the creed – pro-business, yet conscious of the excesses of free markets and the need for state intervention – was never embraced by France's Socialists in the way it was in Clinton's Democratic Party, Blair's Labour, or Schröder's SPD. By and large, the history of the Second Left in France is one of frustration, of unfulfilled potential and time spent on the political margins.

Olivier Mongin, an intellectual with a shock of white curly hair and a deep forceful voice, remembers his first encounter with Macron in this rarefied but peripheral milieu in 1999.

'One day Ricœur invited us to his birthday party in the garden and there was this young man with blondish-brown, rather long hair who was called Emmanuel Macron,' he said from his apartment opposite the Louvre in central Paris. 'He was very discreet, very likeable. His partner was there too.'

At the time Mongin was the editorial director of *Esprit*. Shortly afterwards, he invited the shaggy-haired charmer he had met at the party to write something for the publication. Macron's first article *Historians and the Work of Memory* was published in the August 2000 edition, in which he mused on the difficulty for historians in establishing the truth based on the subjective and incomplete memories of witnesses to past events. Macron's willingness to engage with such complexities would later lead his political opponents to accuse him of failing to express himself clearly or equivocating. He wrote a total of six pieces for *Esprit* and became a member of the editorial board in 2009. He remains a shareholder to this day.

'He was a good team player. The friendship I have with him is linked to that,' Mongin says.

The time he spent with Ricœur had convinced Macron that his future lay in politics but he would not share this idea with his peers just yet. Brigitte would do her best to persuade him otherwise, to the bitter end, convinced that he was better suited to a career in the arts.

'From the beginning, I remember well, Emmanuel said to me that what interested him above all was politics,' Goldenstein recalls.

In his mind, the experience with Ricœur had also helped him rule out the possibility of going into academia. 'In working with Paul Ricœur, I had the time to think a lot about his life:

and I didn't want to have the same type of life as him,' he said in 2010.[1] 'These daily academic routines lacked a form of action, of participation in public life, of interaction with decision-makers.

'I realised one day that he had written all of his great works after the age of 60. I knew that I'd never be able to wait so long.'

Speaking to *Le 1*, Macron confirmed that it was Ricœur who had 'pushed me to go into politics because he hadn't done so himself.' Philosophy would remain important but secondary. 'It's a discipline that is worthless unless it is applied to real life. And real life is worthless without being able to go back to its foundations.'

Macron kept these revelations from his fellow students at Sciences Po, and even from friends like his classmate and drinking companion Aurélien Lechevallier. Though they would talk about current affairs and France's problems together, the depth of Macron's interest wasn't clear. In his highly compartmentalised life, Macron repeatedly used his older friends and acquaintances as mentors and muses, while keeping his intentions and political ambitions hidden from his peers.

'I discovered that politics was his passion somewhat accidentally, as if he didn't dare say it, whereas in fact he knew all about it in detail,' Lechevallier said, recalling a visit they had made to the National Assembly to see a friend doing an internship there. Macron knew all the names of the lawmakers, the heads of parliamentary groups, even arcane details about constituencies. 'He wouldn't acknowledge he had this passion, but he had it already,' Lechevallier said.

In fact, in 2000, at around the same time as Macron began moving in centre-left *deuxième gauche* circles, he also took his first steps into a very different political current. Macron worked for six months as an intern for Georges Sarre, the mayor of the 11th district of Paris who was a close friend of the senior Socialist figure Jean-Pierre Chevènement. Chevènement, a headstrong left-wing nationalist who had resigned three times from the cabinet on matters of principle since the 1980s, was a firm believer in the state's role in the directing of society and the economy. He was also against EU federalism and took a hard line on French identity, seeing assimilation as a necessary step for immigrants. In 2002, he ran unsuccessfully for president as the head of his own *Mouvement des Citoyens* (MDC, or Citizens' Movement) which attempted to bridge the left–right divide.

Macron voted for him, according to the book *L'Ambigu Monsieur Macron* ('The Ambiguous Mr Macron') by the journalist Marc Endeweld, which also claims that Macron took part in seminars and a summer camp organised by the movement. In a sign of Chevènement's appeal across party lines, the 35-year-old far-right strategist Florian Philippot, who in 2017 was one of Marine Le Pen's closest aides, was also a follower.

Macron's time with the MDC was significant for several reasons: it was his first experience of a political organisation which aimed to go beyond the traditional parties and it points to his enduring belief in the need for state activism. Chevènement's euroscepticism and conservative views on French culture, however, appear to have had little lasting impact on him.

Macron has been mistakenly described by opponents (and occasionally in the media) as a free-enterprise small-state liberal. He is not, as he explained to Endeweld. Some on the centre-left among his *deuxième gauche* friends had 'too much of a complex' about state intervention, he said. 'I've always been interested in the role of the state and that's the reason why I turned towards

Jean-Pierre Chevènement as a young man,' he added: 'There's no escaping discussions about the state in an era of globalisation.'

Macron would demonstrate this repeatedly as president, even briefly nationalising a strategic shipyard to retain the state's influence and arguing that strong governments were needed to tame free markets and global businesses.

For anyone with their eye on a career in politics in France, there is one institution that offers a fast track. The obvious choice for Macron after completing his studies at Sciences Po and Paris Nanterre was the École Nationale d'Administration (The National School of Administration, or ENA) in Strasbourg.

Loathed and admired by the public in equal measure, ENA was established in 1945 out of the chaos of post-war France with the laudable aim of creating a new corps of elite public servants to help rebuild the country. Re-staffing a state administration which in many areas had collaborated with the Nazi occupiers was a priority for the post-war government, most of them veterans of the anti-fascist Resistance movement. The institution, which is now housed in a former Revolution-era prison in the centre of Strasbourg in eastern France, was meant to provide young, highly-trained civil servants who would get to work reconstructing the country's shattered public infrastructure. Attracting students from diverse backgrounds was one of ENA's stated objectives.

The ENA model has since been copied by other nations as far afield as Russia and the Democratic Republic of Congo, but in France the initial admiration for its remarkably clever and capable graduates has faded. It has since become a symbol of elitism, discrimination and the ills of the French higher education system.

In addition to Macron, three former presidents have passed through its hallowed halls – Valéry Giscard d'Estaing, Jacques

Chirac and François Hollande – as well as countless ministers, top advisors, and the heads of France's multinationals. The school's graduates, known as *Énarques*, form a network of influence spread across government, finance and business, using links formed as students to advance their careers, and very often (as in the case of Macron, for example) their personal wealth.

Calls to scrap ENA date back to at least 1969 when the idea was raised in an official report, while François Bayrou, a veteran centrist, made breaking up the school a campaign pledge during his unsuccessful bid for the presidency in 2007, calling it 'a weakness of French society.'

As Macron would find out later, being admitted to ENA is both a one-way ticket to success and a stigmatising blemish in the eyes of many voters. While Oxford and Cambridge still produce a disproportionate number of British business and government leaders, and MIT or Harvard perform a similar role in the United States, few democracies do 'elite' in quite the same way as France.

The national education system is 'more like a funnel than an escalator,' the then director of ENA, Nathalie Loiseau, regretted in 2015 as the school celebrated its 70th anniversary.[2] The number of students is progressively narrowed down until only the best and the brightest brains remain in the country's '*Grandes Écoles*' – the elite state institutions – 'We are at the end of the funnel,' Loiseau explained.

As a result, if 'show me the boy at five and I'll show you the man' remains a useful rule of thumb for predicting a child's personality, being shown a French student in their twenties confers one with almost fail-safe powers when predicting their destiny. Top businesses and the senior bureaucracy and government continue to draw from a shallow and narrow pool of the best educated graduates.

Everyone else is playing in a rigged game of catch-up and their jealousy or resentment is understandable, part of a much larger picture of disaffection with France's ruling class. It is made worse by the revolving door between public service and highly-paid jobs in the private sector.

Former President Nicolas Sarkozy, who distinguished himself by not having come from ENA, nonetheless gave half of the positions in his team at the Élysée Palace after his election in 2007 to graduates of the school, according to a study by the CEVIPOF political institute at Sciences Po.

Their report, released in 2015, cited separate research showing that 70 per cent of ENA students from 2005 to 2014 had a father in a senior professional role: an imperfect but telling measure of the sociological background of the intake. This was up from 45 per cent in the 1950s and 1960s.

The now-famous year group of 1980 included François Hollande, his future partner and Socialist heavyweight Ségolène Royal, his finance minister Michel Sapin, the future prime minister Dominique de Villepin and two future chiefs of staff at the Élysée.

Given the fantastic prospects promised by admission to ENA, there are around 1,500 applications every year for the roughly 80 places on offer, with students assessed on their general culture as well as their grasp of politics, economics and international affairs. An emphasis on oral presentation favours those most comfortable with France's highly formal language codes, seen by critics as further reducing the chances of people from working class or ethnic minority backgrounds.

Macron, the keen amateur dramatist who had competed in oratory competitions, held all the cards as he prepared for the entrance exams to this bastion of white male privilege. He was also personally determined to make up for his past failure to enter the École Normale Supérieure.

'What was most important for him at the time was to get into ENA and finish among the top students,' Goldenstein recalled. Macron spent hours revising and discussing with Ferracci, often just the two of them. Entrance exams are a source of intense anxiety for French students, given the competition, the quantity of work and the life-changing stakes. The tears, breakdowns and exhaustion that result are well documented. 'We'd work from 8am to 10pm, sometimes at night too,' Ferracci remembers.

Macron passed the entrance exams, as did Lechevallier, but Ferracci failed and would take a different route, into academia. To comfort him, Macron presented him with a book of poems by the Resistance-era poet René Char with a hand-written note of encouragement.

Some of the first *Énarques* Macron met became his close and lasting friends, like Gaspard Gantzer who would become Hollande's spokesman in 2014. The two hit it off when they met at the physical assessment. Most of the academically brilliant applicants had no interest in sport, turning up in shirts and moccasins, but Macron and Gantzer were keen footballers.

'I was left back, not the most technically gifted,' Macron told *Radio France Bleu* of the student teams he played in.[3] 'The sort who's a bit dirty and quite shouty.' Through fair means or foul, it was early practice in stopping right-wingers. He gave up playing football when he hit 30 but continues to follow Olympique de Marseille, his club since childhood, and he remembers fondly the dribbling skills of the British international Chris Waddle who played for them in the early 1990s.

Although he has given up football, he continues to play tennis, practising against former French professional Patrice Kuchna – 'I let nothing go. I fight every point,' Macron says – and he is a keen fan of the Tour de France, trying when he can to watch a stage in person.

The world's most prestigious cycle race, which ends with the finishing line on the Champs Élysées, is like an election campaign, Macron argued mid-way through his own efforts. 'Geographically you enter into the heart of the country and there are lots of changes in rhythm. No one week resembles another, there are weeks of mountains, weeks of false-flat with the wind from the side, different climates.'[4] But politics nowadays was more comparable to the post-war cycling period, when riders changed their own wheels and sometimes needed to stay at people's homes on the roadside, he added.

Renaud Dorandeu, the deputy director of studies at ENA during Macron's time there and now a politics professor at a university in Paris, remembers him as 'a brilliant student, which was obvious from all of his results' but said he was not among the strongest characters in a year group packed with big personalities.

The 2002–4 intake made waves by rebelling against Dorandeu and his colleagues, denouncing the management in a report signed by every student which was submitted at their graduation ceremony. It called out the 'intellectual vacuity of the teaching' and the 'carelessness of the schooling' as well as the apparent bias towards students who had past family links to ENA. Complaints like these were commonplace from students, but Dorandeu remembers Macron's year as bringing 'a desire for change in the teaching methods of the school that was more thought-through and forceful than in previous years.'

'The teaching all seemed completely out of whack with the need for reforms of the country and the state,' Fabrice Casadebaig, one of several student representatives who had been behind the rebellion, said over coffee near the Palais Royal park in central Paris.

The cleanly-shaven bureaucrat, an image of smart authority in a blue trench coat, said that Macron had participated but that he was not a leader of the insurrection. 'He was someone you saw who was open, nice; he'd talk with everyone, but was quite discreet too. He wasn't at the forefront of things particularly,' he said.

Macron's first year at ENA was spent out of Strasbourg doing work placements. First of all, he headed to Nigeria for the obligatory foreign posting, having chosen West Africa instead of the more obvious places like Brussels or Washington. His first and only stint working abroad was mostly spent in the purpose-built capital Abuja, under the guidance of France's veteran ambassador Jean-Marc Simon.

'This young man arrived, very elegant, classic in a grey suit, very courteous and likeable,' recollected Simon, now retired and back in France after a career that took him to Gabon, the Ivory Coast and the Central African Republic.

'I remember my wife asking him at some point if he had a girlfriend and he replied "yes and she's the same age as you",' Simon chuckled over the phone. 'It was intriguing.'

The two men played tennis together – Macron 'sometimes being kind enough to let me win' – and sat stunned as they watched the results of France's 2002 presidential election on a television at the embassy in April. The far-right leader Jean-Marie Le Pen scored around 17 per cent in the first round and made it through to a runoff vote against the ultimate victor Jacques Chirac, at the expense of the Socialist candidate Lionel Jospin.

But as the country struggled to come to terms with the biggest breakthrough of the far-right since the war, Macron was soon off to have what must have been one of his most wrenching personal experiences.

On 4 May 2002, a plane operated by Nigeria's EAS Airlines nosedived into a heavily populated suburb of the city of Kano shortly after takeoff, killing all but five of the 79 people on board and scores of others in the poor neighbourhood of ramshackle homes built near the airport. A total of 148 people died in the catastrophe – one of the worst disasters for the accident-prone Nigerian aviation sector. Among them were two young French aid workers.

The mangled corpses were taken to three ill-equipped hospital morgues in the dusty and hot city in the north of the country. Two days later, after flying in on the plane of Nigerian President Olusegun Obasanjo who had cut short a regional tour to visit the scene, Simon and Macron got to work.

'We looked through the bodies on the floor for people who might look like our compatriots,' Simon says, recalling the smell of decomposition. 'The air-conditioning wasn't working very well, you can imagine the scene. It was hard, very hard. But he [Macron] did the work with great courage and willingness.

'Our profession isn't only about doing diplomacy. It's sometimes ground work, and sometimes not the nicest of sorts,' he added.

Macron would later recall his six months in Nigeria as an

experience that had toughened him up. One of the embassy's drivers was also shot during his time there. 'It was a hard environment,' said Macron's old friend Marc Ferracci. Shortly after the plane crash Macron completed his internship and bid goodbye to Simon, receiving ten out of ten in his assessment.

'I used to say that I could do without all my colleagues – the first secretary, the receptionist, the driver, the accountant – and keep just one of them: Mr Macron, who would be able to do all the work of the others on his own,' Simon laughed. 'But I'd add that just because he was an excellent intern doesn't mean he'll be an excellent president.'

After returning to France in the summer, Macron headed for his second posting in the local government in the Oise region between Paris and Amiens for six months, where he helped work on plans to develop the local Beauvais airport, which is used by low-cost flyer Ryanair. He received another ten out of ten in his assessment, but his experience there was more notable for his meeting with Henry Hermand, the *deuxième gauche* financier and kingmaker. Hermand was the first but by no means the last billionaire to fall under Macron's spell over lunch.

When Hermand learned that Macron had worked with Paul Ricœur, the two men immediately hit it off. The property developer, then aged 78, was impressed by Macron's intellect and charm. Years of dinners together, as well as holidays in Morocco would follow, and Hermand took to calling him his 'young spiritual son', making no secret of his ambition for Macron (he had failed in a previous attempt to turn former prime minister Michel Rocard into a president).

'I never leave him,' Hermand told *Le Figaro* newspaper in 2016. Before his death in November of the same year, a few weeks before Macron launched his presidential run, he told *Le Monde* that 'Emmanuel has never taken an important decision without speaking to me.'

Their coming together was a critical building block in Macron's career. He already had access to Parisian intellectual circles through Ricœur, Mongin and *Esprit*. He also had the secure emotional foundation provided by Brigitte. 'Unlike the majority of brilliant people his age, he didn't end up accumulating lots of girlfriends. That played an important role in his work,' Hermand said.[5]

The businessman would provide money – a loan of half a million euros for Macron's first apartment in 2007 – and access to a vast network which included Rocard. 'Come to Paris, I'll introduce you to people,' his wife remembers him saying to Macron after the first meeting in the Oise.[6] Macron had a €100,000 loan repayment to Hermand still outstanding in 2017 and another due in 2022, according to a public declaration he made of his assets.[7] Having spent his life bankrolling centre-left think-tanks and media groups, Hermand's death at the age of 92 before the presidential election meant he would never see his most successful personal investment come to fruition.

'He had a sort of tenderness for Emmanuel Macron which was obvious, although he was a hard man and was tough on his own sons,' said Pierre Person, who chatted regularly with Hermand in the final years of his life and later joined Macron's presidential campaign team.

Returning to ENA, Macron balanced his studying with time at a theatre group, football and the odd night out with friends drinking beer or singing in a local karaoke club called *Bunny's Bar*. His repertoire was mostly old classics from his parents' or grandparents' generation – *chansonniers* like Jacques Brel, Stone et Charden or Johnny Hallyday. 'Emmanuel is a king of karaoke,' one of his friends at the time, Mathias Vicherat said.[8] Vicherat, having worked as a top aide to Paris' Socialist mayor Anne Hidalgo, now sits on the board of the state railways group SNCF at the age of 38.

Student buddy Aurélien Lechevallier says he never heard much about Macron's new friendship with Hermand or the networking he was throwing himself into. 'He never talked about him much,' he said. 'I just knew they saw each other sometimes when Emmanuel was travelling between Strasbourg and Paris.'

Macron was also away many weekends seeing Brigitte, meaning that his life was as busy and itinerant as ever. Packing in so much was possible partly because he could survive on only four to five hours of sleep a night, giving him a useful edge over other students. Friends and fellow politicians still marvel at how he is capable of staying up into the early hours socialising or working, only to rise fresh-faced at the crack of dawn.

Macron finished fifth in his year. The final rankings are an ENA tradition, with the highest finishers given the choice of the most prestigious jobs in the civil service.

Among the top students, the year leader Marguerite Bérard, daughter of an *Énarque*, went on to become an advisor to Sarkozy and then chief of staff at the labour ministry. She is now on the board of one of France's largest banks, BPCE. Another top finisher, Sébastien Proto, also joined Sarkozy's presidential team, became a ministerial chief of staff and is now a senior banker at Rothschild in France. Among Macron's friends from ENA, Sébastien Veil, the grandson of the late pioneering feminist minister and Holocaust survivor Simone Veil, is a director at a private equity fund. Boris Vallaud, who married the Socialist education minister Najat Vallaud-Belkacem, became an advisor to Hollande and was elected to parliament in 2017 for the Socialists. Macron's year boasts so many illustrious stories that they are frequently compared to ENA's famous intake of 1980 which included President Hollande.

Macron has been repeatedly pushed to defend his time there.

'Before ENA, what was it? It was recruitment through crony-ism, a competition in good manners, or because you had a parent or cousin who was already in public service,' he said in January 2017, referring to the dominance of wealthy upper-class families in the pre-war civil service. 'I prefer the Republic's exams, they're meritocratic.'[9]

He acknowledged that the selection process served as an unfair social filter for entrants, but insisted that the institution was the wrong target. 'The real scandal isn't ENA. The scandal is that there are fewer children whose parents are farmers or work-ers who arrive at ENA [compared with 30 years ago],' he added. 'That's what I want to fight against.'

Dorandeu, the former ENA professor, also believes that 'we have been very unfair to this school', pointing out that it has educated more than 6,000 French students and 3,000 foreigners in its 70 years of existence, most of whom went on to careers in obscurity.

With his final position in the top five of his year, Macron had the luxury of taking his pick among available positions at the most prestigious state bodies, opting for the *Inspection Générale des Finances*, a powerful corps of civil servants tasked with auditing and analysing the state bureaucracy. 'I chose the inspectorate because it was the most alien to what I was – I wanted to be involved in the decision-making process on a political-administrative level,' he told the Sciences Po student magazine in 2010.[10] 'I always make choices in life this way, in a contrarian way, in the belief that I'll learn more by turning over new ground.'

It was also, as he would have known, the most direct route to power. ENA-*Inspection* alumni included ex-president Giscard d'Estaing, former European Central Bank governor Jean-Claude Trichet, ex-prime minister Alain Juppé, Rocard, and the chairman of the insurance giant AXA, Henri de Castries. When Macron joined, it was headed by Jean-Pierre Jouyet, an old ENA chum of Hollande and husband of an heiress to the Taittinger champagne fortune.

'The French state has various bodies inside it. It's like a troop of macaques, ordered in terms of strength,' says veteran sociologist Hervé Le Bras, who has known Macron for years. 'Those below must obey those slightly ahead of them. There's a type of hierarchy which functions like that.'

Arriving at the inspectorate, Macron joined as a powerful macaque at the top of the tree. Using a different metaphor, a colleague of his at the time called the *Inspection*, only half-jokingly, 'the mafia within the state mafia', pointing out how its members stayed in touch and helped each other throughout their careers.

Macron made an immediate impression on Jouyet, whose political views were similarly centre-left. And, as was customary for young inspectors, he paid a courtesy visit to another celebrity member of this elite caste, the former ENA-*Inspection* graduate Alain Minc.

Both were members of the ultra-exclusive and secretive Parisian club *Le Siècle*, which brings together the wealthy and influential power set across politics, business and the media once a month for dinners at a private club. A kind of French version of the Bilderberg Group, it can be joined by invitation only and keeps its membership private (although a guest list leaked online in 2011).

Minc, a small wiry man now aged 68, has spent decades working on the edge of French business and government: at once political advisor, consultant and HR manager, always ready to recommend a talent, grease a business deal or advise on policy. He is also a writer and historian, with one of the deepest contacts books in Paris. The reception room of his office on Avenue George V, a short walk from the Princess Diana memorial, is decorated in hues of purple and grey. Entering it is like walking into a Rothko painting.

'I always ask when I see these young folks "where do you see yourself in 30 years?",' Minc said, sitting in the lounge area of his large office with its impeccable mid-century furnishings and modern art. 'And [Macron] answered me "I'll be president".'

Minc was taken aback. 'I've only had a reply like that twice,' he said, the other being from the *Énarque* and successful banker Matthieu Pigasse, who is now focused on building up a portfolio of investments that include *Le Monde* newspaper and several music labels.

For Macron, the comment seems out of character. He had otherwise demonstrated extreme caution in showing his political ambitions and had relied on modesty and good humour to win over his mentors. Had he allowed the mask to slip, or was this a deliberate attempt to grab Minc's attention, knowing his influence and ability to open a door by placing a call when needed?

'I found him unusually interesting,' Minc explained. The two men still chat regularly. 'I've followed him a lot in his career,' he added.

Like the provincial social climbers that so fascinated him in novels by Stendhal and Balzac, who gained access to high society through a mixture of charm, manipulation and the co-opting of sympathetic aristocrats, Macron had a rare skill for identifying and winning over modern-day gatekeepers. Minc was one of his early benefactors.

CHAPTER 5

Marriage and Machinations

WHEN MACRON LEFT FOR HIS PLACEMENT IN NIGERIA IN January 2002, for what would be the longest time that he and Brigitte would ever be separated, she offered him a ring with three intertwined bands of silver which he stills wears on his right hand. It signalled their engagement. After years of enduring resistance from their families, their life together was now established.

The role of Macron's adored grandmother Manette had been crucial to the couple, with her initially being less opposed than Macron's parents to their alliance and then offering her endorsement. 'It didn't happen immediately. Initially, she took it badly and then it went quickly,' Macron recalls.[1]

'Nothing would have been possible without her blessing,' admits Brigitte.[2]

Throughout his student years, Macron made no secret of his unusual romance, presenting Brigitte to his close friends while enduring gossip and innuendo behind his back from others.

With his first salaries arriving as an *Inspecteur* and with Brigitte's divorce finally concluded in 2006, Macron began pushing for them to get married, for the 'official consecration of a love that was at first clandestine and often hidden, misunderstood by many, before finally imposing itself on them.'[3]

The Macrons have fascinated both France's celebrity press and the public since they first emerged as a couple on the public stage. Long gone are the days when the French media considered reporting on a politician's private life to be in poor taste – famously enabling ex-president François Mitterrand to keep a mistress and child housed in a government apartment away from public view.

The editors of *Closer* magazine, *Gala* or *VSD* had plenty to feast on under the previous two presidencies. Sarkozy campaigned and won in 2007 alongside his second wife Cécilia, who appeared on the trail intermittently, when she was required to project an image of family unity. At her husband's victory party in May at the Place de La Concorde, she joined him and supporters on stage, doing a poor job at hiding her evident discomfort: less than six months later they were divorced. In February the following year, Sarkozy married the model and singer-songwriter Carla Bruni in a gift to tabloid newspapers worldwide.

In the same election year, François Hollande was putting on a brave face like Cécilia Sarkozy, alongside his long-time partner Ségolène Royal, who was the Socialist Party candidate. Behind the scenes, Hollande and Royal were no longer together. Hollande had even started a new relationship with a political journalist from *Paris Match*, Valérie Trierweiler.

When he was elected in 2012, Hollande took office with Trierweiler at his side, but two years later he was caught cheating on her with the actress Julie Gayet. In one of many memorable low-points of his presidency, *Closer* published pictures of him partly hidden behind a helmet riding pillion on a scooter, being driven to their love nest by a security officer.

As they followed their presidents' love lives in the media, many French voters felt embarrassed and duped, seeing the dishonesty and undisguised libido as further debasement of the presidential office. But others were fascinated, and the media got a taste for intruding further than ever before into politicians' lives.

In France, the public reaction to the Macrons went from 'what?!' to 'how?' and then 'is it real?' On the latter question, dozens of interviews with friends, family members from both sides and associates bear witness to an unusual but loving marriage. The Macrons' chemistry together in public and their frequent gestures of affection, strikes everyone who has spent time with them as genuine. During his campaign speeches, Macron could often be seen making eye-contact with Brigitte in the crowd and she was a constant presence around his headquarters.

Nonetheless, some still find this unconventional relationship too hard to believe in, leading to the persistent rumours that Macron is gay, bisexual or even asexual. It's a key part of the difficulty people have in grasping a complex and unusual character who seems to delight in defying easy classification. 'He's a bit male, a bit female ... androgynous,' ex-president Sarkozy said in 2016 at the start of a campaign in comments designed to discredit him.

These suggestions amount to a refusal to believe that a handsome, successful young man could be physically satisfied with a woman 24 years older than him. The relationship challenges our common understanding of male sexuality. Donald Trump, ageing male Hollywood actors and a host of France's glitterati have younger wives separated by the same age gap, or more, and barely anyone raises an eyebrow. It seems to be an obvious double standard.

But there is another double standard from which the Macrons undoubtedly benefit: if their roles had been reversed, with Macron the teacher and Brigitte an infatuated schoolgirl, he would be considered a predatory creep or borderline paedophile.

'There are some things you can't explain. It's about someone aged sixteen or seventeen who falls in love with his teacher and then has the kind of character which means he follows his logic through to the very end,' says long-time friend Ferracci, who was a witness at their wedding.

'It's an extremely intense relationship because it began as the coming together of two minds: through their relationship to literature and their writing of the play together,' he said. 'It's complementary. Brigitte is a bit more exuberant, extroverted, whereas Emmanuel is more controlled. They're good foils for each other.'

Others describe being struck by the difference in age at first encounter, but then quickly forgetting about it because of how natural and attuned the couple appear. 'Brigitte is very likeable, smiley: like Emmanuel in that way,' says Catherine Goldenstein, who first met them over dinner when Macron was working with Paul Ricœur. She remembers him announcing with an air of amusement that one of Brigitte's daughters had given birth. 'I'm a grandfather!' he said.

Olivier Mongin, the philosopher and former editor of *Esprit* who has been in regular contact with Macron since his early twenties, describes Brigitte in terms that again suggest a mixture of wife, mother and coach. 'She has a very positive role. He's so political, so quick, so nervy, but he's supported by someone who channels him,' he explained.

Listening to Brigitte talking about her husband, it's still possible to catch a sense of her admiration for the star pupil he once was, the 'Mozart' she worked with when he was sixteen years old. 'My husband, a workaholic, is a knight, someone from another planet who mixes a rare intelligence with exceptional humanity. Everything is in the right place in his head. He's a philosopher, an actor who became a banker and a politician, a writer who has still never published anything,' she has said.[4]

Macron clearly sees his relationship with his wife as a testament to the triumph of their willpower, under the always curious and often critical gaze of others. 'We needed to battle to have it accepted, to deal with the difficulties and build a life that looks nothing like anyone else's,' he said.[5]

An account of a wedding in the book *Les Macron* provides an insight into the difficulties of being a taboo breaker, particularly in conventional French society.

In 2006, the couple attended the marriage of Macron's friend Sébastien Veil: a wealthy former fellow-student at ENA of impeccable manners and pedigree. At the reception at a château among the gentle hills of the Burgundy wine-growing region, Macron arrived with Brigitte on his arm: him in a suit, her in a short white dress and with her trademark blonde highlights.

In front of them was a crowd of young Parisians, immaculately turned out, as beautiful as they were haughty. One man standing in a group asked 'who's this not very classy fifty-something on Emmanuel's arm?' Another confessed to the authors that she 'had a slightly trashy look'.

As well as their age difference, Brigitte is identifiably not from the same background as Macron's Paris friends and contacts. With her dyed hair, love for flashy sunglasses and taste for not-so-subtle designer clothes, there is still something un-Parisian about her even now. Old-money Parisians and their imitators value under-stated style, preferably rendered in muted natural tones. For them, beauty and fashion should be carried off effortlessly, while wealth is to be displayed with discernment, not flamboyance. Brigitte might be from a bourgeois family in Amiens, but she's a bit too brash, too direct to ever be mistaken for a product of the capital's elite social classes. 'She doesn't respect the codes of high Parisian society, that's obvious,' said the editor of *Paris Match* magazine Olivier Royant. That may also explain her enduring popularity.

The Macrons' wedding was organised the year after Veil's in 2007 in Le Touquet, one of the most exclusive seaside resorts on the Channel coast, 50 kilometres from the port of Calais. The town was founded on a large sandy stretch of beach in the early 1900s, attracting wealthy families from Amiens, Paris and Britain who could relax among fellow socialites, gamble and promenade at their leisure. The Trogneux chocolate magnates have owned one of the many large four-storey villas in the centre of the town for generations, worth €1.4 million at current prices, which Brigitte herself inherited.

Once he had convinced Brigitte of his intentions, Macron broached the subject of marriage with her three children, whom he'd known since their time at school together. Brigitte's son, a media-shy statistician called Sebastien, is three years older than him. Her eldest daughter Laurence was in his year at school, while the youngest Tiphaine, a lawyer, is six years his junior. 'He came to see us and told us that he wanted to marry our mother,' Tiphaine explained.[6] 'It was a moving gesture. Not everyone would have taken his precaution to come to ask for her hand. He wanted to know if we would accept it.'

The couple chose Le Touquet for the ceremony, undeterred by the fact that Brigitte's first nuptials had taken place there in 1974, coincidentally in the same year that Macron's parents were married. For her second marriage, she wore heels and white again, and a dress with a cape that dropped to the level of her very short hemline. The ceremony was at the town hall and the reception was held afterwards at the imposing Westminster Hotel, whose name recalls the town's heyday in the 1920s when Britons would take the short trip across the Channel to come and play the casinos, which were banned at home at the time. In its architecture and pubs, Le Touquet still retains an obvious British influence.

As witnesses, Macron chose Ferracci, as well as the billionaire property developer Henry Hermand, who would become so close that Macron supposedly never took an important decision without speaking to him first. Ferracci and Hermand sat together close to the couple. The guest list also included ex-prime minister Rocard, as well as Macron's friends from ENA and Sciences Po and relations from both families, including Emmanuel's grandmother Manette. Macron's parents were there, but were now divorced. His father had remarried and had another child by then, giving Macron a half-brother who was a teenage schoolboy at the time of his election.

During the speeches over dinner, Ferracci delivered a moving tribute to Macron and to the newly-married couple's love story, which opened with a dig about his old friend's eccentric student hair-do which on first impression suggested he was a 'Czech student on a university exchange.'

With the guests rapt with attention, Macron rose to speak in his dark suit and pink tie. Despite the weight of the occasion, his voice stayed strong and clear, his emotions controlled, a smile on his face as he reflected from the height of his 29 years on a decade and a half of knowing Brigitte.

'We're very happy that you're here to be with us at this moment,' he began. 'All of you here have been witness to what we have lived through for the last fifteen years and you've made us what we are, something not entirely common, a not entirely "normal" couple, even though I don't like this adjective, but nonetheless a couple which exists.

'It's thanks to you. I wanted to thank you – for accepting us, for loving us for what we are – in particular Brigitte's children because if there's anyone for whom it might not have been easy, it's them. It [our marriage] became, thanks to them, sort of obvious.'[7] There was a roar of cheers and applause. 'Bravo!' 'More!' shouted guests. The couple took to the dance floor for a waltz.

Writing much later about his relationship of more than two decades (and marriage of ten years), Macron considers that it was Brigitte who displayed the 'real courage', not him, the amorous schoolboy.

'She had three children and a husband. I was just a pupil and nothing more. She didn't love me for what I had, for my situation, for the comfort or security that I brought. She walked away from all that,' he wrote.[8]

The couple still have their holiday home in Le Touquet, known as *Monejan*, which was renovated extensively in 2011. Its central location on a narrow busy shopping street is far from ideal given their public profile now and the heavy security that surrounds them at all times. But the town remains an important retreat from the Parisian political bubble, somewhere to recharge, to admire the constantly-changing light and the wide open skies. They both enjoy long walks in the dunes along the blustery coastline from where Napoleon once viewed the distant cliffs of the British coast and contemplated an invasion.

Over the course of the wedding weekend, as well as discussing matters of the heart, Macron also found time to talk about politics with his firmly established mentors, Rocard and Hermand. After his experimentation with Chevènement's MDC in the early 2000s, he had taken out what would be a very brief membership of the Socialist Party and had tried to stand in the 2007 parliamentary elections as a candidate for the region surrounding Le Touquet.

Rocard had spoken to some of his contacts in the local Socialist network about the chances of parachuting in his young apprentice. Macron later claimed he had done 'a lot of local politics' in the region. An exaggeration, according to the 2015 book *L'Ambigu Monsieur Macron*.

Macron's overtures were rebuffed and Rocard, the centre-left moderniser, was given a brutal lesson about his weight in the party. 'Among Socialists, my name is still suspect. I annoyed them for too long,' he admitted.[9] From that moment he decided to become a mere 'observer' of Macron's career, a supportive friend in the background.

It was another important junction in the future president's life, an instant when his political trajectory might have changed. What would have happened had he been offered a berth by the Socialists? There's no guarantee he would have won, given that he was unknown locally and perceived as an outsider. On top of this, Le Touquet voted overwhelmingly for right-wing candidates in 2007.

But it would have brought Macron inside the tent, perhaps instilling in him a sense of loyalty and affiliation to the Socialist

Party machine. Some of his allies think that would have been the case, but there are nonetheless reasons to be sceptical: Macron has proved over and again to be loyal only to his own ideas, and in any case, he would wreak his revenge, and serve it ice-cold, ten years later when he virtually destroyed the entire party.

2007 would be a year of decisive change in Macron's life, a sudden acceleration in his personal and professional development. As well as getting married, he also bought his first apartment in the 15th district of Paris and moved in with Brigitte for the first time. She moved to the capital from Amiens to take up a job at the private Lycée Saint-Louis de Gonzague (the 'Franklin' school) in western Paris, which educates the children of diplomats, senior civil servants and business people.

It was also the year Sarkozy was victorious in the French presidential election, which led to unexpected opportunities. Firstly, the newly elected right-wing president named Macron's boss Jean-Pierre Jouyet as minister for European affairs, and Jouyet chose the number two in the *Inspection des Finances*, Pierre Cunéo, as his chief of staff. The abrupt high-profile departures suddenly led Macron to be named interim head of the powerful service, aged just 29.

Then in August, President Sarkozy called upon the econ-omist, sage and political advisor Jacques Attali to head a cross-party panel called the 'Commission to Liberate French Growth', one of the headline announcements of the opening part of his mandate.

Sarkozy, then 52, wanted 'practical and pragmatic solu-tions to get things moving' and he set a six-month deadline for the panel to deliver results. 'Today the situation is fairly easy to describe: we must increase our potential for economic growth by one point, to return to full employment and safeguard our social model,' Sarkozy said.

The world economy was enjoying a historic boom, having recovered from the dot-com crash of 2001, and was being led upwards by the United States and emerging markets in China, India and Latin America. France's economy, by contrast, had grown by a rather lacklustre 1.7 per cent annually on average since 2000 even though the government had run large public deficits throughout the period.

Attali, another ENA graduate and *Le Siècle* member, insisted on being able to pick his own assistants and set about looking for bright young bureaucrats to help. Thanks to his prior work as an *Inspector* – auditing French tax services, social housing policies and the effects of competition policy – and having been named interim head of the service, Macron had by this stage forged a stellar reputation both inside the civil service and in left-wing intellectual circles. He had been doing work in his free time for the Jean-Jaurès Foundation, a Socialist Party-affiliated think-tank, producing a report for them on globalisation and inequalities which saw him travel to Chile. 'He already had an aura around him, there was a sense of "watch out he's someone exceptional",' remembered Gilles Finchelstein, the boss of the Foundation, in an interview.

Jouyet eagerly recommended Macron for the Commission to Liberate French Growth. 'He seduced me immediately,' Attali told *Paris Match*.

Attali's intellect ('I don't need a computer, I've got Attali,' President Mitterrand once said) is matched by his ego and he has stated in the past that he 'discovered' and 'made' Macron. Although he has since backtracked slightly, he's one of many people with a claim on the current president's political paternity. Jouyet, Rocard, Hermand, Minc and latterly Hollande all fathered him to different extents.

The commission chairman did, though, tip Macron early on as having the qualities to become president, as well as predicting that the 2017 election would be won by someone previously unknown to the French people. In a recent book, he also warned about the risk of a Third World War between 2025 and 2035. Fortunately like all futurologists, his record with predictions is mixed ...

Attali's panel was an extraordinary opening for Macron. Its more than 40 members featured the bosses of major companies like Nestlé, AXA and the global consultancy group Accenture, bankers, top lawyers, think-tankers and writers, as well as one or two trade union representatives. Luminaries from all sections of society attended its more than 400 hearings.

'Attali put very right-wing people and left-wing people together,' remembered Hervé Le Bras, the sociologist, who was named as a member. The spectrum went from businessmen like Nestlé boss Peter Brabeck – 'no softie', as Le Bras remembers – to a strong centre-left contingent and a small minority of leftists.

'The measures all needed to be adopted unanimously, and there were two people who built that consensus: Macron and Orsenna,' Le Bras said, referring to the writer Érik Orsenna who became a friend and political supporter. 'I think he [Macron] perhaps understood that even if a right and a left existed in politics, there was a way to get them to co-exist together. He knew how to do it and that's where he experimented with the idea.'

It was also something akin to speed-dating for Macron. One by one, in the course of meetings, titans of industry and slick no-nonsense moneymen fell under the charm of the energetic *rapporteur*, who was always ready with a quick joke to lighten the atmosphere or a tweak to the language to gather support. 'At the beginning no one knew Emmanuel Macron, but very quickly he became central to the endeavour,' said top Paris financier Serge Weinberg, another graduate of ENA and former political advisor who was on the panel.[10]

After five months, Attali delivered his findings in a report entitled '300 Proposals to Change France.' No-one could accuse him of lacking ambition as he handed it over to President Sarkozy and half a dozen ministers. 'We believe these measures need to be implemented quickly, and we believe there is a limited window of opportunity to do so,' Attali said.

Together the proposals would slash unemployment from 7.9 to 5 per cent, create 2 million new jobs and cut French public debt from 66 to 55 per cent of gross domestic product. They included recommendations to deregulate protected sectors such as pharmacies, legal services and the taxi business, and to restructure local government. Funds for life-time learning were proposed to help re-train adult workers. They recommended an easing of immigration rules to attract foreign talent, as well as reforms to pensions and cuts in charges for companies, compensated for by an increase in sales tax.

On the whole, they were pro-growth and pro-innovation, aiming to produce a leaner, more business-friendly France. Some were also politically toxic for Sarkozy, notably the recommendation to ease immigration rules, while the proposals to slash public spending and to reform the civil service were anathema for the left.

In retrospect, the report's optimism about the world economy and the debt-fuelled Western consumer boom was naïve, but at the time there were far worse culprits than Attali and his colleagues in governments around the world, above all the then US Federal Reserve chairman Alan Greenspan.

'If political, economic, commercial, environmental, financial and social governance is organised properly, global growth will be maintained above 5 per cent per year consistently,' the report said. Less than one year later, the global financial crisis provoked a worldwide recession.

Addressing the findings of the report, Sarkozy replied that 'some may find your proposals frightening, I find them basically quite reasonable ... Our country needs an intensive course of modernisation.' He added: 'By seeking to regulate everything in the smallest details, we have created a straitjacket that prevents growth.'

As president, Sarkozy adopted some of the recommendations, such as a hard-fought pension reform that he passed in the face of mass street protests in 2010, while others like the immigration, local government or deregulation proposals would go largely unheeded.

Sarkozy's presidency, built around his promise of a 'break' from France's underperforming past and the halving of the unemployment rate, was upended by the financial crisis that unfurled after the bankruptcy of Lehman Brothers in September 2008. Now his time and energy was consumed by helping to save the eurozone from a banking and public debt crisis, but he reacted by recasting himself as a protector of the French from dreaded free-market capitalism.

Having started his term in office flaunting his connections to the rich and powerful and as an open admirer of American-style capitalism, Sarkozy now led the fight against bankers' bonuses and declared that 'the idea that markets are always right was a mad idea.'

'Laissez-faire is finished,' he announced in a speech in the southern port of Toulon. Attali's 300 recommendations seemed to have come from a different era, but many of them would be given a second life ten years later when they re-appeared in Macron's election manifesto.

CHAPTER 6

The Banker

'YOU'LL HAVE NOTICED HOW BRILLIANT MY FEELING FOR
an opportunity is by my having become an investment banker on
1 September 2008, ten days before the fall of Lehman Brothers
– which shows a real sense of timing,' Macron recalled. 'Being
an investment banker after Lehman is not really the same thing
as before.'[1]

'It's a profession where you're not master of your own time,
where you need to be prepared to work a lot for something that
might not happen. All the same, bankers make a lot of money …
I don't fetishise money but at the same time I do not have a
hypocritical relationship with it. I don't consider earning it to
be scandalous.'

After his experience on the Attali Commission, Macron had
access to a gold-plated network and numerous job opportunities.
Many of the businessmen who had served on the panel would
gladly have recruited him. He was also approached by members
of Sarkozy's new right-wing government, who were hunting for
talented civil servants to serve in ministerial cabinets.

A few months before Macron took up a job at the French bank Rothschild & Cie, Julien Aubert, an ENA peer who was among the most politically ambitious of the year group, had lunch with him. 'I asked him if he was going to join a cabinet under Sarko and he replied "no, no way",' said Aubert, who won a parliamentary seat in 2012 for the right-wing UMP party.[2] Aubert felt that Macron's decision to snub the then-government revealed his political identity: 'It was the first time I realised he was from the left,' he said.

Prime Minister François Fillon was among the politicians interested in Macron at this time. Taking a government job at this stage would have been the classic next step for many ENA graduates: senior experience in a cabinet which is then leveraged for a high-paying job in finance.

'I suggested to him, and I wasn't the only one, that if he wanted to go into politics he should go into banking, because it's better to have made yourself some money before going into public life,' Alain Minc, the consultant, remembered. Serge Weinberg, the financier and influential businessman from the Attali Commission, had similar advice for Macron. They and others suggested Rothschild.

'Above all, at Rothschild you can still be involved in politics, it's a very open workplace,' Minc explained.

The House of Rothschild, as it was dubbed in the 1934 Hollywood movie of the same name about the family, has become synonymous with international wealth and finance. It traces its roots back to five remarkable Jewish brothers who left the ghetto in Frankfurt in the early 1800s to start banks across Europe.

The French arm of the Rothschild banking dynasty, founded by James and now headed by David de Rothschild, shares the same privileges (and dislike for the limelight) as its British wing under Lord Jacob. The French family enjoys a similar position as a unique sort of aristocracy, owning banks, racehorses and the famous Bordeaux vineyards of Château Lafite.

But the French Rothschilds have had a far more turbulent modern history than their British counterparts. Subject, like their other relatives, to anti-Semitic propaganda before the Second World War, including the Goebbels-commissioned film *Die Rothschilds*, the French family were among the first to be dispossessed by occupying German forces after the fall of Paris in 1940. Their art collection and furniture was pillaged, and much of it was sent back to Germany for senior Nazi leaders such as Hermann Goering, and Hitler himself.

Under the French collaborationist government led by Philippe Pétain, Rothschild family members had their French nationality revoked and their assets stolen. Compensation after the war restored only a fraction of their wealth.

Forty years later they were dispossessed again. In 1981, after the election of the Communist-backed Socialist candidate François Mitterrand as president, the Rothschild bank was among 36 lenders that were nationalised. Late patriarch Guy looked on with distress as the state took ownership of the bank's modernist headquarters on Rue Laffitte, built on the site of the old family home. 'Jew under Pétain, pariah under Mitterrand,' he wrote afterwards.

Macron's four years at the bank, which was rebuilt by Guy's son David during the 1980s, was one of the most widely commented periods of his life in the run-up to the 2017 election. He would find it impossible to shake this association, with most descriptions in the press starting with 'former banker':

something that never ceased to irritate him. As he constantly pointed out, he had been a civil servant for longer. But for Macron's opponents – from leftists all the way to the far-right – it was a fitting designation, something which underlined his elitism, his dubiousness and his complicity with the world of money and business.

On the internet and at far-right meetings, conspiracy theorists and anti-Semites held up proof that their theories about global domination by a clique of Jewish financiers were true. In March ahead of the election, the right-wing Republicans party of candidate François Fillon published a cartoon of Macron looking like a hook-nosed Jewish banker from 1930s propaganda on its Twitter feed, leading to uproar and, eventually, apologies.

Defending himself, Macron repeatedly stated that attempts to slur him through his association with Rothschild 'takes us back to the worst moments of our history.' His claim was true to a certain extent in the case of the vicious, unfounded and anti-Semitic campaign conducted by far-right trolls online.

But the focus on Rothschild also reflected a more widely felt hostility to banks, stemming partly from ongoing resentment over their role in the global financial crisis and the still-enormous salaries being paid to their employees. More than 150 people working in the French financial sector earned more than a million euros in 2015 alone, compared with the national average wage of about €2,200 a month.

There are also genuine questions to be answered about conflicts of interest, given Rothschild's longstanding access to power, with the bank being emblematic of a certain *capitalisme à la française* with its tentacles spread between the private sector and the all-powerful state. It has long recruited ministers, influential aides and often past *Inspecteurs de finances*, because of their access to the Élysée or to the economy ministry. Georges Pompidou, a surprise choice for prime minister in 1962 by de Gaulle, was plucked directly from the bank. Nicolas Sarkozy worked for it as a lawyer in the mid-1990s.

'Is it Rothschild that cultivates a certain proximity with people in power or people in power who cultivate a proximity with Rothschild?', Édouard de Rothschild, David's brother, asked cryptically in a documentary broadcast in 2016.[3]

Ever eager to recruit the finest of Paris's talents and having now heard Macron's name from the lips of several trusted sources, Rothschild vice-president François Henrot set up a formal interview with him in one of the bank's meeting rooms at the low-key headquarters in central Paris.

'It was an immediate revelation. We stayed two hours together,' he said, lauding Macron's 'literally extraordinary intellectual capacities', but also his character.[4]

'At the end of the interview, I said to him "Don't look any further. Consider yourself an associate of the company".' Henrot added: 'It's astonishing to say that to someone who you've only met two hours previously. It was the first time it ever happened to me and it hasn't happened since.'

After four and a half years as a civil servant, Macron jumped at the chance to work in the private sector.

But after the Henri IV school, ENA and the *Inspection des finances*, he was accumulating the insignia of the Paris elite. 'He wanted to know what it was like to be an investment banker,' his old friend Ferracci says. 'He was fascinated by a career that he didn't know at all and one for which he didn't necessarily have all the skills.'

There was a new world of business jargon and spreadsheets to learn. Macron, who always considered maths to be his weakest subject, had been hired without possessing any technical knowledge. At its most basic level, investment banking involves valuing companies by analysing their balance sheets and profit and loss statements, as well as the strength of their underlying business and management. Recruits are normally thrown quickly into work advising on issuing bonds or shares to raise capital or on how to structure an acquisition.

'He was the guy who would constantly say thank you,' a former colleague told *The Financial Times*.[5] 'He didn't know what "EBITDA" [Earnings Before Interest, Tax, Depreciation and Amortization – a measure of profitability] was. He didn't try to hide it. And instead of looking it up in a corporate finance book, he asked around, which was disarming.'

The four years at Rothschild are a period when some of the traits that help explain Macron's rise are clearly visible. To begin with, there's the first meeting with Henrot which concludes with an immediate job offer. It's remarkable the number of times grizzled, older figures like Henrot, Minc or Hermand – hardly showbiz luvvies – describe their first meetings with him with almost star-struck wonder.

Christophe Castaner, one of the earliest political figures to back Macron's presidential run, and the future boss of his party, admitted to an 'amorous dimension' in their relationship. The heavy-set and bearded MP from the Alps courted ridicule with his comments on Macron by sounding like an infatuated schoolgirl. 'He's got every-thing: the background, the intelligence, the vivacity, even the physical strength,' the 51-year-old married father-of-two admitted in an interview.[6]

All that knowledge of literature and philosophy, combined with the analytical skills of an *Énarque*, seems to be particularly intoxicating. 'It's a mixture of intelligence and charm,' says Minc. 'I often describe him as a nice Giscard d'Estaing,' he added, referring to the centrist president who was in power from 1974 to 1981, a famously cerebral master of detail and policy who left office unloved and with a reputation for being cold and snooty.

Macron the investment banker also drew on his sponge-like ability to suck up new knowledge, while making no attempt to disguise his ignorance. François Heisbourg, a former diplomat and veteran security and geopolitical advisor, says 'he's not a guy that is going to pretend that he knows.'

Heisbourg, now the chairman of the UK-based International Institute for Strategic Studies, advised Macron during his presidential campaign, and saw similarities between him and late British prime minister Margaret Thatcher, with whom he also worked during talks about German reunification after the fall of the Berlin wall. 'She would make people speak up, listened and eventually made up her mind,' Heisbourg recalled of conferences held at the British prime minister's country house, Chequers. 'Of course once she'd made up her mind, she was not for turning.'

Macron 'also has that quality, which is more unusual in politicians than you think: he knows when he doesn't know, and what he doesn't know he wants to know,' he added.

What is clear is that Macron was taken on by Rothschild in spite of his lack of experience and his major technical shortcomings. From the beginning, his obvious value was in his contacts book and ability to bring in business. The number-crunching could be done by the army of analysts employed by the bank. Reflecting on the profession in an interview with the *Wall Street*

Journal, he was under no illusions. 'You're sort of a prostitute,' Macron said.[7] 'Seduction is the job.' A former colleague described him as a 'lubricant'.

Sophie Javary, a partner at Rothschild at the time and a corporate finance specialist, was assigned by François Henrot to show the ropes to Macron after he arrived. 'François rang me to say that he had just hired a particularly brilliant *inspecteur* who was coming to learn the business,' Javary explained. 'He asked me to include him on assignments and came to introduce us personally.'

She was immediately struck by the new recruit, who took over a corner office from an associate who had left the bank. Not only was he upbeat and enthusiastic, he had interests that immediately marked him out among the financiers. 'His general cultural knowledge was extraordinary. We didn't see it that much, but when it came out it was impressive,' she said. 'He always used words and references that no one had heard of.'

Javary's division – helping companies find financing – was one of the busiest of the whole bank at the time because of the severe credit crunch that had struck the global economy after the collapse of Lehman Brothers. Banks began hoarding their reserves and refusing to make loans. Javary's task was helping find alternative sources of money, or making use of emergency loan facilities provided by the government. Insider information on the state's intentions amid a wave of nationalisations in the European financial sector and multi-billion-euro bail-out funds for banks was vital.

'He had highly placed sources when we had cases that were linked to the state,' Javary remembered. As well as his network of former *Inspecteurs* and *Énarques* to gather intelligence from in the finance ministry, Macron's friend and mentor Jouyet had a seat at the cabinet table. 'He always had a good reading of who to contact and who was taking the decision,' Javary added.

In the private sector, his Attali Commission contacts also stretched across the close-knit business community in Paris and into Europe and America. 'He was identified as being a very singular person with lots of contacts,' recalled Cyrille Harfouche, another veteran banker who helped Macron through his early years.[8]

Among Macron's first projects at Rothschild was a business plan for a new film studio complex backed by *The Fifth Element* director Luc Besson which needed financing. He was also involved in the acquisition of the consumer loans group Cofidis by French bank Crédit Mutuel and several media group transactions, including one for the newspaper distributor Presstalis and another with publisher Lagardère.

'We were all convinced early on that he would have a meteoric career in the bank,' Javary remembered. He soon earned a reputation as someone who was quick to reply to emails, hard-working and friendly with both secretaries and the number-crunchers. 'He'd remember all their names and spend a few minutes with everyone to pay them some attention,' Javary added.

He also had a skill in remembering personal anecdotes about colleagues' children or family illnesses. 'It gives the impression that he's really interested,' Javary said. 'For someone so young, I found it remarkable.'

His charm also worked its magic during meetings with finance directors and chief executives. 'He's got this ability to be the son everyone would have liked,' Javary said. 'It's a mixture of maturity and an almost juvenile, joyous side.' Macron is 'always trying to seduce,' she added.

After about a year and half working with Javary, his impact in client meetings and ability to bring in business led to a transfer to the mergers and acquisitions (M&A) division of the bank, where the challenge was to identify companies that could be bought or sold and then recommend a transaction. Fortunes and reputations could be made with a major deal, though as a rookie in a tough market Macron's initial success was limited. Mergers and acquisitions fell by 50 per cent in France in 2009 compared with the year before and by 30 per cent globally.[9]

As well as a succession of work lunches and dinners around Paris, he was in perpetual motion in his private life, now a member of the board of *Esprit* magazine and a participant in think-tanks and other associations. 'We could see that he wasn't only doing investment banking. He had two mobile phones for a start,' one co-worker told the journalist Marc Endeweld.[10]

Gautier Daniel, a colleague for several years in M&A, remembers Macron's unusual working hours which allowed him to pack so much into his days. 'Normally in banking we work late at night but it wasn't the case for him,' he said. 'He'd leave pretty early but would then start work very early in the morning. We'd get messages at 3–4am when he was beginning his day.'

Despite the time pressure, lack of sleep and the workload of investment banking, Javary says she never saw him lose his cool. 'I never saw him stressed,' she explained. 'He has incredible self-control.'

Two years into his banking job and still without a major deal to his name, Macron was reintroduced to François Hollande. The two men had met several times previously, notably at a dinner party at Attali's house in the elegant Parisian suburb of Neuilly-sur-Seine in 2008.

Hollande, who was now 56, had decided to run in the Socialist Party primary which was being organised the following year, and was searching for an economic advisor. He had started his career in the early 1970s while still a student, when he began working for the Socialist Party leader François Mitterrand. When Mitterrand became the first left-wing leader of the Fifth Republic in 1981, he gave the ambitious young man his first break, with a junior role on the presidential staff.

A stellar future beckoned for Hollande, a man known for his quick wits and easy humour. At 26, he set off to build himself a political fiefdom in the isolated rural region of Corrèze in central France where he was elected to parliament for the first time in 1988.

But Hollande was always in the shadow of his more successful partner Ségolène Royal, the mother of his four children. They became a famous power couple after graduating from ENA together, and they joined Mitterrand's staff as a duo. But Royal went on to become a three-times minister and presidential candidate.

Hollande, by contrast, took the party route, becoming head of the Socialists in 1997, a position he held for eleven years. Known for his love of gossip as well as his indecision, few saw Hollande as presidential material. His unfortunate nickname '*flanby*' – a wobbly vanilla and caramel dessert – was hardly a character recommendation. It was a cruel dig at his chubby physique that underlined his lack of authority.

As head of the Socialists, Hollande was in charge of their calamitous campaign for the 2002 presidential election when his ally, the former prime minister Lionel Jospin, was defeated in the first round. In 2005, the party tore itself apart during France's referendum on a new European Constitution. Hollande backed a 'yes' vote, while his number two Laurent Fabius openly defied him to campaign for 'no'.

In 2007, the party lost the presidential election again, this time with Royal as the candidate running against Sarkozy. Hollande's term as first secretary ended with an acrimonious congress in the city of Reims in 2008 where the Socialist Party's internal divisions and ideological splits, which he had battled so long to paper over, burst into the open once more.

'The key weakness of François Hollande is inaction. Can the French people point to a single thing that he has achieved in 30 years in politics? One single thing?', Ségolène Royal asked, once the couple had split.[11] A comment from an estranged partner and embittered political rival perhaps, but a question that was difficult to answer nonetheless.

By late 2010, Hollande had dropped ten kilograms, had found the 'woman of my life' in the shape of *Paris Match* journalist Valérie Trierweiler and was about to start a grassroots campaign across the country to build support for his presidential bid. His mantra – 'to be liked, one needs to be likeable' – had been taken from Mitterrand.

He was a rank outsider, most people seeing International Monetary Fund (IMF) boss Dominique Strauss-Kahn as the far better candidate from the centre-left of the party. While Hollande was a mere MP and head of the Corrèze region, Strauss-Kahn had bolstered his reputation in Washington as a firefighter on the frontline of the global financial crisis.

Now that he needed an economic advisor, Hollande was brought together with Macron again at Jean-Pierre Jouyet's urging, and the two hit it off. The Socialist candidate had no pretensions to be an intellectual, but both men shared a similar love of humour, as well as an interest in football and broadly compatible views – or so it seemed – on the country's economic and social ills.

While his colleagues at the bank were working themselves to exhaustion, catching up on sleep or seeing their neglected families when they could, Macron took on a new project offering policy advice to Hollande. Only two years after having left the public sector, he now had his first opportunity in frontline politics.

'I didn't really have a battle plan. In 2010, I was convinced that François Hollande was the best candidate,' Macron said.[12] 'I didn't think that Dominique Strauss-Kahn would win the primary, notably because money in France is taboo.'

Indeed, Strauss-Kahn's flashy watches, vast holiday home in Marrakech and the gaudy lifestyle he led with his millionaire television presenter wife Anne Sinclair attracted negative attention. A widely published picture of the IMF chief getting into a Porsche in Paris didn't help and led to an article in the left-leaning *Libération* newspaper which asked: 'Can a man from the left be rich?'

But there are reasons to doubt Macron's claims to clairvoyance. Alain Minc offers a different theory. 'He didn't want to be just one among 50 or 100 people working with Strauss-Kahn. With Hollande, he was the only one, the star,' he said.

In the same year, Macron had lunch with a journalist contact from *Le Monde* and found himself another sideline. France's most respected newspaper faced yet another financial crisis and was in danger of running out of cash over the summer. Staff representatives, acting on behalf of the employee cooperative which owned the majority of the paper, were desperately searching for new investors and needed professional advice.

'He said he'd do it in his free time, he'd do it for no fee and that he'd let his bosses [at the bank] know about it,' one of the cooperative's representatives, the senior staff economics writer Adrien de Tricornot, remembered over a coffee in south-west Paris. 'He was exactly the sort of person we needed, someone who wanted to help and was willing to lend us a hand in the name of the public good.'

Over the course of multiple meetings, occasionally out of hours in his office at Rothschild or in cafés around Paris, de Tricornot and his colleague Gilles van Kote got to know Macron while talking about possible solutions to the crisis at the paper. 'He told us he had worked in the *Inspection de finances*, but that now he was at the bank and was making lots of money but the job didn't have much meaning,' de Tricornot explained.

'You read about how he used to take time with people underneath him at Rothschild, the secretaries and others. I don't know if it's because he knew he was going into politics or if he's genuinely just a nice person, but it was the same feeling that we got from him,' he added.

Macron also made an early impression at a meeting with *Le Monde* chairman Louis Schweitzer, who had been promising to bring new investors on board. Van Kote felt that Schweitzer was keeping the staff in the dark and again asked – without success – for more details. 'Emmanuel slapped his hand on the table and said "I've never heard anyone talk to shareholders like this",' de Tricornot said. 'It was a moment of empowerment for us.'

Things became more difficult over the summer. Despite Macron's assurances to the staff of the newspaper, he hadn't yet produced any results. And a deal for *Le Monde* was taking shape with Pierre Bergé, the billionaire co-founder of the Yves Saint Laurent fashion house, telecoms and internet tycoon Xavier Niel and the banker Matthieu Pigasse from Lazard, Rothschild's Paris-based rival.

Macron urged de Tricornot and van Kote in increasingly forceful terms to delay agreeing with this trio, saying they should wait to see if a better deal would take shape. The only other possibility was a rival and still incomplete bid by a consortium led by the Spanish media company Prisa, which was viewed as being too risky. Furthermore, Prisa was being advised by Minc, who had become a bogeyman for many at *Le Monde* after an ill-fated period he had spent on the board of the company. Nonetheless, Macron continued to play for time.

Le Monde's staff voted in favour of talks with Bergé, Niel and Pigasse about their deal over the summer and on 3 September de Tricornot and van Kote had a meeting with one of Bergé's lawyers on the Avenue Georges V, coincidentally in the same building as Alain Minc's office. That day would change their perception of Macron forever.

As they stood in the street outside after meeting the lawyer, the heavy wooden door to the building swung open again, and de Tricornot was sure he spotted Macron about to walk out with Minc. But the figure doubled back and disappeared.

'You won't believe me but I'm sure I just saw Macron with Minc,' de Tricornot said to van Kote and the others standing with him on the pavement. He headed in to investigate, first ringing the bell at Minc's office, which was empty, everyone having gone out to lunch. He climbed the richly-carpeted stairs, checking each floor one by one. Finally, on the last level, he saw Macron standing with his back to the staircase starting a conversation on his phone. The lift had been blocked to stop anyone from coming up.

'Hello Emmanuel? You're not saying hello to us anymore? My colleagues are waiting for you below,' de Tricornot said. Macron carried on talking into his phone but had lost his composure. 'He was gulping for breath. His heart seemed to be going at 200 beats a minute,' de Tricornot remembers.

The two men walked down the stairs together and by the time they reached the outside door Macron's ashen face had regained signs of his trademark self-assurance. Why had he hidden? For Macron to meet Minc, given the businessman's role in mounting a rival bid, would have been legitimate – but only if he had informed his 'clients' at *Le Monde*. They expected him to be an impartial advisor. He had also neglected to tell them about his long-standing relationship with the consultant despite the potential for a conflict of interest. Suddenly his opposition to the Bergé-Niel-Pigasse deal seemed to make sense.

De Tricornot remembers van Kote saying during the early days of working with Macron that 'we've been betrayed by so many people that if Emmanuel betrays us then we should give up on humanity.' Later that day, he sent a text message to his colleague reading: 'What a shame for humanity.'

'He's such a seducer, a real professional, what he really thinks at heart I don't know,' de Tricornot concludes. They broke off contact at that point. The sale was ultimately completed with the staff's preferred choice of Bergé, Niel and Pigasse two months later for €110 million.

Despite this embarrassment, back at the bank Macron was going from strength to strength. He had started initially as an

associate on a €130,000 pre-tax annual salary before being promoted to director in 2010, which tripled his income. In February
2011, he bounded ahead, this time being made partner, which
gave him a share of company profits each year.

Former colleague Sophie Javary says that this was no surprise
given his reputation, but it created a sense of envy among some
of his colleagues, particularly more experienced bankers who
were waiting for promotions. Benefiting from having supporters
right at the top of the bank in David de Rothschild and François
Henrot, Macron would also short-cut his immediate managers
at times, speaking to his boss's boss if he wanted to, and would
occasionally call clients directly without consulting. This pattern – not respecting the immediate hierarchy while benefiting
from patronage at the top – would be repeated in 2014 when he
became a minister.

'The only fault, which could lead to a certain jealousy, was
his ambition,' Javary says. 'It was clear he was really driven.' She
assumed he had given up on the public sector when he joined
the bank. 'I thought to myself that he'd do something exceptional
before he was 40. I was sure he'd be the boss of a CAC 40 company,' she said, referring to the 40 firms which make up the blue
chip index on the French stock exchange.

Gautier Daniel said he and his colleagues started speculating
about Macron's future behind his back from 2010. 'We'd joke
about how he'd be president one day. Investment banking for him
was a staging-post,' he said. 'It was obvious given his background
and his character.'

Had his links with Hollande from 2010 also turbocharged
his career in the bank? Given Rothschild's manner of operating,
quite possibly. The bank was the subject of an investigative book

by the French journalist Martine Orange in 2012 which looked into the revolving door between the bank and politics, which enabled Rothschild to benefit from lucrative government contracts. It noted how the group had unearthed another new talent – a 'brilliant but unusual banker' called Emmanuel Macron – and included an interview with David de Rothschild discussing the most likely winner of the Socialist primary. 'Hollande, don't you think?', he said, tipping the rank outsider.

CHAPTER 7

Ahead of the Pack

IN MACHIAVELLI'S BOOK *THE PRINCE*, WHICH MACRON studied closely in his twenties, the Italian writer contemplates the role of *Virtù* (prowess) and *Fortuna* (luck) in the fate of Italy's warring rulers in the 16th century. 'I believe it is probably true that fortune is the arbiter of half of things we do, leaving the other half or so controlled by ourselves,' he wrote. In such circumstances it was 'better to be impetuous than circumspect.'

Besides his evident qualities, Macron has been repeatedly favoured by fortune, but the first major stroke of it came years before the 2017 election campaign.

On 14 May 2011 at around midday, Dominique Strauss-Kahn walked naked out of his bathroom in suite 2806 in the Sofitel hotel in New York, and came face-to-face with hotel cleaner Nafissatou Diallo, a 32-year-old immigrant from Guinea.

A sexual encounter took place – according to Strauss-Kahn a consensual one, a forced one according to Diallo – which left traces of saliva and semen on the carpet of the $3,000-a-night VIP room.

The silver-haired IMF boss checked out half an hour later, had lunch with his daughter and then boarded a plane heading to Paris where he was due to have meetings about the launch of his imminent presidential run. Polls still showed him as the favourite to clinch the Socialist Party candidacy and defeat Sarkozy in the election the following year.

Ten minutes before his flight was set to leave Kennedy airport, he was hauled off by two police officers acting on a complaint by Diallo. He was taken to a station in Harlem and charged over-night with sexual assault and attempted rape, which he denied.

Leaving the police station the following evening, looking hag-gard and with his hands cuffed behind his back, the presidential frontrunner was paraded in front of the world's media in images that shocked France.

He had only narrowly kept his position at the start of his term as IMF boss after claims that he had pressured a Hungarian economist at the Fund to sleep with him at the World Economic Forum in Davos in 2008. This time, while in custody in Rikers Island jail, he resigned from his job almost immediately.

His political career was in tatters too, even though a poll taken a few days later found that 57 per cent of French people believed he had been set up. The scandal would keep conspiracy theo-rists busy for years. As media commentators united in declaring the end of his prospects, the French philosopher Bernard-Henri Lévy was one of few people to defend Strauss-Kahn – his friend – saying it was 'absurd' to depict him as 'this brutal and violent individual, this wild animal, this primate'.

In the end, the case never went to court. New York pros-ecutors dropped the charges several months later after Diallo was judged to have lied to them about some of the details.

Strauss-Kahn settled a civil case in 2012 for an undisclosed amount.

His legal woes continued for years at home, however, after his name cropped up during a separate investigation into a prostitution ring in north-east France. After a trial that exposed his liking for rough sex and champagne-fuelled orgies across the world, he was acquitted of pimping charges in June 2015. Other women stepped forward to tell of his predatory advances.

Reacting to the Sofitel scandal over the same weekend, Hollande said modestly that he did not see the scandal benefiting anyone. Internationally, France's image, not to mention the IMF's, was widely sullied by the revelations, leading to new questions about the problem of lecherous behaviour in French politics.

Hollande had been slowly closing the gap on Strauss-Kahn for the presidential nomination in previous weeks, but the arrest transformed his prospects. A survey by the OpinionWay-Fiducial pollsters published on 18 May showed that Hollande was up a staggering 27 points compared with April, and 62 per cent of respondents planned to vote for him in the Socialist primary.

Almost immediately, hundreds of CVs flowed into his campaign headquarters as desperate Strauss-Kahn aides scrambled for a lifeboat. Some were taken on. But Macron had been there since the beginning and had already built a privileged relationship with Hollande. The young banker stepped up his advisory work, convening meetings with eminent economists including Jean Pisani-Ferry at one of his favourite Left-Bank restaurants, *La Rotonde*.

In October, Hollande clinched the Socialist Party nomination, beating the left-winger Martine Aubry by 57 per cent to

43 per cent in a second-round run-off. 'Macron coordinated the working group on the macroeconomic and financial elements of Hollande's programme for the primary,' Aquilino Morelle, one of Hollande's top advisors and his speechwriter, said in an interview. 'When Hollande was chosen, [Macron] withdrew himself so that in the autumn and spring of 2012 he didn't appear in the official campaign hierarchy. He was continuing to advise Hollande outside of working hours though. We knew he was there.'

At the bank, Macron was working to reel in a huge deal that, if successful, would justify his decision to seek his fortune there. It had been entirely enabled by the old Attali network.

Through regular trips to the headquarters of Nestlé in the Swiss town of Vevey, Macron had managed to persuade the boss of the cash-rich food giant, Peter Brabeck, to consider making an offer for the baby milk unit of US pharmaceutical group Pfizer. The sales pitch – or 'equity story' – told over expensive lunches on the edge of Lake Geneva was that the Pfizer unit would give Nestlé greater presence in fast-growing emerging markets, particularly in China where it had so far been weak.

Nestlé had never made a transaction of the size Macron was suggesting and had never worked with Rothschild. But the otherwise brusque and generally unapproachable Brabeck was receptive to Macron, holding fond memories of the banker since their time together with Attali four years earlier.

As discussions heated up, the Pfizer unit attracted bids from the US manufacturer Mead Johnson and French food group Danone, which was being advised by Lazard and Pigasse, that threatened to scupper Macron's plans. Mead Johnson dropped out early as the price climbed and then Nestlé looked to have clinched the acquisition with a bid of $9 billion, which was leaked to the *Wall Street Journal*.

But there was another flurry of bids and counter-bids from the Swiss group and Danone over a final frenetic weekend, with Macron and Pigasse working behind the scenes to encourage their clients to raise the stakes.

On 23 April 2012 – the day after the first round of the French presidential election – Nestlé made an announcement to the media and its shareholders. It had won the battle, clinching the acquisition for a higher-than-expected $11.85 billion. The takeover will 'complement our existing infant nutrition business perfectly,' the group said.

Gautier Daniel, Macron's colleague, was far from alone in being impressed. 'Honestly speaking, he was not among the best-qualified partners to take on a deal like that from a technical perspective. But he had the confidence and the contacts and the relationship with Peter Brabeck which meant he got taken on and then had the emotional intelligence needed to handle that relationship,' he explained. 'He also surrounded himself with extremely good people who could handle the financial aspects and make up for any of his weaknesses.' Macron couldn't have cut it any finer. At the 11th hour of his banking career, he had bagged a gigantic transaction and could now look ahead to a possible government job with Hollande. But was it big enough to give him the financial independence he craved before going into politics?

Overall for 2009–2012, Macron declared a pre-tax income in bonuses and salary payments from Rothschild of around €3 million. His income in 2012, the year of his greatest triumph at the bank, was €991,000 pre-tax. Not bad for five months work, but there was no major bonus for bringing in a new client and clinching a massive cross-border transaction. He received a share in the bank's overall profits like all the other partners. His income in 2011 had been higher at €1.4 million.[1]

In any case, he was now wealthy, which by his own admission was difficult for a politician in France, particularly one from the left. His nest egg wasn't enough to see him through for the rest of his days, but he was rich beyond the dreams of most people in their early thirties.

Hollande finished top in the first round of the presidential election with 29 per cent, ahead of Sarkozy, who won 27 per cent. In the second-round run-off between them two weeks later, Hollande won with 52 per cent.

Macron's deal-making skills would be called on again. He wasn't part of the official victorious campaign team, and as an informal advisor he wouldn't normally have been at the front of the queue for important jobs at the Élysée; but he made his feelings clear to Hollande that he would only leave Rothschild for a major role.

'Of everyone in the team around Hollande, he was the only one who knew what position he was going to take,' remembered Hollande's advisor Aquilino Morelle, a doctor by training. 'He knew he was going to be the deputy chief-of-staff, the president's Sherpa.'

To give such a crucial position to an investment banker was an incongruous choice for Hollande. The president had shifted progressively further left during his campaign, which is remembered chiefly for a speech he made at Le Bourget near Paris in front of thousands of cheering supporters in January.

'In this battle ahead of us, I will tell you who my opponent is, my real opponent,' Hollande said at the start of the most memorable passage of that speech. 'It doesn't have a name, a face, or a party. It never proposes a candidate. It is never elected. And yet, it governs.'

As the suspense rose in the giant arena packed with 25,000 flag-waving activists, he delivered the punch line: 'This opponent is the world of finance.' The world 'which has seized control of the economy, of society and even our lives,' he thundered, standing in front of his slogan 'Change Is Now'.

In February on the same campaign trail, Hollande made another proposal that fired up the Socialist Party base, promising to introduce a tax of 75 per cent on income over €1 million a year to soak the rich. 'I have seen the considerable progression of the pay of the CAC 40 bosses: €2 million a year on average. How can we accept that?', he said of France's biggest bosses during a television interview.

It seemed to take his budget spokesman by surprise and apparently Macron was not aware he was going to say this either. 'Cuba without the sunshine,' he wrote to Hollande dismissively in an email that revealed the candidness of their exchanges. Sarkozy, meanwhile, mocked Hollande for appearing to make up policy on the fly.

The country with the highest top rate of tax in the European Union at the time was Sweden, with 56.4 per cent. Hollande said the levy, which would fall on 3,000–3,500 people, would raise €200–300 million in extra revenues and called on the rich to show 'patriotism'. Instead many left for Belgium, Switzerland or Britain.

Hollande's pitch to voters was also a change in presidential style. In contrast to the hyperactive and ostentatious behaviour of Sarkozy, Hollande promised to be 'a normal president' in his pre-election book *Changing Destiny*. One of his first acts was cutting his own salary as president.

His other promises included renegotiating a new EU budget austerity pact, which had been adopted at the urging of Germany in March 2012 and committed members to introducing laws on balanced budgets and accepting sanctions if they violated deficit rules. Europe needed growth, and a tax on financial transactions, Hollande argued.

In January, he visited workers protesting at a refinery which was threatened with closure in northern France, telling them encouragingly that 'more than your jobs today' they were 'defending a national industry'.

In almost every presidential election, a factory threatened by job losses somewhere in France offers candidates an opportunity to grandstand alongside angry workers in hard hats, as they burn tyres and hold up placards. In 2007, it had been Airbus factories; five years previously, a biscuit maker.

The refinery was the prelude to the much bigger showdown at the Florange steel mills in eastern France which risked being shuttered by their owner, the billionaire Indian steel tycoon Lakshmi Mittal. Standing on the back of a truck with trade union flags fluttering behind him, Hollande pledged to prevent job losses and pass a new law obliging companies to find buyers for any sites they wanted to close. The former industrial heartland was an electoral priority for the Socialists where they and the Communists had progressively been losing votes to the far-right party of the Le Pens, the *Front National*.

'This is the great ambiguity of Hollande,' said his former political advisor Morelle, a left-winger who wrote a book on his presidency after stepping down in 2014. 'He got himself elected with his speeches saying no to finance, no to unbalanced relations with Germany, and yes to a tax on financial transactions, but in reality he didn't believe a word of it.'

As well as appointing the recognisably left-leaning Morelle, Hollande's first government also included the leftist firebrand Arnaud Montebourg as minister for industrial production. He spearheaded a 'Made in France' drive and repeatedly stirred controversy with his attacks on business owners. Amid negotiations to save the Florange mills, Montebourg declared 'we don't want any Mittals in France because they haven't respected the country,' provoking anger in India where some deemed the comments to be xenophobic.

The cabinet was balanced up by members of the centre-left wing of the Socialists, Hollande's traditional habitat, meaning that the government straddled the ideological split that had erupted so often in the party since the 1980s: from what the French call *Colbertistes* – those committed to state intervention and public ownership – through to free-market liberals. Although they had been appointed to give a sense of even-handedness to his cabinet, the seeds of Hollande's future problems had been sown.

It was clear from the start where Macron's sympathies lay, however. The 34-year-old took up his role as deputy chief-of-staff at the presidential palace, accepting a salary that was only 10–15 per cent of what he had been making at Rothschild. He moved into a corner office with a view of the lush garden behind the Élysée Palace, which had been occupied during Sarkozy's term by François Pérol, another former Rothschild employee. As the youngest member of the team he was dubbed affectionately 'little Macron'.

Even though Morelle and he were ideologically on different ends of the spectrum – the 'yin and yang', as Morelle puts it – they quickly developed a relationship of mutual respect: 'The advantage of Emmanuel is that he has his ideas, it's a real framework of quite coherent liberal ideas which is rare in politics,' Morelle explained. 'And he had the courage to defend them. He wasn't trying to second-guess the boss by aligning his views in advance. He said what he thought. And when he didn't agree with the President he'd say so.'

Within a few months, Macron was attracting media attention. He gave an interview to *Libération*, posing for a photo looking tanned and relaxed in pin-striped trousers, white shirt and tie. The spread, headlined 'The Little Genius at the Élysée,' included testimony from friends and former banking colleagues. 'An extraterrestrial,' said one.

Macron's otherness crops up regularly in descriptions of him by colleagues and friends – even Brigitte described him as being 'from another world'. It seems to be an admission that even those closest to him are never sure they've completely worked him out. It points again at the difficulty in defining a person who moved from investment banking to help a Socialist president, who comes from Amiens and Paris, but neither in particular, who has youthful looks but old-fashioned tastes.

Macron's role as a crucial gatekeeper to Hollande was established early on in his time in the Élysée, with heads of ministerial cabinets recounting exchanges with him by phone or text message at 2–3am. Tension with his colleague Philippe Léglise-Costa, a presidential advisor on Europe, was already causing trouble, with both men holding different views about how to negotiate in Brussels. Léglise-Costa, a former high-ranking diplomat in

Brussels was 'nervy and experienced,' while Macron was 'calm, strategic but doesn't know the European machine,' a diplomat told *Libération* on condition of anonymity at the time. But overall Macron sounded delighted with his new role. 'I've got the chance here to take part in a collective endeavour which aims to have meaning,' he told the newspaper.

There were also remarks from less-admiring colleagues who painted a picture of a slightly saccharine courtier who was difficult to pin down – a description that would stick. 'When he talks it's not with real conviction, but he's very aware of the power games between people,' the Socialist lawmaker Karine Berger said. The two would later work together – and clash – on a law which Hollande had promised, separating retail and investment banking activities at France's biggest lenders.

The article concluded with a prescient quote from an unnamed friend. 'I'm sure that deep down he dreams of becoming President of the Republic,' the friend said. Other profiles followed in *Le Monde* and the business newspaper *Les Echos* before his over-exposure in the public eye eventually annoyed colleagues and Hollande.

Macron's main responsibilities were in handling important economic dossiers and liaising with the foreign and finance ministries over the eurozone crisis, where Greece was again in need of a new bailout. He also welcomed investors or business groups worried about legislation or seeking guidance.

At closed-doors meetings with Hollande and private dinners between the two, he continued to champion efforts to improve French competitiveness by lowering taxes on companies or loosening labour laws.

The two men 'had a very strong relationship, very friendly,

very aligned at a political level because they had a lot of ideas in common,' Morelle says.

But Hollande, whose tendency to dither had been remarked on since his time as head of the Socialist Party, was stuck with his campaign pledges which he now needed to show he was trying to implement. However great his sympathy with Macron's proposals, he had both public opinion and Socialist MPs in parliament to keep onside.

The 75 per cent super-rich tax was unveiled – before being struck out by the country's highest court at the end of 2012. Hollande also went to Berlin to champion a loosening of the German-imposed budgetary rigour, where he retreated meekly when faced with resistance from Chancellor Merkel.

On Florange, Montebourg took on the challenge of trying to find solutions to save the steelworks. The global steel industry was suffering from chronic overcapacity after a contraction in demand following the global financial crisis. No private buyer was prepared to stump up the investment needed to save the plant.

Backed by the unions, Montebourg proposed nationalising the site to modernise it. Hollande acknowledged this as a possibility, before opting for a negotiated settlement with Mittal who closed the foundries but pledged not to make any forced lay-offs. Workers and unions cried treachery, seeing the end of steelmaking at the site as an irreversible blow for the industry. 'For me, it was a personal humiliation and a political defeat,' Montebourg said later.[2]

Montebourg accused Macron of leading him to believe that he could count on the support of the president in nationalising the plant if necessary. 'I remember this remark from Emmanuel Macron: "we'll jump with you",' said Montebourg bitterly.

'Except I didn't have a parachute and I had all the people from ArcelorMittal with me. We all splattered together, me included.'

The economic and political climate was becoming ever more difficult. Hollande had started his term promising to tackle the chronic French problem of high unemployment, which stood at 9.3 per cent when he took office. But his rhetoric on his 'enemy' in finance, the tax measures and talk of nationalisations had taken a toll on business sentiment, leading to a fall in private investment.

Speaking at around this time, the late head of oil giant Total, Christophe de Margerie, spoke for many company bosses when he said France had become 'its own caricature' with the resurgence in state interventionism. 'Because of the incoherence, the timidity, public statements from our leaders no longer inspire confidence in anyone,' he said.[3]

By the end of 2012, six months into Hollande's term, the unemployment rate in France had risen to 9.7 per cent and would continue to rise quarter over quarter until the middle of 2013 when it reached 10 per cent.

On the social front, a seemingly safe left-wing measure of passing a new law authorising gay marriage and adoption turned into another ordeal. Few saw number 31 of Hollande's 60 pre-election promises provoking such a large national protest movement. Nine other European countries including Spain and Portugal had passed similar legislation without major resistance from Catholics.

But France's normally dormant churchgoers, as well as far-right sympathisers, mobilised countrywide, sending hundreds of thousands of people into the street for a series of demonstrations that often ended in violence. 'The current climate and rising anger is the responsibility of the President and the government which refuses to listen to the people,' said Frigide Barjot, the leader of the *Manif pour Tous* movement which sprung up nationwide to defend traditional family values.

The bill needed more than 130 hours of parliamentary debate and proceedings were disrupted by protesters, who often gathered noisily outside the National Assembly during hearings. Gay charities reported a spike in homophobic incidents.

As if this wasn't enough, Hollande's credibility was sapped further by the resignation of his budget minister, Jérôme Cahuzac, a former plastic surgeon who had promised to lead the fight on tax evasion. Press reports revealed that Cahuzac had a Swiss bank account where, with the help of his wife, he had stashed millions of euros from their lucrative hair transplant business.

Only one year into his term in office, the President had an approval rating of 26 per cent, the lowest of any French leader at that stage of their mandate. 'For a year, I've lived through difficult moments,' he confided to visitors to the Élysée in April, listing his challenges.[4]

In addition to his domestic woes and problems in the eurozone, Hollande had sent French troops into northern Mali to stop the advance of jihadists in January. It was up to him to be a 'responsible president in an exceptional period', he added.

Macron was growing increasingly frustrated. There was little sign of the bold leadership he felt France needed nor the vital role of explaining policy to the public to prepare them for the changes. In private, Hollande's love of gossip and palace intrigue were further sources of concern.

Above all, the President showed little appetite to take on structural reforms – for which no elected mandate existed. In late 2012, Macron had a reason to cheer when he helped push through a corporate tax cut plan which handed businesses a tax break worth €20 billion aimed at increasing their competitiveness. It was financed partly by a rise in sales tax, which Hollande had previously promised not to increase.

Given the business climate at the time, and the sense that Hollande's leadership was weak and confused, the package of measures had little immediate impact and remained controversial through to the end of Hollande's term. Many questioned its effectiveness, while companies complained about the complicated forms they needed to complete to qualify for the tax breaks.

'He reached a point of being frustrated about his ability to influence things, that there was actually little room for manoeuvre,' Macron's friend Ferracci said of the period. 'And on top of that, Hollande is not easy to work with. It's very difficult to know what he thinks.'

Personal events in 2013 also led Macron to reassess his relationship with the president. In April, the health of his grandmother Manette, the most important person in his life along with Brigitte, began to deteriorate. Macron spent every evening on the phone to her and dashed to her side in her final hours in Amiens.

Her death in April at the age of 97 was devastating for him. Manette had spoiled and educated him as a child, influenced him with her left-wing politics and transmitted her love of literature. She had offered support for his relationship with Brigitte when others stood in their way. Even when her darling 'Manu' had grown up, as well as keeping in touch via regular phone calls, she continued to cut out newspaper articles she thought would interest him and send them by post.

'Hollande was very off-hand [about Manette's death], very unpleasant. He knew perfectly well the importance of this woman in Emmanuel's life,' Morelle remembers. 'It really hit him.'

Macron acknowledges this moment as a turning point in his relationship with Hollande, in his interview with Anne Fulda,[5] saying that Hollande's words of condolence were along the lines of 'yes, I was very sad when I lost mine'. 'I'll never forgive him,' Macron told Morelle afterwards.

Manette was buried after a funeral in her family village in the Pyrenees, with a memorial service held later in Amiens. Having pushed her grandson to learn, stretch himself and aim high in life, her death would influence his decision-making too.

In early 2014, the Élysée was in chaos again after the revelations about Hollande's affair with the actress Gayet came to light following the publication of pictures of him arriving to meet her on a moped. At the end of January in a terse statement, he announced the 'end of my shared life' with his partner Trierweiler, who would go on to write a book called *Thank You for This Moment* which claimed among other things that the President disdained the poor and called them the '*sans dents*' ('the toothless ones').

The book, which was a bestseller when it came out later that year, was a shockingly intimate account of the First Couple's explosive relationship, in which Trierweiler claimed Hollande became 'dehumanised' as he closed in on power and that he even mocked the modest background of her family. When she discovered Hollande's affair, she recounted attempting an overdose of sleeping pills, leading to a struggle in their bedroom which left tablets strewn all over the floor. She ended up in hospital.

The lurid details even seemed to spark something approaching sympathy for Hollande in the far-right leader Marine Le Pen who said it was a 'profoundly indecent settling of scores.' A front-page headline by *Le Parisien* newspaper screamed 'Pathetic' over a picture of the couple, which summarised the tone of the sniffy – but voluminous – French media coverage of the book. A reviewer in the *Guardian* newspaper described Trierweiler's writing as 'an uninterrupted wail of pain' and said that parts read like a teenager's diary. In March, in the first nationwide test of Hollande's presidency since he had come to power, the Socialists were pummelled in local elections, leading to huge gains for the far-right National Front under Marine Le Pen which won control of eleven towns. 'A black Sunday,' said one leading member of Hollande's party.

In a seemingly unending stream of bad news for the Socialists, the investigative website *Mediapart* claimed a month later that Morelle had done unauthorised work for pharmaceutical companies while working as a senior civil servant, a charge he denied. More memorably, it said he kept a collection of 30 pairs of hand-made shoes at the Élysée which were professionally cleaned every two months. Convinced he had been forced out by a leak designed to purge the government of left-wingers, Morelle bowed to the inevitable and resigned as Hollande's advisor in the face of the 'shoe shiner scandal'.

In this context, Macron began thinking about the exit too. On the campaign trail in 2017, he would make a virtue of his decision to leave the Élysée without securing himself a senior well-paid role in a public institution. His immediate boss at the Élysée, chief of staff Pierre-René Lemas, was named as the head of the French state bank *Caisse des Dépôts* at around the same time.

Macron and people close to him later suggested that he had only ever intended to do two years in the presidential team. His decision to leave appears to have been driven by a mixture of personal difficulties with Hollande – since the death of Macron's grandmother, their relationship had cooled – and the realisation that his opportunities for progression looked limited.

When Hollande changed his prime minister in March, promoting the young centre-left moderniser Manuel Valls from his role as interior minister, Macron was touted as a possible budget minister, but Hollande vetoed the idea, much to Macron's frustration.

Hollande's logic – Macron didn't hold an elected office, so he couldn't be in the government – seemingly blocked his chances of a promotion. As Macron discussed leaving in the late spring of 2014, Hollande never proposed the golden parachute which he would have expected, according to Morelle. 'Macron realised that when he told the president that he was thinking about leaving ... that in reality Hollande wanted him to leave and did nothing to keep him,' Morelle said.

Speaking while packing his boxes at the Élysée on 16 June 2014, Macron said he was happy to 'find a form of freedom again,' to 'be able to say things,'[6] in one of several interviews he gave at the time. He was leaving after two years of service to the most unpopular president in modern history. Only 21 per cent of voters now had confidence in Hollande.[7]

Ironically though, he was on the way out just as his ideas were gaining traction in government. Hollande pivoted to the centre-left under Valls, promising structural reforms and cuts to public spending of €50 billion, which split the Socialist Party and provoked a rebellion in parliament. In one of his valedictory interviews, Macron dismissed the Socialists as being stuck in the past. 'There's never been a fundamental update in their thinking,' he said.

Macron had various plans for the future: he'd been in talks about doing some teaching at the London School of Economics, a return to the academic world that he had once dismissed as lacking in a 'form of action'. He also flew to California as part of plans to create a start-up in e-learning with Ismaël Emelien, a former PR and think-tank whizz in his twenties who had been an advisor to finance minister Pierre Moscovici.

Emelien and Macron had first crossed at the left-wing Jean-Jaurès Foundation think-tank in Paris, where Emelien worked after finishing his studies at Sciences Po. He then took a job at the Euro RSCG communications agency (now known as Havas Worldwide). This led him to advise Moscovici as an outside consultant but he also contributed to the 2013 election campaign of the Venezuelan strongman Nicolas Maduro, who succeeded the late leader Hugo Chavez that year.

In addition to the e-learning project, Macron made progress in starting a political and investment consultancy, along the lines of Alain Minc's business. He showed a logo for 'Macron Partners' to a few close friends on his iPhone.

'I thought it was a very good idea to start a boutique advisory business. I told him he'd need to find a client to get some working capital but he seemed pretty relaxed about that, probably rightly,' said Sir Simon Robertson, a senior London-based British banker, who Macron had contacted for advice.

'I thought that either it could become a profession for him or a place to park himself which would give him independence and flexibility if something else came up,' added Robertson, who after a career in senior roles at Goldman Sachs and HSBC now runs his own advisory firm.

Robertson had already encountered Macron several times at the Élysée while acting on behalf of clients – having been introduced by Minc – and was struck by the depth of his network when they met again in the tea room of the five-star Bristol Hotel, a dealmaker's haven a stone's throw from the Élysée.

Macron went round the tables shaking hands. 'It reminded me of being in Iran back in the 1970s. All of us bankers went over there trying to get business off the Shah or the Shah's acolytes,' Robertson recalled. 'We were all put in a huge room and then they came round talking to us one-by-one in a sequence. It was rather like that. He's obviously very popular.'

Macron's partner in the nascent business, Ismaël Emelien, said that the consultancy enterprise was intended to raise capital. 'The main project was the start-up,' he said, explaining that it was going to be a learning website for French-speakers.

But before they could get any further, an insurrection in Hollande's government would change both of their destinies.

CHAPTER 8

Into the Spotlight

ON 26 AUGUST 2014, SIX WEEKS AFTER HE HAD LEFT THE
president's staff, Macron's phone rang while he was on holiday in
Le Touquet during a break from organising his new career. It was
Hollande's chief of staff on the phone. The president had another
mess on his hands. Did Macron want to join his government and
become the economy minister?

At the end of Macron's leaving party at the Élysée Palace,
Hollande had made a speech, joking that his young aide would
soon end up back in politics: 'I'm sure we'll see Emmanuel again,'
he'd said with a smile.[1] No one expected to see the 36 year old
back again before the end of the summer holidays.

Over the telephone, Macron tentatively agreed, albeit setting two conditions: he wanted assurances that he would be able
to carry out major economic reforms, and of course he'd need
Brigitte's consent before accepting. Hollande assented to the first
request and Macron headed off to discuss the move with his wife.
This was his ticket to the big-time.

Tensions within Hollande's government under the Spanish-

born Prime Minister Manuel Valls had been growing steadily
since the spring of 2014. Valls' nomination in March had signalled a definitive change in economic policy: a clear pivot away
from Hollande's leftist campaign pledges of two years previously,
in favour of cutting corporate taxes and business regulations.
It was also the end of Hollande's half-hearted and unsuccessful
efforts in arguing for greater budgetary leeway in Europe, with
German Chancellor Angela Merkel and her conservative allies as
committed as ever to cracking down on deficits.

Hollande had spent the first two years of his presidency and
his eleven years as head of the Socialists attempting to contain the
divergent currents within the party on the economy, on Europe,
on tackling inequality or on the role of the state. Skirmishes were
frequent and major fighting would occasionally flare up in the
open, but the ideological war was an attritional series of battles
in which no side ever came out convincingly on top.

The government under the disciplinarian Valls was a ticking
bomb. The new centrist prime minister had been appointed to
push through cuts to state spending of €50 billion and reductions of €40 billion in business taxes as part of Hollande's
'Responsibility Pact' to tackle overspending and to spur
employment. But Economy Minister Arnaud Montebourg, the
flamboyant left-winger who had repeatedly tussled with company
bosses, wanted stimulus efforts for consumers and was known
to be a fierce critic of austerity. He had once accused Merkel of
wanting to impose 'Bismarck-style' policies on Europe, a reference to German chancellor Otto von Bismarck who humiliated
France in the 1870–1 Franco-Prussian war.

The tensions exploded in the open on the last weekend of
August. Montebourg fired an opening public salvo against his

government on the Saturday, telling *Le Monde* in an interview that 'you have to speak up. Germany is trapped in an austerity policy that it has imposed across Europe.' Hollande read the comments with fury during a trip to the Comoros Islands off the coast of Africa. Only days earlier he had said publicly that he wanted to avoid a confrontation with Berlin.

The last thing he needed was a minister challenging his authority. The annual return to work at the start of September after the country's long August holiday was already shaping up badly. The government had recently halved its growth forecast for the year to 0.5 per cent and unemployment was at a record high. The debate about public spending in Europe remained unresolved. The left of the Socialist Party, backed by influential economists such as the Nobel Prize for Economics winner Paul Krugman, saw budgetary rigour as a German-imposed straitjacket that had caused unnecessary harm to southern European countries, particularly Greece. They proposed higher public spending to spur economic growth. But so far France had hardly been a victim of austerity.

The country's public spending was the equivalent of 56 per cent of its annual economic output (GDP), the second-highest in Europe behind Finland, and was four points higher than it had been during the economic boom years a decade ago. France's budget deficit in 2014 was nearly 4 per cent, while extra spending would bloat the public debt – which had shot up to nearly 95 per cent of GDP – even further.

Act two of Montebourg's insurrection came the following day at a local Socialist Party event in his constituency in the Burgundy region of western France. The Rose Festival in the village of Frangy-en-Bresse brings hundreds of local activists together each year for an afternoon of speeches, games and hearty meals of local sausage or chicken washed down with lashings of the region's renowned local wines. Montebourg had been the star attraction since being elected from the area in 2007 and he arrived in front of the assembled reporters in visibly high spirits, dressed down in jeans and a white shirt. He was accompanied by Benoît Hamon, a fellow-traveller from the left-wing of the Socialist Party who had been promoted to education minister only four months before. The meal was eaten under a giant tent, with Montebourg flamboyantly opening bottles of crisp white wine in the late muggy heat of summer. 'I'm going to send the President a good bottle of vintage economic recovery,' he joked in front of reporters, sounding like a man who might need a lie down and a glass of water soon.

But he was just warming up for his speech. In it, Montebourg reprised some of the inflammatory comments he had made to *Le Monde*, but this time in front of the waiting television cameras which relayed the unfolding drama live on the rolling news networks. Hollande was following events in his office in the Élysée. Montebourg did not hold back after mounting a stage to deliver his remarks. 'France is one of the founding members of the European Union and it's not in her interests to align with the obsessions of Germany's right-wing,' he said in an open attack on Hollande's Europe policy.

Then he launched his second scud. 'I have asked for and urged the president to make a major change in our economic policy,' he said. 'After helping companies with their competitiveness ... it's equally important now to help families and households.'

Hamon, serving as sidekick, said he agreed with Montebourg, adding that being in the government was not a 'chain or a muzzle' and they were free to express their convictions.

The defiance was a gift to Hollande's political opponents. The same evening, Valls sent out an aide to brief the press, saying that Montebourg had 'crossed the line'. He and the President were resolute that such an obvious challenge to the government could not go unpunished. The search began immediately for a new economy minister.

Their first choice was Louis Gallois, the one-time head of the state railways, SNCF, and the European aerospace and defence giant EADS (and an *Énarque* naturally), who had prepared a report for Hollande in the first few months of his term recommending a 'shock' reduction in business taxes to revive France's declining industry. But Gallois had been appointed to a high-paying job as chairman of the board of car maker Peugeot only a few months earlier. He declined.

What about Emmanuel Macron? He was young, and dynamic. Wouldn't his background and politics send out a strong signal to reassure the business community that Hollande was serious about reform after his false start in power? No one would see him coming and he was bound to provoke some positive headlines. Valls backed him, as did Jean-Pierre Jouyet, Macron's old boss at the *Inspection des finances* and his long-time ally and friend. Jouyet had been brought in as chief of staff in the Élysée earlier in the year, and had briefly overlapped with Macron.

Despite having vetoed Macron for the role of budget minister in March on the grounds that he had no elected mandate, this time Hollande was prepared to bend his rules. It had been 48 hours since Montebourg and Hamon's outburst and the press and his right-wing opponents were having a field day.

Once he was offered the position, Macron was under pressure to make a decision quickly. Having talked it over with his wife, he accepted. 'We really weren't expecting this,' Brigitte told her local newspaper *Les Echos du Touquet*. To take up the job and be ready to be unveiled in the morning, Macron would need a government car to get back to Paris and a suitable pair of shoes, having no footwear worthy of a new minister in his holiday home, he said.

'It's exhilarating, isn't it, being in charge of the economy, companies, industry, all of that at your age, no?', Jouyet asked Macron paternally over the phone from the Élysée after his decision.[2] 'It's everything I would have liked to do. I thought I was the boss at the *Inspection des finances*, now it's you who's going to be the boss,' he added.

The new government was announced the same evening. Montebourg's sacking was confirmed, as was Hamon's. The latter earned the dubious distinction of being an education minister who was fired without ever overseeing the start of a new school year. The fellow leftist rebel (and Montebourg's partner) Aurélie Filippetti, the culture minister, was also replaced.

Prime Minister Valls called the reshuffle an 'act of authority' in a prime-time television interview in the evening and reminded ministers that they were expected to toe the government line. The nomination of Macron had the intended effect in the media: he was quickly leading news bulletins and was the top item on all the major websites where quickly-written profiles of the new face in government mentioned his reputed brilliance and culture, but also focussed on his past at Rothschild. Valls leapt to his defence: 'So what?', he shot back when asked about Macron's banking background: 'Can one not be an entrepreneur in this country? Can't one be a banker?'

Macron's nomination also deepened the estrangement between the government and the serving leftist Socialist MPs.

One of them, Laurent Baumel, called the move an 'obvious provocation'. Montebourg went out of government in a blaze of glory, calling austerity a 'financial absurdity' that had extended France and Europe's economic crisis, which he said was the worst since the Great Depression in 1929.

In their final meeting, Montebourg also had some personal advice for Valls. The Barcelona-born 51-year-old prime minister was by then the most popular politician in the country, helped by his confident prior performance as interior minister, as well as his intense Iberian looks which saw him consistently voted among France's most handsome politicians. He was also notoriously abrasive and had earned the nickname 'Pepe' from some cabinet colleagues after a stubborn Spanish boy who features in the Asterix comics.

Valls' ambitions were barely concealed. He had sought the nomination to stand as the Socialist presidential candidate in 2011 and no one doubted that he saw himself as a future head of state, perhaps as early as 2017. 'You're making a huge error,' Montebourg told Valls in his warning about Macron: 'He's going to kill you. He'll steal your position as the modern face and you'll be left with nothing.' Montebourg had sized up Macron at the Élysée and correctly foresaw that there was only room for one dashing young reformer in the government. Macron and Valls held broadly similar views on the need for greater flexibility in the French economy, lower public spending and more efforts to stimulate private enterprise. Both had been close to former Prime Minister Michel Rocard, the figurehead of France's moderate reformist Socialism.

Macron's arrival in government was an entirely unexpected opportunity, borne like so much of history by the chance coming together of events and circumstances. As with his backing of Hollande in 2010 before the implosion of Dominique Strauss-Kahn's presidential run, Macron could count on the vigorous backing of influential people and was in the right place at the right time – Virtù *and* Fortuna.

Taking over at the economy ministry – housed in an ugly modernist building on the bank of the Seine in eastern Paris – gave him his first national platform and the opportunity to put into action some of the reforms he had championed for so long behind the scenes. He held responsibility for industrial policy, managing the state's broad and powerful interests across the economy, as well as overseeing the regulation of the internet. But in keeping with his attitude to every role he'd ever had, he would not see the initial job description as a constraint. He had a direct line to the president: too bad if he overstepped his brief occasionally and squashed some of his ministerial colleagues' toes in the process.

Macron's time in office got off to the worse possible start, however. At the beginning of the week, on the day of Montebourg's theatrics, he had agreed to talk to a journalist from *Le Point* weekly news magazine about the economic reforms that France needed. Not imagining that he was about to be called into government, Macron spoke freely and candidly of his earlier experience in the Élysée.

The article was published on the Thursday, while he was still arranging his new office in the ministry. In it, he had taken aim at one of the totems of the left: the 35-hour work week that had been introduced by the Socialist Prime Minister Lionel Jospin in 2000. In the interview, Macron proposed letting companies negotiate working time and conditions directly with their employees, rather than having to follow the top-down national labour code which imposed everything from working hours to the placement of water coolers. France needed 'to get out of this trap', he said, although this concept was 'difficult to explain … especially when one is on the left.'

If his appointment was a 'provocation' in the eyes of many in the Socialist Party, then this statement was a red rag. Although the pro-business lobby group Medef sounded delighted, trade unions immediately denounced him as trying to undermine workers' rights. 'The left loses its credibility when it starts trying to unpick part of its own heritage and what it has achieved in the past,' warned the head of the Socialist group in parliament, Claude Bartolone.

The government moved quickly to try to extinguish the fire. The prime minister's office issued a statement saying that the 35-hour working week legislation would be respected, adding that Macron's three-day-old interview had been conducted 'well before' his appointment. This first controversy was certainly not deliberate, but Macron would nonetheless make a habit throughout his time in government of attracting the spotlight. Sometimes intentionally, by daring to break with Socialist Party orthodoxy or by criticising government policy; sometimes by accident, with a slip-up or fumble. But the effect from day one, quite apart from the public interest in his unusual personal life, was to make him into a political celebrity – a role he fuelled with regular media interviews. The irony would not be lost on Manuel Valls when, once Macron was elected president in 2017, he told his ministers in their first cabinet meeting that he expected discipline, collective responsibility and for them to stay away from the press.

Three weeks after his nomination as minister, Macron's first media outing was an unmitigated disaster. Speaking on the *Europe 1* radio station, he brought up the example of a bankrupt abattoir in a village in the western Brittany region to illustrate the difficulties of getting laid-off workers back into jobs.

'One of my briefs is this abattoir [called] Gad; it's a company where the majority of employees are women and a lot of them are illiterate,' he said. 'We come along and explain to these people that they don't have a future at Gad, that they need to go to work 50–60 kilometres from there,' he said. He explained that the problem was that many couldn't read or drive and couldn't pass the tests to get a driving licence which was needed to travel to other factories.

The comments were picked up on social media immediately and a furore quickly snowballed. Macron had named-and-shamed the most vulnerable of the abattoir's employees and tarnished many of their literate colleagues. His use of 'these people' added insult to the injury by seemingly confirming everything his opponents suspected about him: that he was a snooty, over-privileged ex-banker and *Énarque* who had no idea about real people. 'If you don't know anything about it, shut your mouth,' one of the abattoir's employees remarked to reporters as she drove in for work. 'It shows clear contempt for us,' local trade unionist Jean Marc Detivelle said.

Ministerial colleagues and media advisors quickly realised they had a crisis on their hands. To try to douse the controversy, Macron agreed to go before parliament in the afternoon to offer his apologies. 'My main regret, and my most abject apologies go to the employees [of Gad], whom I upset with my words for which I can never say sorry enough,' he said. 'My focus will be to help them, which was what I was saying this morning.'

He was barely audible above the sound of booing. An opposition MP from Brittany was on his feet waving his arms and leading the shouting, which would have been intimidating for anyone, not least a 36-year-old minister with only three weeks of experience.

But Macron was in a combative mood, defending himself against accusations by another MP that he shared Hollande's reported view of the poor as the 'toothless ones'. 'My regret today is that you are so appalled by words but you're not so appalled by the reality,' he said before being drowned out by the noise.

It was an early lesson in how every one of his statements would now face a level of scrutiny he had so far not been accustomed to. He prided himself in talking frankly, in naming problems as he saw them. Illiteracy was a reality in France, afflicting 2.5 million working-age people in 2012, according to government statistics. He continues to think he was right to have raised the issue, but has conceded in interviews since then that it was a mistake to personalise it with people who were humiliated by the attention.

The episode highlighted one of the persistent questions about Macron: how much does he know and understand working-class people? In France's professionalised political class, there are few who could point to any authentic experience of struggle or deprivation. Though his family background is resolutely middle-class, since arriving at the age of sixteen at one of Paris's most exclusive schools Macron has inhabited a world of privilege, wealth and influence. He is naturally curious about people of all backgrounds and a master at making them feel important on a one-to-one basis, but his social and professional life has been spent in the company of life's winners.

Of course, there's nothing intrinsically wrong with being surrounded by well-educated, successful friends, but during his time as economy minister, and in his first months as president, Macron consistently offered ammunition to critics who saw in him signs of the sort of snobbishness that is so prevalent among France's elite classes.

He appeared conscious of this during the presidential campaign of 2017, letting slip in front of a camera during a badly-organised meeting with trade unionists that 'we've been *bourgeois.*' Admonishing his campaign staff, he added: 'I can't afford to look like a banker.'

Macron blundered again at the end of his time as minister in May 2016 while visiting the southern town of Lunel in the sunny Languedoc wine-growing region, a mix of both picturesque narrow streets and run-down concrete housing estates. It had gained notoriety as a breeding ground for jihadists with about twenty local youths having left to fight in the Syrian civil war since 2013.

Macron was visiting an IT training centre there, designed to help tackle local youth unemployment which was up to 40 per cent in some areas and particularly prevalent among the town's large Muslim population. As was customary during all of his visits around this time, a handful of protestors gathered outside, using loudhailers to denounce the government. Macron, impeccably tailored in a dark suit and flanked by his security guards, decided to go outside to talk to them. In his lexicon this is called 'going into contact': something he professes to love and does repeatedly, and is the opposite of 'bunkerising yourself' which means avoiding protestors at all costs.

This time, though, it went badly. At the end of a lengthy discussion with a 60-year-old local agitator and an unemployed 21 year old about his government's planned labour reforms, Macron lost his temper. He claimed the men failed to show respect by addressing him as *tu* instead of the formal *vous* required when talking to a minister. Though highly informal with work colleagues, Macron likes to see the hierarchy respected when he is addressed by a member of the general public.

The younger protestor, Jordan Michaux, who was dressed in a black and white 'Free Palestine' t-shirt, harangued Macron over the labour reform and the lack of job opportunities for people like him. Michaux had started but hadn't finished a catering qualification and was stuck between odd jobs and handy work. 'I wanted to tell him that we're fed up. That all these short-term contracts, they're dividing society,' he told the *Libération* news-paper afterwards.[3] In the part of the conversation not shown on news bulletins that night, a witness from the scene claimed that Michaux had said something along the lines of 'with your cash you can buy yourself suits.'

Macron became visibly angry and let rip with a phrase that became an instant social media sensation. 'You're not going to scare me with your t-shirt!' he said. 'The best way to buy yourself a suit is to work.'

Michaux replied: 'But I can only dream of working Mr Macron.'

As well as sparking an immediate craze for t-shirts that mocked Macron, and the Twitter hashtag #atshirtforMacron, it led to a deluge of commentary about the damage he had done to the government and to his own reputation. 'The words of the economy minister from a left-wing government, especially when he has never been elected and is a former banker with a personal fortune, ooze a sort of class contempt,' said a column in the left-leaning *Libération* newspaper. It was 'suits against t-shirts. The elite against the proles. Workers against the workless.' The head of the hard-left CGT trade union, Philippe Martinez, compared Macron to the French advertising guru Jacques Séguéla who famously said in 2009 that 'if you haven't got a Rolex by the time you're 50 you've messed your life up.' Even if he had the money, Michaux said he wouldn't buy himself a suit, adding: 'We don't all want to be bankers.' 'It was taken completely out of context and I don't regret it,' Macron said of the clash.[4] 'I'm sure I'll make other mistakes; sometimes I get carried away, but the beauty of politics is to try to persuade people, to meet them, and I'll continue to do that.'

At the end of his first month in office, once the furore over his criticism of the 35-hour week and the row over the illiterate abattoir workers had died down, Macron set to work in the economy ministry reorganising its own way of working to make it less hierarchical. 'Everything was done to make sure that ideas quickly flowed up from the bottom to him,' remembers Eric Dupas-Laigo, who worked there at the time. Macron's office door was often open and using *tu* to address the minister was, within the ministry at least, commonplace.

In between giving interviews to the *Financial Times*, the *Wall Street Journal* and the *Economist*, he and his team of senior policy advisors began preparing a new reformist law, which was billed as the centrepiece of the government's economic policy at the end of yet another terrible year for Hollande. The number of unemployed in France had climbed by around 5 per cent over 2014 to a record 3.5 million.

Unveiled on 10 December, the new law aimed 'to improve the lives of French people concretely and rapidly,' Prime Minister Manuel Valls said. Drearily named the 'law for growth, activity and the equality of chances,' it was quickly dubbed 'Macron's law' in the media.

Despite all the sound and fury it would provoke, its scope and ambition were relatively modest. This wasn't 'big-bang' structural reform, but a series of proposals designed to deregulate specific sectors of the economy. It would allow the creation of private long-haul bus companies which Macron had said would help 'the poor' travel more easily (another verbal faux-pax which earned him more criticism); it would open up the highly-regulated legal services business to more competition with the aim of lowering prices; it proposed a modest extension of Sunday shopping and would tweak labour law, as well as the functioning of labour courts and the regulations for driving schools. There were also provisions to help start-ups. Even President Hollande would later concede that it 'wasn't the law of the century'.

Nonetheless, tens of thousands of lawyers and solicitors descended into the streets immediately to denounce the proposed changes. Macron received anonymous death threats and there were strikes in regional labour and commercial courts. Protesters chanted '*Macron, patrons, même combats!*' (Macron, bosses: same demands!')

'These [Macron's proposed changes] are all the old demands of the European Commission,' said the Eurosceptic far-right leader Marine Le Pen dismissively. The far-left critic Jean-Luc Mélenchon called the plan to open shops on Sunday the 'sanctification of our consumer society'. Left-wingers in the Socialist Party said the law was too right-wing and the right-wingers said it was too timid. News website *Mediapart* declared it 'neoliberal': a dirty word in French politics.

The intensity of the reaction was partly explained by the targets of the measures. Sunday trading had been a hot-button political issue in France for decades, fought against by the left not for religious but for social reasons, as a way to guarantee a day of rest for all workers. Others saw in the law a weakening of the paternalist force of the French state: it was best, they thought, to prevent people going shopping lest they be tempted to go on a consumerist binge when they should have been at home with their families.

New bus lines meanwhile would compete with the state-run SNCF railways, which occupies a special place in the French psyche given its employees' role in the Second World War Resistance movement and its symbolic value as a demonstration of the country's state-backed industrial might. It was also one of the country's biggest employers with around 150,000 workers.

Macron worked hard behind the scenes throughout December and January, meeting lawyers' representatives one day, rebellious Socialist MPs another as he tweaked some of the measures in the draft law. To succeed, he needed to build consensus and a parliamentary majority to get the legislation through the national assembly.

He didn't help his cause with the Socialist Party in early January 2015 when he told *Les Echos* newspaper that the internet was an 'industry of superstars'. 'We need young French people who want to become billionaires,' he said, immediately antagonising left-wingers. It was classic Macron, pushing the boundaries while grabbing attention. It was also sincere: he genuinely believed France needed to celebrate success more and get over its suspicions about wealth. The spat recalled some of Tony Blair's struggles with his Labour Party over income inequality in Britain. Macron's views can be summarised as being broadly in line with Blair's wingman Peter Mandelson, who famously stated that he was 'intensely relaxed about people getting filthy rich as long as they pay their taxes.'

Socialist Party boss Jean-Christophe Cambadélis sniffed that 'the lure of profit for billionaires is not exactly my cup of tea' and wondered aloud if Macron was offering the right advice to young people.

When he rose to present his bill in parliament on 26 January, Macron and Prime Minister Valls were confident they would have a majority to pass it at the end of the two weeks of scheduled debate. 'This country has its back to the wall, the status quo is no longer an option,' Macron told the few lawmakers present on the largely empty red velours seats of the assembly. 'This law will allow us to prove that we are capable of moving forward.'

To keep a watchful eye on the young moderniser, the Socialist parliamentary group assigned a brusque left-wing MP from western Brittany, Richard Ferrand, to assist Macron with the drafting of the final version of the bill.

But Ferrand soon fell under his charm, becoming an apostle for the legislation, and even some opposition MPs from the right-wing UMP admitted to admiring Macron's ability to spend hours answering questions in parliament. Some sessions lasted until the early hours of the morning. There were thousands of amendments tabled. But article by article, through compromise and persuasion, the bill ground its way through parliament with the debate overrunning its allotted time and stretching into a third week. At her home, Macron's mother Françoise was watching events on the parliamentary channel, sending him encouragement and suggestions by text message.

On Sunday 15 February, during a marathon examination of the final bill that went on until 6am, the leader of a faction of left-wing Socialist rebels in the parliament, Benoît Hamon, declared that he would vote against it. The former education minister, who had been sacked along with Macron's predecessor Montebourg, argued that the bill failed to make enough concessions on Sunday working hours. The leader of the right-wing UMP party, ex-president Nicolas Sarkozy, also instructed his lawmakers to oppose it. (Sarkozy, who had taken to the lucrative conference circuit after being beaten by Hollande in 2012, had returned to front-line politics after being voted head of the UMP in November the previous year.)

'Mr Macron is a tap of lukewarm water that has run for fifteen days and someone even forgot to turn it off over the weekends,' the head of the UMP parliamentary party, Christian Jacob, said in a withering verdict on Macron's performance in parliament. The law was worth 'between nothing and not much,' he added.

As the final vote loomed on 17 February, Prime Minister Valls faced a dilemma. The government had so far never lost a vote in parliament under Hollande but their majority in this instance was estimated to be razor-thin at three to six votes and success depended on about a dozen opposition MPs crossing the line and supporting the government. About 25 Socialist MPs were preparing to follow their rebel colleague Hamon and vote against the law while another twelve or thirteen would abstain, the PM's office estimated.[5]

After consulting with Hollande, Valls decided to use an

authoritarian constitutional weapon contained in article 49, point three, of the French Constitution (known as '49.3' in shorthand) which allows the executive to ram a law through parliament without it being voted on. It had last been used in 2006 by a right-wing government (Chirac's), which had led Hollande, then head of the Socialist Party, to denounce its 'brutality'.

This was a humiliating lesson in party politics for Macron. The bill passed through parliament and became law, but the use of the 49.3 mechanism meant it lacked legitimacy in the eyes of many voters. 'When I saw his face on the bench of the assembly I thought he was going to resign that night,' his mother Françoise remembered.[6] All those hours spent patiently arguing his case in a near-empty parliament, meeting MPs privately, making changes to the bill. All that lack of sleep and effort in the noble cause of democracy and reform. Few forces had stood in his way so far in his life: he'd conquered Paris on his own like a young *Rastignac*, convinced his school teacher to leave her husband for him, brokered a multi-billion-euro transaction at Rothschild that few thought him capable of. But the use of the 49.3 felt like defeat, even though the bill had passed. This was a bitter taste he'd experienced only a few times before: when he failed the entrance exams to École Normale Supérieure or when he was knocked back by the Socialist Party in northern France.

As he rose to speak in parliament, Macron's eyes had lost some of their piercing blue and looked dark and tired. His bubble of confidence and superiority had sprung a small but perceptible leak. But this was not enough to stop him, an unelected political appointee, giving the assembly a lesson in democracy: 'What our country expects from us, and I say this to all of you … is that we make progress,' he said to jeers. He returned to the economy ministry that night and barely spoke, instead playing the piano, Brigitte remembered.

In his own analysis, a clear majority existed in the assembly in favour of the law, including many MPs from the UMP who were supportive. But Sarkozy had instructed them to vote against the legislation for tactical reasons: to weaken the Socialists ahead of upcoming regional elections. And the rebel Socialist Hamon and his acolytes were merely posturing ahead of an imminent Socialist Party conference where Hamon was eager to emerge as the leader of the left-wing of the party. Hamon had also seen an opportunity to bring the golden-boy Macron down a peg or two. 'This bill was taken hostage, it was sunk by political games,' Macron told *Le Monde* a few days later.

It was a crucial moment in his reflections about what ailed France, why it seemed immobilised and so resistant to change. 'The 49.3 was a failure and he experienced it as a failure,' his old friend Marc Ferracci said. 'It was an important moment.' Macron's decision to launch his own political movement can be traced back to this day in mid-February 2015. His bruised ego would be the driving force. And when he launched his presidential bid, saying that he had seen the 'vacuity' of the political system and wanted to change it, what he meant was that he had experienced first-hand how political games and personal ambitions could thwart legislation. He was convinced he was working in the national interest, while Hamon and Sarkozy were acting in theirs alone.

CHAPTER 9

The Precocious Minister

'MACRON'S LAW' SIGNALLED THE START OF AN OPEN BAT-
tle between the government and Socialist rebels in the parliament
that would lead Valls to use the 49.3 six times in total. Despite
Macron's sense of failure, the episode helped raise his public profile and earned him sympathy from many right-wing voters who
liked the law's pro-business objectives. In a poll published the
following week, he was now the 14th most popular politician in
the country, with 45 per cent of French people holding a positive
opinion of him, up six points and five places in a month. Valls,
meanwhile, had tumbled to sixth place.[1]

Furthermore, when the results of the legislation filtered
through and began to be felt in daily life, many voters associated the convenience of more Sunday shopping with Macron.
Similarly, the thousands of colourful shiny buses which began
trundling between previously unconnected towns and cities from
the summer of 2015 also became known as 'Macron's buses'.

'I think people know where this new opportunity came
from,' Roland de Barbentane, the chief executive of one of the

bus companies, OUIBUS, said at a campaign stop for Macron in January 2017. 'You only need to go online and look at the positive reaction.' He continued that it was 'amazing to see how a law can free up a new sector of activity and create new jobs in such a short space of time.' Nearly 5 million people travelled on 'Macron buses' in their first year, demonstrating the latent demand for the new services by consumers who were lured by the low prices or the convenience of being able to reach new parts of the country from their homes. It was an undoubted consumer success, which garnered most of the attention, but as a job creation scheme it fell abysmally short of expectations: there were only 1,430 direct recruits at the bus companies by the end of the first year, compared with a government report which had forecast up to 22,000 new positions in total.[2]

But Macron's first year and half in the economy ministry were not just about producing new legislation. He also became an enthusiastic flag-waver for 'French tech', the vibrant start-up scene centred around Paris which included the world-leading online publicity group Criteo and the car-sharing service BlaBlaCar. He travelled to tech conferences around France, to New York and notably in 2016 to the huge industry show in Las Vegas, where the giant French delegation spent €300,000, including around €100,000 for hotel bills. Macron appeared, uncharacteristically, with a three-day stubbly beard, perhaps in order to blend in among the tech start-uppers. This trip is now the subject of a fraud investigation, having been organised in a hurry and without respecting public procurement procedures. (The probe does not target him personally.) He also sponsored competitions for entrepreneurs to seek funding from the state investment fund Bpifrance, which had been created early in Hollande's term.

In Macron's view, France had flunked its adaptation to the first wave of globalisation in the 1980s and had missed the surge of investment in robotisation by leading manufacturing nations which had begun in the 1990s. It could not, he thought, afford to miss out on the industries of tomorrow in the new sharing economy, alternative energy, online learning or artificial intelligence.

A row that broke out over the expansion of app-based taxi firm Uber into France was emblematic of Macron's drive to embrace modernity, underlining his core message that France needed to be 'turned towards the future'. The American company began seriously disrupting France's highly regulated taxi business in 2015, particularly with its now-banned UberPOP service that allowed anyone to start using their car to pick up passengers. It led to blockades around Paris airport as well as on other roads in June of that year which saw taxi drivers burn tyres and set fire to several cars being used by their competitors.

Macron agreed that UberPOP should be banned, but he took on the powerful taxi lobby by defending the US company's right to exist. 'It's normal that there is innovation, new ways of doing business in the driving sector,' he said. He was dubbed 'the Uber spokesman' by protesting taxi drivers who complained in large cities that they had paid hundreds of thousands of euros for their licences which were now falling in value.

Pascal Beneganos, a 42-year-old driver, took out a ten-year loan in 2012 to pay the €350,000 for his licence in the southern city of Nice. 'I bought it because there were rules and then suddenly there weren't any,' he said during the presidential campaign. 'I wouldn't suddenly set up a stall in front of the tobacco shop and start selling cigarettes cheaper, would I?' He said he didn't know any taxi drivers who planned to vote for Macron. 'He's bad news for us. Maybe we're part of all the regulated professions that need to disappear, eh? Like solicitors and pharmacies,' he added, referring to previous targets of 'Macron's law'.

There were other concerns too. Uber paid very little in tax in France thanks to an accounting sleight of hand which saw it reduce its profits to almost zero. Drivers had no job security in this new 'gig economy'. Some complained about working 60–70 hours a week for less than the minimum wage.

But the benefits for the wealthier consumers who used the service were felt instantly. In Paris, the city's notoriously rude drivers were suddenly friendlier. Frustrating long waits for a taxi on street corners during rush-hour, rain or in the early hours of the morning were a thing of the past. And Uber was recruiting a large proportion of its drivers from the ranks of the unemployed or under-employed, often African-origin Frenchmen.

Macron made this latter point repeatedly in candid, and reductive, terms: 'Go to Stains [a deprived area north of Paris] and tell young people there who are willingly working for Uber that it would be better to do nothing or deal drugs,' he said. 'Our collective failure is that we have offered these people nothing … [Uber] gives them self-worth, they're entering the workplace, they're putting on a suit and tie. What have we offered them that's better in the last 30 years?'[3]

Macron's attachment to the suit can be judged by his repeated references to it as a status symbol, as well as his own insistence on wearing one for almost every public appearance. Like most young men, his suits have improved immeasurably with time, having graduated from baggy off-the-peg numbers in his first few years in the workplace to the dark tailored trousers and jackets he adopted from his time at Rothschild. Nowadays he gets his tailoring done at a small and moderately priced boutique in central Paris called Jonas & Cie where a *jacket sur mesure* costs under €350. It's Brigitte, not him, who comes to choose the colour and material, co-owner Laurent Touboul said. 'Mr Macron has kept his shape. In two years, his dimensions haven't budged an inch,' he told *L'Express* magazine.

During the presidential campaign, staffers unsuccessfully urged Macron to go casual occasionally to try to mix up his look. 'Emmanuel has a sort of syndrome of being the top of the class, the best pupil,' one of his close aides, Ludovic Chaker, said. 'For him, he wants to be president of the Republic and being president means looking a certain way. It [the suit and tie] is his uniform, it's in his head.'

In the economy ministry as a pro-business champion of innovation, Macron not surprisingly became a hero of French tech entrepreneurs, among them the telecoms and internet tycoon Xavier Niel, whose partner Delphine Arnault is from the family that controls the LVMH luxury goods empire. Her father Bernard is France's richest man, with a fortune estimated at nearly €50 billion in 2017.[4] Niel and Arnault became friends of the Macrons, with Arnault offering fashion advice to Brigitte during their later campaigning, as well as loaning her outfits from her favourite label Louis Vuitton.

The economy ministry was a formidable platform for networking. Brigitte had moved into Macron's top-floor government apartment with views over the river Seine and had given up her teaching job at Franklin in 2015. She took on a role as his social organiser, but also sat in on meetings occasionally and regularly chatted with staff. It was highly unusual for a minister's wife to be so implicated in the workings of the ministry. But as Macron has repeatedly stated, she is a 'non-negotiable' part of his life, an advisor and muse in private, as well as an unobtrusive but highly vigilant presence in his working life who makes sure he is eating healthily and that staff are not overloading his diary.

She had become a minor celebrity in her own right since Macron's elevation to minister. The celebrity press latched onto their unusual marriage quickly, leading to the unwanted attention of paparazzi, some of whose first pictures appeared in *Closer* magazine a month after he was named minister. 'Emmanuel Macron, married to his ex-teacher!' screamed a front-page headline over a picture of them holding hands in the street, him in jeans and jacket with an unbuttoned white shirt. 'Exclusive photos: she's twenty years older than him!' it added. The Macrons' lawyer sent a threatening letter, pointing out that the pictures infringed their privacy rights.

Brigitte made her first official public appearance the follow-ing summer in June 2015 at the Élysée during a state dinner in honour of the Spanish royals King Felipe VI and Queen Letizia. The photos of the Macrons walking through the perfectly-raked gravel forecourt of the palace – her in a short black dress and red and gold stilettos, him in a classic dark suit – attracted wide press attention.

'Having never bought celebrity magazines and not being particularly interested in them, I can only observe, without entirely understanding why, that they are interested in my pri-vate life,' Macron told the journalist François-Xavier Bourmaud in December. Despite apparently being perplexed at the success of glossy magazines popular with housewives and working-class women, Macron was quick to latch on to how they could help him reach voters who didn't read the daily press or watch the news channels. And the Macron couple were certainly interested in getting to know some of the other people who featured in their pages.

Having been brought together twenty years before by their love of literature and the theatre, the Macrons were regulars at shows around the city, but they began going backstage at the end to meet the musicians or actors. Their circle soon included the prolific actor Fabrice Luchini, recognisable from many French art-house movies that have had international success, who lent Macron his holiday villa on the exclusive Île de Ré off France's western coast in the summer of 2016 while he was writing his pre-election book. They also got to know the veteran leathery rocker Johnny Hallyday and his wife, as well as the writer Philippe Besson.

The book *Les Macron* recounts how they met their loyal showbiz friend Stéphane Bern, a television presenter and historian. Macron's car apparently nearly knocked Bern down as he was leaving a lunch at the Senate in central Paris. As he called out of the window to apologise, Macron recognised the host of *Secrets of History*, a popular show on the France 2 channel. 'Ah Stéphane, my wife loves you,' Macron hollered. 'She talks about you all the time ... she would absolutely love to have dinner with you.' The Macrons' networking included many such bold invitations extended in person, or a discreet card sent by Brigitte to suggest a date for a dinner party.

Brigitte began to attend shows during Paris Fashion Week and the economy ministry was the scene of regular catered dinners for the great and the good. Entrepreneurs, journalists, academics and writers were invited, often being struck by the easy company of the chatty down-to-earth couple and marvelling at Macron's endurance in a social context. Some guests would make their excuses and leave late at night while he stayed up talking. In their investigative book on the economy and finance ministries (*Dans L'Enfer de Bercy*), the French journalists Frédéric Says and Marion L'Hour claimed that Macron spent €120,000 out of his annual entertainment budget of €180,000 in the first eight months of 2016. Staff were reportedly amazed that some nights would feature two sittings for dinner with different guests.

'He used to have a lot of people over for dinner, the power set in Paris across all the networks, and not necessarily people relevant to his work in the ministry,' his former cabinet colleague, Budget Minister Christian Eckert, remembered. Eckert's and Macron's offices were in the giant Bercy ministry building on the bank of the river Seine in eastern Paris, along with those of Finance Minister Michel Sapin. 'You used to cross a lot of people in his ministry and near the ministerial apartment. Everyone knew about it,' Eckert added.

There was an earlier time when Macron had needed mentors to open up Paris high-society for him, like the billionaire centre-left businessman Henry Hermand, ex-Prime Minister Michel Rocard or the super-fixer Alain Minc. But after the Attali Commission, his four years at Rothschild and two as an aide at the Élysée, he was now networking under his own steam, propelled by his own reputation. As another of his patrons, ex-minister and senior civil servant Jean-Pierre Jouyet, had told him at the time he took the job as economy minister: 'You're the boss now.' Still aged only 37, Macron was a media darling, a man with a major reforming law to his name and influential supporters across the business and entertainment worlds.

His position also offered another stage on which to perform: the international one. In his first months in the job, he visited Brussels, Berlin and Tokyo, vaunting France's new willingness to reform and its sudden business-friendly approach. Other trips would take him to Madrid, Rome and London. After Macron had quit as deputy chief of staff at the Élysée in July, Hollande had joked during his leaving speech that 'when I go abroad I often introduce myself as the man who works with Emmanuel Macron.'[5] As minister now, Macron could be more than just the popular back-room assistant. On each trip, he'd give local media interviews and press conferences, often opining on foreign policy issues far beyond his mandate. The focus throughout was Europe, its need for reform, and most particularly the role France and Germany had to play in reinvigorating the EU.

On 20 October 2014, two months after taking office, Macron set off for Berlin with Finance Minister Michel Sapin. Relations between the two men at this stage were still friendly, although Sapin, now aged 65 and an old ENA friend of Hollande's, would eventually grow infuriated with Macron's love of the limelight and the frequent statements he made beyond his remit that conflicted with government policy. Sapin was reported by *Libération* to have privately called him a 'dickhead', although he denied this.

The pair arrived in the German capital with a proposition: in exchange for the €50 billion in cuts to public spending that the French government had pledged, Berlin should agree to increase its public spending by the same amount. This extra spending would help spur economic growth elsewhere in stagnant Europe, particularly in Germany's biggest eurozone trading partner, France. Berlin had run a balanced federal budget since 2012 and had the capacity to spend more through borrowing.

French cuts and German stimulus was a 'good balance', Macron told the German newspaper *Frankfurter Allgemeine Zeitung*. The increased spending by Germany would be 'still compatible with a serious budget policy,' he argued.

Chancellor Angela Merkel and her conservative and powerful Finance Minister, Wolfgang Schäuble, were unmoved. The profligate French were on track to run a budget deficit of around 4.0 per cent of GDP, way above EU budget rules that set 3.0 per cent as the upper limit. How many times had different governments in Paris pledged to rein in spending and proved themselves incapable? France was again in the process of negotiating a derogation of EU rules because of its bloated public sector.

Schäuble fobbed off the French emissaries with a promise 'to draw up a joint paper'. He had made his views abundantly clear before their arrival: Germany was aiming for another balanced budget in 2015. He didn't want 'growth through debt' and Europe needed to clean up its public finances to restore investors' confidence. German austerity would remain in place.

Throughout his time in office, Macron continued to argue, unsuccessfully, for a 'new deal' for Europe that would see Germany raise its public spending to help stimulate growth across the EU area.

On the presidential campaign trail more than two years later, he carried an identical message, but one informed by his chastening experience of negotiating with the hardliner Schäuble. 'If we want to dance the tango, we have to take the first step given everything that's happened over the last fifteen years,' Macron told an audience in March 2017, arguing that France had repeatedly promised the Germans it would cut its public spending and reform its economy without following through.[6] 'If we don't take the first step by accepting our responsibilities, we'll never convince the Germans to make changes,' he added.

The next government would need to start with major economic reforms such as overhauling its labour legislation in the summer of 2017 to 'restore France's credibility' by the time Germany had finished with its federal election in September, he argued.

While he was economy minister, Macron also locked horns with Schäuble repeatedly over Greece, which was in crisis again for the first half of 2015, after the election in January of that year of the leftist Greek Prime Minister Alexis Tsipras, who came to power pledging to re-negotiate the terms of the country's international bailouts.

Greece had been the first eurozone country to require financial aid in 2010 when the global financial crisis left the government unable to borrow money on international markets. Greece had been forced to admit that its public deficit for 2009 was more than double the 6.0 per cent of GDP it had officially declared, leaving investors worried about the country's solvency and unwilling to extend more credit.

The first package of emergency loans it received in May 2010 was worth €110 billion, financed by the troika of the EU, the European Central Bank and the International Monetary Fund. In return, Athens pledged severe public spending cuts and painful economic reforms of its social security system and corruption-ridden public sector. The measures led to a collapse in Greece's domestic economy, triggering ever higher claims for welfare payments.

Again in crisis in 2011 and unable to meet its repayments, Greece sought a second rescue package in which the troika stumped up another €130 billion and private holders of Greek public debt agreed to write off a further €100 billion.

By 2015, an economic depression had led Greece's economy to shrink by a quarter; unemployment was at 25 per cent; public debt was 177 per cent of GDP and thousands of young Greeks had gone overseas in search of jobs. Despite progress in balancing its budget and the fact that the country was once again able to borrow on international markets, Tsipras and his hard-left Syriza party tapped into widespread public anger that citizens were being punished for the mistakes of past governments by the country's over-zealous creditors, chief among them Germany. Merkel and Schäuble were portrayed in Nazi-era military garb in Syriza-aligned newspapers. Tsipras also publicly raised the issue of forced loans by the Greek central bank to the Third Reich during the country's war-time occupation. Proper compensation now would help alleviate the country's dire financial problems.

In Germany, Greece was seen by the government as reaping what it had sown when it cheated on its public finances and failed to reform both its stagnant industry and its overly generous welfare state which it could not afford. *Der Spiegel* magazine put Tsipras on its front page after his election with the headline 'Europe's Nightmare'.

Every time the Greek premier raised his demands for debt cancellation, Germany pointed to the danger of moral hazard: letting Greece off would encourage others to spend irresponsibly (the German word for debt, *Schulden*, is the plural of *Schuld*, meaning guilt or fault).

France, with Macron in a secondary role, attempted to bridge the gap between Greece and Germany. In the game of brinkmanship that developed over the first half of 2015, Greece risked being ejected from the eurozone and defaulting on its debts. Tsipras knew that if his country was forced to leave, many investors would wonder if debt-ridden Italy or Spain might be next, undermining confidence in the whole shared currency area. But he was clearly in the weaker position, with the effect on the Greek economy of the country's sudden exit likely to be devastating, while the eurozone as a whole was now seen as much more solid than at the start of the decade. 'Hand over the money or I'll shoot!' said a headline in the German *Handelsblatt* newspaper showing Tsipras holding a gun to his own head. Ultimately, the Greek premier blinked first, agreeing to a new set of reforms in return for a third bailout worth up to €86 billion in July.

Greece's finance minister, the erratic and hard-left Yanis Varoufakis who antagonised many eurozone partners during months of negotiations, revealed during the 2017 campaign that he felt a grudging respect for Macron, despite disagreeing with his liberal politics. 'Macron was the only minister of state in Europe that went out of his way to lend a helping hand,' the former university economics teacher wrote.

Having worked in debt restructuring while at Rothschild, Macron had some experience in the area and had long felt that Greece's debt pile was unsustainable and would need to be partly cancelled. This view was shared by the IMF and a host of senior economists too, but was strongly contested by Berlin. In June, with investors and EU governments growing increasingly anxious that Germany was prepared to see Greece tumble out of the single currency area, Macron texted Varoufakis: 'I do not want my generation to be the one responsible for Greece exiting Europe.'

In his 2017 book *Adults in the Room*, Varoufakis recounts how Macron unilaterally proposed himself as a mediator, offering to fly to Athens to speak with Tsipras to find a solution. Never mind that neither President Hollande nor France's main negotiator with Greece, Finance Minister Michel Sapin, were aware of this offer. Macron suggested via his backchannel to Varoufakis that Tsipras call the Élysée to confirm he was ready for a meeting. When Tsipras did so, he was met with incomprehension. 'Hollande's office replied that they have no idea about a possible mission by Macron to Athens. They referred us to Michel Sapin.' Tsipras asked Varoufakis angrily. 'Is he pulling your leg?'

Macron explained events to Varoufakis four months later in October of that year, saying he had been frozen out of the negotiating process – apparently at the insistence of Merkel. The German chancellor had not appreciated Macron warning that the bailout deal with Greece risked being another 'Treaty of Versailles' – the crippling First World War settlement imposed on Germany that contributed to the rise of fascism. He might also have failed because he was clearly trying to muscle in on sensitive multilateral negotiations and his opinion that debt relief needed to be on the table clashed with both Hollande's and the German government's view.

When Tsipras capitulated and accepted the EU's demands and signed a new bailout deal, Macron observed that this final agreement was 'the best deal possible'. 'We succeeded in putting the issue of Greek debt on the table – which is progress when compared with the start of the discussions.'

Elsewhere, over the summer of 2015 at a time when Europe's established parties and leaders were terrified by the steady march of Eurosceptic left and right-wing populist parties, Macron fleshed out his views that 'more Europe' was needed, not less. The young dreamer dared to raise ideas that would require treaty changes, which sent shivers through Eurocrats after the debacle of the 2005 referenda to ratify the European Constitution. There was almost no appetite among leading politicians in France and Germany for further European integration.

If it didn't budge, Europe would be condemned to 'populism and national egotism,' Macron argued.[7] The eurozone needed its own parliament, and a finance minister who would oversee a new budget to transfer money from wealthy members to those in need of stimulus: like Greece. But objections to funding Greece were why negotiations over the country's third bailout were so protracted and bad-tempered. Other financial transfers were already in place in the form of so-called EU structural funds, which are used for everything from road-building to professional training in poorer member states, but Macron argued that more was needed.

In August 2015, he stated this view in a joint article with his ally Sigmar Gabriel, the German vice chancellor from the centre-left SPD party. The SPD was part of the German coalition government dominated by Merkel and Schäuble's conservative CDU. 'The eurozone needs new institutions to which national governments transfer more sovereignty: a strong European economic government in control of its own budget,' they wrote. They argued that the issue of treaty changes would have to wait until 2017, however, after the French and German elections.

Macron made this latter point again in London in September 2015. 'We shouldn't make changing a treaty into a sort of trauma or taboo,' he said in front of the French press. But he offered little encouragement for the British Prime Minister David Cameron, who was trying to convince his EU counterparts of the need for major reform ahead of an in–out referendum on whether Britain should stay in the EU.

Cameron wanted changes to one of the four founding pillars of the EU project: the freedom of movement of workers between member states. This had been responsible for a surge in EU nationals living in Britain (around 3 million in 2015, according to official statistics)[8] and the Conservative government wanted to be able to restrict their access to benefits such as tax credits and child support payments.

The Brexit negotiations showed how Macron's and Cameron's visions of the EU were fundamentally at odds: Cameron was suspicious of greater integration between eurozone countries and wanted an assurance that Britain, as a non-euro member of the EU, would not be sidelined. He also held the traditional view from London of the bloc as primarily a free-trade area, not a political project of shared sovereignty. Cameron wanted a promise that Britain would not be forced to accept the EU's stated goal of 'ever closer' union between its members and that London would not have to contribute to future bailouts of eurozone members.

In the spring of 2016 ahead of the referendum on 23 June, Cameron half-heartedly attempted to sell the British public a series of concessions granted to him by EU members, including a new mechanism allowing Britain to restrict benefits to EU migrants if they could be shown to be 'putting excessive pressure on the proper functioning of its public services.' Britain's status as a peripheral but full EU member, not committed to future integration, had also been endorsed.

At a conference organised by the *Financial Times* before the referendum, Macron urged Britain to see that its interests lay in being a full member, not a distant associate country. 'If you want an efficient and powerful relationship with the European Union, why do you want to leave the club?', he asked. 'You will take two years to renegotiate something new, for what? The sort of relationship that Norway or Switzerland have.'

The shock vote in favour of Brexit, cheered by the then US presidential candidate Donald Trump and the French far-right leader Marine Le Pen, served to deepen Macron's conviction that politicians needed the courage to make the case for Europe with greater clarity and passion. And Europe's people needed to see the benefits in their own lives of a political project which was too often seen as distant, bureaucratic, high-handed and unwilling to stand up for struggling workers. It needed a 'positive project,' he argued. His views on Brexit, and his contempt for leading Brexiteers, would become clear during the presidential campaign.

Presidential Dreams

CHAPTER 10

Presidential Dreams

THE EXACT POINT AT WHICH MACRON BEGAN CONSIDERING a 2017 run for the French presidency is difficult to pinpoint. Over the course of the summer of 2015, polls showed that he was having a major impact on public opinion. Right before the Socialist Party's summer conference at the end of August there had been another example of his ability to make himself the centre of attention by speaking either too candidly or deliberately provocatively, when he declared that the 35-hour working week was one of the 'false good ideas' of the left. Introduced by the government of Socialist Prime Minister Lionel Jospin in 2000, the reduction in the working week was intended to generate more jobs and raise wages by forcing companies to recruit higher numbers of workers or pay greater amounts in overtime. It was also seen on the left as another victory for workers' rights that provided greater leisure time.

Government policy was to leave it alone and the subject remained a raw nerve in the Socialist Party. As angry left-wingers reacted to his comments and the media devoted most of the attention they would otherwise have spent on the conference talking about Macron, exasperated Prime Minister Valls issued yet another call to order. 'When you're in government, every word, every attitude, every phrase is important,' he said.

Valls' fortunes had turned for the worse. Although he had recently been the country's most popular politician, his approval ratings had been sliding for months and took a further hit in June when he flew two of his children on his government jet to watch the final of the Champions League football competition in Berlin. Polls at the beginning of September suddenly showed Macron ahead. A survey by the CSA polling group identified Macron as France's second-most popular politician, and suggested that he was particularly appreciated among right-wing voters.

Around this time, the Socialist Party chief Jean-Christophe Cambadélis went to see Macron at the economy ministry at Hollande's urging. Cambadélis wanted to discuss recent tensions within the party and to size up Macron's political intentions. Recalling the meeting from an armchair in his office in the party's grand headquarters in central Paris, Cambadélis said he was struck by the effusiveness of Macron's welcome. 'He was very warm, open, all enveloping, touchy-feely. You'd have thought we'd known each other since kindergarten,' he said. 'All of that leaves me a bit cold, but I noted I had a complex character in front of me and started to talk to him about his future.'

Cambadélis, a large-framed 65 year old, was looking ahead to presidential and parliamentary elections in 2017 and saw Macron as a potential asset for the party. There was a possibility for him to run for safe Socialist seats in Lyon or Marseille, he said. Or to head a regional government in northern France. Less than ten years after he had failed in his efforts to run as a Socialist candidate around Le Touquet, Macron had the head of the party in his office offering him a choice of opportunities!

'He considered what I was saying but I could tell he wasn't completely convinced,' Cambadélis added. At which point he said he asked whether Macron would be interested in starting a new centre-left political movement under the Socialist Party umbrella, which could be used to energise voters for Hollande's re-election bid. 'To connect with the people the Socialists have trouble reaching out to: start-uppers, people outside of traditional politics,' Cambadélis remembered.

Macron replied that he had been considering it. 'Three times I said to him "in support of the President's re-election?" and not once did he reply yes,' Cambadélis said. 'A few days later I saw the President and said to him "Macron has an idea in his head, watch out" and he dismissed it with a wave of his hand.'

Hollande remained convinced of Macron's loyalty. Yes, the inexperienced minister had a tendency to speak too frankly and perhaps enjoyed being the centre of attention too much, he believed. But he knew his place and knew who his patron was. Hollande was just the latest older man to fall for Macron as the 'ideal son', charmed by his mix of wit, intelligence, eagerness to learn and faux-naivety. The president had certainly developed almost paternal feelings for his underling, a mixture of pride and protectiveness. Some allies wondered if Hollande had wanted to create the sort of relationship with Macron that he would have liked to have had with President Mitterrand when he started out in politics.

'Macron is not someone who is seeking his own political space at the expense of the government … that's not true,'

Hollande told the journalists Gérard Davet and Fabrice Lhomme for their book *Un Président Ne Devrait Pas Dire Ça* ('A President shouldn't say that'). 'There might be some clumsiness but there's nothing perverse.'

Showing signs of frustration with his frequent outbursts, many ministers in the cabinet had taken to showing French reporters text messages that they had received from Macron saying sorry for his 'screw ups'. Hollande would receive abject apologies in person each time he tried to discipline his protégé, normally in his characteristic indirect and unconfrontational way. Macron would invariably claim that he hadn't intended to overstep the line or that his words had been taken out of context by the press. 'There's a childish side to him,' Hollande reflected.[1]

In October, in the utmost secrecy, Macron asked his two most loyal lieutenants in the economy ministry to begin thinking about creating a new political movement. He had been a minister for just fourteen months.

The first person taken into confidence was 28-year-old Ismaël Emelien. The political strategist and communications expert, who was a fan of the *West Wing* TV series and boxing, had been named as an advisor in the ministry by Macron after the pair had abandoned their plans to launch an e-learning start-up together in 2014.

The second was 34-year-old Julien Denormandie, who like Emelien was a former advisor to Finance Minister Pierre Moscovici and had first met Macron when the latter was working as deputy chief of staff in the Élysée.

Their brief was to look into how Macron could leverage his burgeoning public profile and popularity ahead of the 2017 presidential election. There were several possibilities. 'One way was to join the Socialist Party and create a new movement, or to set up a political foundation or association, or to propose a sort of contract that we'd get the main candidates to sign,' one of the men said in an interview conducted on condition of anonymity. Both of them are notoriously media-shy.

From October, Emelien and Denormandie widened the circle slightly. They brought in friends who they had first met ten years earlier while working as junior staffers on the unsuccessful campaign of Dominique Strauss-Kahn when he was seeking the Socialist Party nomination for the 2007 presidential election.

Brought together by politics, the group had stayed in contact, frequently dining out, spending weekends away together with their families and taking holidays. Apart from Emelien, they were all in their mid-to-late thirties, they had all attended either Sciences Po or the top business school HEC, and all had experience in centre-left politics and business. The 'Macron boys' as they were later dubbed in the French media were remarkably similar to their leader.

This inner core included Benjamin Griveaux, an HEC graduate who had started out in local politics in his Burgundy region before taking a highly-paid job doing PR for property developer Unibail. There was also Cédric O, who had been an advisor in the economy ministry until 2014 before he switched to working for the defence company Safran. He had also graduated from HEC, as had Stanislas Guerini, who had worked for Strauss-Kahn before setting up his own renewable energy company. Convened by Emelien and Denormandie, they began meeting in the evenings at each other's homes, often gathering at 9.30pm to eat pizza or take-out food accompanied by a decent bottle of wine. 'We're all hard-workers and we all had very busy lives,' said Guerini, who like Denormandie and Griveaux has young children. 'One of the features of our group of friends is that we're able to separate out time for socialising and for work when we're together. When we met for these meetings, we were very focused.'

Macron only attended when there were major decisions to take or conclusions to present. Otherwise, Emelien and Denormandie, who saw him every day at the economy ministry, acted as go-betweens. Philippe Grangeon, a 60-year-old strategic advisor at the Cap Gemini consultancy who knew Macron from Hollande's campaign team in 2012, also joined the discussions, adding some experience to the team of young guns.

The working-group discarded the idea of joining the Socialist Party and starting a movement, as party boss Cambadélis had suggested to Macron during their meeting in Macron's office over the summer. The discussions were soon focused on launching Macron's own movement, a political party in all but name. But they would need an identity, a clear ideological offering, staff, money and an electoral strategy.

In November, the team brainstormed possible names for their organisation at a meeting attended by communications and marketing expert Adrien Taquet, who had also come on board. As the hours ticked by, they drank whiskey and tossed around ideas in another intense but good-humoured session. Later on, Taquet, whose own advertising firm had worked on campaigns for Eurostar, Martell cognac and Mikado biscuits, had a flash of inspiration: *En Marche*.

It is most commonly translated as 'on the move' but can also mean 'on the march' or 'moving forward' depending on the context. It conveys movement, progress and has echoes of '*marcher*' which means 'to walk'. Best of all, its initials were the same as

Emmanuel Macron's. It was given an exclamation mark for extra emphasis: En Marche!

Over the autumn as these meetings took place in the evenings and at weekends, the economy ministry was also abuzz with work as Macron and his team prepared what was intended to be his second reformist act of parliament: the law for 'new economic opportunities' or *Noé* for short. The media dubbed it 'Macron II'.

At a major press conference on 9 November with the heads of companies like the car-sharing group BlaBlaCar and biotech firm Eligo Bioscience, Macron unveiled his plans for this law with typical fanfare. The proposed legislation contained a series of new measures intended to encourage start-ups and widen their sources of funding. It also would abolish compulsory qualifications for dozens of professions such as hairdressing, which Macron viewed as both unnecessary and an obstacle for people wanting to start a business. At the same time, it would increase adult professional training to help workers adapt to the new digital-focused workplace. But before serious discussions about Macron's latest attempt to modernise the economy could take place, France was struck by catastrophe.

The country had been traumatised once already in 2015 when two brothers in their early thirties, armed with Kalashnikov machine guns, attacked the offices of the satirical magazine *Charlie Hebdo* shortly before midday on 7 January. After storming its morning editorial conference with shouts of *Allahu Akbar* ('God is greatest'), the gunmen murdered eleven people including some of the country's most famous cartoonists: Cabu, Wolinski, Charb, Tignous and Honoré. As they fled, the gunmen executed a Muslim policeman at point-blank range outside the magazine's headquarters near the Bastille monument in central Paris. 'They're dead, they're all dead, come quick!' Patrick Pelloux, a doctor and contributor to the magazine, screamed down the phone to his friend President Hollande after arriving on the scene.

The attack had been carried out as revenge for the magazine's decision to repeatedly publish caricatures of the Prophet Mohammed – considered blasphemous by many Muslims. In 2011, with a headline reading '100 lashes if you don't die of laughter,' an issue invited Muhammad to be a 'guest editor' for the weekly. It was one of the numerous deliberate provocations in defence of free speech that had led to lawsuits, an office fire-bombing and frequent death threats.

The attack horrified France and turned *Charlie Hebdo* into an international symbol of press freedom. The *#JeSuisCharlie* ('I am Charlie') hashtag became a global phenomenon and hundreds of thousands of people marched in the streets of France in solidarity.

It also sparked a debate about whether *Charlie Hebdo* stigmatised Muslims in particular among its frequent and merciless depictions of religious figures of all types. Some French Muslims declared themselves 'Not Charlie'. And followers abroad were left wondering what to think of this eccentric and previously niche brand of French humour, which was often in poor taste and nasty in the service of the higher ideal that nothing and no one should be above satire. In the public rallies of support afterwards, some participants held aloft copies of *Treatise on Tolerance* by the French Enlightenment philosopher Voltaire, whose views published in 1763 were summarised by one of his biographers as 'I disapprove of what you say, but I will defend to the death your right to say it.'

The gunmen, radicalised Muslims who claimed that they had been financed by Al Qaeda in Yemen, were killed in a shoot-out with police two days after their attack. A third gunman, an ex-convict, took hostages at a Jewish supermarket, killing four of them and claiming in an interview aired live on the BFM channel that he was a terrorist from the Islamic State group. He was shot dead when anti-terror police raided the building.

Macron largely kept out of the ensuing public debate about the state's security failures, the spread of extremism in prisons and the blind eye France had turned as fundamentalist interpretations of Islam had been taking hold in mosques and communities in parts of the country. One of the gunmen, abandoned like his brother by his Algerian parents as a child, had spent time in jail with known radicals and had been a member of a Paris-based jihadist group which had sent fighters to Iraq after the US-led invasion in 2003.

Days after Macron had unveiled his second reformist law, a far bigger and more devastating attack took place. This atrocity led to a much more divisive debate in which the sense of national unity that had emerged after the *Charlie Hebdo* murders was lost. It would damage irreparably Macron's already-strained relationship with Prime Minister Valls at a time when he was already thinking of striking out on his own.

The first sign of the night of carnage on 13 November was early in the first half of a friendly football match at the French national stadium in Paris between France and Germany where President Hollande was watching from the VIP enclosure. The sound of a large explosion, audible to the millions watching on television, surprised the players, but led to cheers in the 80,000-strong crowd where many thought it was a firecracker. A first suicide bomber had detonated his explosive belt just outside the stadium after being refused entrance, killing a passer-by.

Simultaneously, in the trendy 10th district of Paris, gunmen in a black Seat car pulled up outside the *Carillon* bar and a Cambodian restaurant, both popular hang-outs packed with locals laughing, drinking and smoking on a typical Friday night out in the capital. Fifteen people died in bursts of automatic gunfire. Another five were killed at a different nearby café. A second, then a third, then a fourth bar was attacked where dozens more lost their lives.

At the Bataclan concert hall, three gunmen with suicide vests burst into a sold-out performance by the American rockers *Eagles of Death Metal* and began firing indiscriminately into the crowd of 1,500 people. They took hostages and told police negotiators over the phone that the attack was revenge for French military action in Syria and in Iraq against the Islamic State terror group. Three hours later, after the gunmen had issued threats to kill their captives, elite anti-terror police raided the venue, bringing an end to the siege. A total of 89 people had died inside. The scene was so gruesome that later in the evening a police investigator came out of the concert hall vomiting.

A total of 130 people died and more than 300 were injured in the course of the evening in the worst violence on French soil since the Second World War. The coordinated attack on young people out enjoying themselves had involved nine gunmen and had apparently been planned and executed from Syria.

While the *Charlie Hebdo* attack provoked disgust and defiance, the 13 November atrocities left France shell-shocked and scared. People wept at makeshift shrines at the venues where pictures of the young, smiling victims were placed among the flowers and candles. Takings in restaurants and bars plummeted. The violence was a turning point, both in awareness about how the metastasising Syrian civil war posed a direct threat to the French people but also about how the country had entered a new era of insecurity. France grappled for answers to why it was being singled out for attacks and why, with French Muslims again among the attackers, second-generation immigrants were turning against their own country.

President Hollande, having been evacuated from the football stadium, declared a state of emergency, sent troops onto the streets and called the attacks 'an act of war'. Three days after the bloodshed he convened a special joint session of parliament at the former royal palace in Versailles outside Paris to deliver a speech that was to be one of the defining moments of his presidency.

In it, he struck a martial tone, promising to 'destroy' Islamic State, ordering the country's *Charles de Gaulle* aircraft carrier into action against the terror group and promising thousands of new police, customs and judicial jobs. He planned to extend the state of emergency for three months, which would simplify police work and diminish judicial oversight. All of these measures could count on broad support under the circumstances. But Hollande also proposed that any French person convicted of a terror offence with dual nationality – a Franco-Moroccan, for example – should have their French citizenship revoked.

This would require a change to the French constitution and it immediately created unease among the Socialists and cabinet. Not only did it have unfortunate echoes of France's collaborationist past when the Pétain regime cancelled the citizenship of around 15,000 opponents (including that of General de Gaulle), but it had also been a longstanding demand of the far-right.

'I was tempted to leave [the government] over the issue but it [revoking passports] wasn't part of my ministerial responsibilities,'

Macron explained during campaigning.[2] He lobbied against the proposed constitutional change along with other cabinet colleagues including Justice Minister Christiane Taubira and Interior Minister Bernard Cazeneuve.

The measure was wildly popular with the public. Some polls showed that nine out of ten people backed it. The far-right National Front pointed out that they had been proposing this for some time, with the party's vice president Florian Philippot adding that common criminals should have their nationality revoked for serious offences, not just terrorism.

But the logic against the measure was compelling. Macron objected to it partly on a philosophical level: in removing citizens' nationality, France was expelling people from its society without trying to understand their actions. There were also serious doubts about its efficacy: a suicide bomber was unlikely to be worried about his passport being removed. And on a practical level, there would be difficulties expelling French-born terrorists. Why should other countries accept them? Even Manuel Valls wondered aloud 'is the symbol worth all the trouble, for three or four people?' But showing loyalty to the President, he agreed to push it through cabinet and into parliament.

Justice Minister Taubira, the country's most senior black politician, resigned at the end of January, saying she had a 'major political disagreement' with the government and wanted 'to be true to myself, to my commitments, my battles and my relationships with other people.' Different versions of the draft law then bounced between the lower and upper houses with no sign of agreement. Hollande eventually abandoned the measure at the end of March 2016 after four months of bitter debate. It was his 'only regret' during his time in office,' he later said.

'I thought it would bring us together. Instead it divided us,' he conceded.[3]

The week after the attacks Macron addressed the left-wing think-tank Les Gracques. It was another demonstration of his willingness to expound the full range of his beliefs. France was in mourning, many were baying for revenge and the focus was on the police busting down doors to arrest terror suspects and close radical mosques. Macron backed the state of emergency decreed by President Hollande but 'only because it is temporary'. (One of his early acts as president would be to extend it for a sixth time in July 2017 and propose a new security law making many of its provisions permanent, however.)

But Macron also told the think-tank that the country needed to look inwards and had to face its 'share of the responsibility' for why young French men, mostly from poor Muslim backgrounds, were joining the terrorists of the Islamic State group. Around 1,500 were estimated to have travelled to the territory it controlled in Syria and Iraq.

The idea of *égalité* (equality) lay at the core of French identity, yet the country failed to offer opportunities for its newest arrivals, notably Muslims, Macron explained. 'Someone who has a beard or who has a name that could sound Muslim has four times less chance of getting a job interview than someone else,' he said. 'I'm not trying to say that all these things are the cause of jihadism. It's human madness and it's a sort of totalitarian manipulation of people. But there is a breeding ground and this breeding ground is our responsibility.'

Macron had publicly raised the sense of alienation felt among France's large community of African-origin Muslims, who arrived in large numbers in the 1950s and 1960s to fill job vacancies after the Second World War. This feeling of alienation was evident in the way that many of their children continued to view themselves as second-class citizens 50 years later due to their experience of racism and discrimination. In the most deprived areas, often desolate high-rise, out-of-town housing projects in *les banlieues* (the suburbs), police, firefighters and even postal workers faced threats of violence as symbols of state authority. Hatred of the Republic was a recurrent theme in French rap music of which the 2010 song 'Fuck France' by ZEP was a vivid example. The resentment and anger so vividly captured in Mathieu Kassovitz's 1995 film *La Haine* ('The Hatred') burned just as brightly ten years later when huge urban riots swept France. In 2016, a noxious mix of global terror propaganda was spreading via the internet and combining with underlying social and religious tensions to devastating effect.

In a destructive cycle of mutual incomprehension, the far-right National Front fed on the disgust felt by many white French people at the violence, anti-social behaviour and lack of gratitude shown towards the nation by the angriest, most disaffected residents in *les banlieues* despite the provision of free education, health care and public housing.

The attempt by Macron to explore some of the deep and complex social problems at the heart of France's terror problem at such a sensitive time went down badly with Prime Minister Valls. 'I've had enough of people who are permanently trying to find excuses or cultural and sociological explanations,' he said shortly afterwards in the Senate. At the beginning of January, Valls made his thinking clearer: 'There can't be any valid explanation. Because to explain is to excuse a bit.'

The Prime Minister, who had fought as much as anyone to have Macron made a minister, was coming to his wits' end. On a personal level, the prophesy from sacked Industrial Minister Arnaud Montebourg that Macron would steal Valls' space as the modernising figure in the Socialist Party had been correct (Montebourg had said Macron was going to 'kill' Valls). And Macron continued to make the Prime Minister's job difficult by causing tensions in the cabinet and parliamentary party with his indiscipline and lack of solidarity.

'I follow the rules but he doesn't,' Valls complained to Hollande.[4]

But Valls still had control, along with Hollande, over the bills that the government planned to introduce in parliament. After the attacks, Macron began updating his proposals for his *Noé* law, adding in new suggestions for reforming labour law to make it easier for companies to hire-and-fire. 'It was a series of ideas to respond to the economic and social state of emergency raised by the attacks,' a close advisor explained on condition of anonymity. 'It was a shock package of ideas, but it was refused [by Valls].'

Macron had joined the government on the strict understanding that he would be given licence to reform the French economy. But less than eighteen months in, his first law had been forced through parliament in what he saw as a personal defeat. And now Valls had snubbed his second effort, opening a clear rift between the two men. He'd reached the same stage as he had in the Élysée under Hollande: all avenues for further progress looked blocked. It was time to consider a new move.

Behind the scenes, he was widening and deepening his network of media, entertainment and business contacts. During his secret late-night dinners, he and the Macron boys were drawing up plans for the next stage in his meteoric rise.

Other older mentors like the nationalist left-winger Jean-Pierre Chevènement, whom Macron consulted, or Alain Minc, urged him to take his time and build his career the traditional way.

'I was saying to him that he should lay the groundwork for a run in 2022, that he should run a large city for example,' Minc explained. 'But he replied "you've no idea. You're talking about yesterday's world. It doesn't work like that now".'

CHAPTER 11

On The Move

ON 7 JANUARY 2016, THE FORMER DIPLOMAT AND CHINA specialist Ludovic Chaker was taken on as the first official employee of En Marche. Chaker was a long-time friend of Ismaël Emelien, Macron's top advisor at the economy ministry. After returning to France at the end of 2015 from a stint working alongside the French army in Iraq, Chaker met Macron and accepted a new mission. The stocky and well-groomed martial arts expert, then aged 36, was tasked with managing the logistics and initial groundwork needed to get the movement going.

He joined the ongoing and regular late night dinners and weekend meetings with the other founding members, with the group sometimes eating at restaurants like *Le Square Gardette*, a trendy bistro in north-east Paris. 'We'd go to different places so that we didn't have the same patterns,' Chaker says. 'We were all a bit paranoid at the time.'

The group had made major progress in defining some of the most important issues. 'We wanted it to be an inclusive movement, which had two direct consequences,' Stanislas Guerini, one of the members of the inner circle, said. 'Firstly, signing up would be free, so there was no financial barrier for people. And the second was that you could be a member of another political group and be a member of our movement.' Becoming a member would be as easy as filling out a basic form on a website; less oner-ous than buying a train ticket or a book online.

The members of the team had also taken on different roles. Emelien and Denormandie were the main strategists, assisted by Griveaux. Guerini was the HR manager, in charge of identifying the skills and people the organisation would need. Chaker did operations, while Cédric O would be in charge of fundraising. The latter teamed up with Emmanuel Miquel, another HEC graduate who worked for the French private equity fund Ardian. 'We're all from the same generation,' Chaker said. 'We speak to each other as mates, all very informal. The relationships between us are simple.'

Others included Stéphane Séjourné, another advisor from Macron's cabinet, who would be responsible for reaching out to potential political allies once the movement was launched. Macron would also regularly consult his former chief-of-staff at the economy ministry, Alexis Kohler, a former Énarque who had left to take up a job at a shipping company in Geneva. 'Alexis is the last person he speaks to every day,' one of his team said on condition of anonymity.

Another crucial stage was in defining what would be offered to members once they filled out the form on the En Marche website. The team wanted each of them to sign up to a charter of values as they joined. 'We wanted a clear commitment from people,' Guerini said. 'The charter was aimed at clarifying some of the things that the traditional parties were divided over.

'We made it clear that we had an obviously pro-European vision. We also stressed that for us work was a value, which was a problem for some on the left, which had abandoned this as a theme. Our view was that work should be something that liberates people and we put liberty at the same level of priority as equality,' Guerini added. 'We also wanted to state that we believed in progress – we were progressives, as opposed to conservatives – and we believed that kindness was a fundamental value.'

Despite this, En Marche would be criticised consistently for being vague and for lacking a clear programme. Guerini disagrees. 'The charter was very clear,' he said. Pro-European, committed to work, and progressive on both social issues and the role of innovation. The fourth founding value – kindness – was a nebulous but attractive concept that recalled the motto adopted by Google's founders: 'Don't be Evil.' It was impossible to disagree with, but difficult to define in practice.

'Without wanting to be immodest, it was something that we felt defined us. We were all people who knew the political world and we all found that kindness and benevolence was completely absent,' he said. 'It had struck all of us individually.'

Was En Marche intended to lead to a presidential run in 2017? 'Yes, absolutely,' said Chaker in one of several interviews he gave at campaign headquarters. 'We approached it [creating the movement] with the idea of winning the election from the beginning.'

Others have claimed it was not clear whether all this would culminate in an election run. All agree that it was intended to turn Macron into a major national figure who would have an influence on the vote, either directly as a candidate or as someone who might offer his support to someone else in exchange for clear commitments on policies. It was an extraordinary escalation in Macron's ambitions: only eighteen months previously, he was footloose, having just resigned from his first job in politics, and was preparing to launch a start-up and begin some university lecturing. Now he was eyeing the highest office in the land, having never before stood for election.

What is certain is that in early 2016, a presidential run looked utterly fanciful. The first round of the election was scheduled for the following year on 23 April. Anyone was free to enter, providing they garnered 500 endorsements from elected figures around France.

Under the electoral system, the top two finishers in the first round would go through to a second-round run-off vote, scheduled for 7 May, when whoever of them won more than 50 per cent would be declared president.

At this stage, the polls showed the far-right leader Marine Le Pen and the centre-right moderate Alain Juppé, a 71-year-old former prime minister from the Republicans, qualifying for the run-off. Juppé, then the country's most popular politician, was forecast to easily win the second round.

Juppé, however, would first need to win a primary vote to stand as the Republicans candidate in November, almost certainly being pitted against party boss and ex-president Nicolas Sarkozy. There were other uncertainties: no one knew if President Hollande would try to defy his catastrophic approval ratings and seek re-election. If so, Hollande would need to win a primary that was being organised by the Socialists in late January 2017. Would the veteran centrist François Bayrou run for the presidency for the fourth time?

Nothing about Macron's intentions leaked in the press for months, but in early March *L'Obs* magazine reported that he was preparing to launch his own party. Macron swiftly denied it, calling the story 'a journalistic fantasy'. He then called the author of the article to ask for the sources of the article (a request which was naturally declined).

The main political news in early 2016 was a new labour law, presented by Hollande's inexperienced Labour Minister Myriam El Khomri, which included some of Macron's suggestions for changes to the rigid work code. It was instantly watered down in the face of resistance from trade unions, but still sparked massive street demonstrations when it was introduced in parliament.

Changes to labour law are among the most sensitive reforms in France, striking at the heart of what are known as '*les acquis sociaux*' – social benefits and protections. These are the fruits of two centuries of struggle between French workers and often abusive business owners. Among them are advances such as the ban on child labour, while others are measures that have improved working conditions for everyone: the progressive reduction in working hours, guaranteed paid leave, pensions, rights to redundancy compensation, protective labour contracts, and improved health and safety measures. For trade unionists and many on the left, making it easier for companies to fire workers, and undermining their contracts or any of these hard-fought rights, is an assault on this march of progress.

In early April, En Marche moved into its first offices, a small ground-floor space on the Rue des Plantes in the south of Paris with a large bay window which Chaker covered up for security reasons. The space belonged to the wife of a director of the pro-business think-tank the Montaigne Institute (which was set up in 2000 by the founder of the AXA insurance giant, Claude Bébéar). The link was revealed by the left-wing investigative website *Mediapart*, which said that En Marche had 'received important but discreet logistical help from one of the most influential business groups'. En Marche replied that the owner of the space, the wife of Laurent Bigorgne, was a 'personal friend' of Macron's.

Chaker got to work setting up the office. He had to take on the first volunteers to help with the workload. 'I'd organise a meeting point and then go to fetch them rather than give out the address,' Chaker remembers. 'It was all a bit James Bond.'

There was a huge amount of logistical work. The founding members and Macron had decided that the movement would be self-organising. Members would sign up and then be directed initially to regional committees and then local sub-committees which would organise to bring people together physically. The team at headquarters needed to select the regional leaders and coordinators, but then each local committee would be encouraged to organise autonomously.

Also in the first days of April, Macron went to see Hollande to inform him about the creation of En Marche, unsure how the president would take the news. He was preparing to go public the following week. As the most popular minister in an unpopular government it would be difficult for Hollande to sack him. However, if he was cut loose then he would lose the prestige and platform of his ministry.

'I want to do something – there are people asking me to do it,' Hollande remembers Macron saying to him as he described his plans for En Marche. 'I can reach voters who are outside of normal politics.'

Hollande listened and then replied: 'OK, do it. But be careful not to take any politicians on board because then it will look as if it's a move inside the Socialist Party or worse, like competition.'

'No, no, it's going to be a people's movement,' Macron reassured the President.[1]

Chaker remembers the feeling within En Marche afterwards. 'His [Hollande's] reaction was pretty positive which made us think "that's a bid odd",' Chaker said. 'Some reports afterwards claimed that Hollande was pushing Macron and that he was behind the movement, which wasn't the case at all.'

It was true that nine months previously Hollande and the Socialist Party boss Cambadélis had already discussed the idea of Macron launching a political movement to help the president's re-election campaign. Cambadélis had warned Hollande that it would not ultimately be to his benefit, but the head of state still seemed convinced that Macron would remain loyal, or at the very least, that his efforts could be co-opted at some point.

The launch date was set for 7 April and organised on a 'shoestring budget,' according to Chaker. The team booked a hall at the *Mégacité* conference complex in Macron's home town of Amiens, which was meant to underline his credentials as a man from the provinces, rather than the Paris elite. The minister, along with Brigitte, was driven to Amiens from Paris in the afternoon in his black Renault saloon car, stopping to eat sandwiches in a motorway lay-by. The events were captured by the French documentary film maker Pierre Hurel who had been invited by Macron to shadow him for the next six months.

Hurel's presence was the first indication that Macron had started to put in place an image management strategy, which would be crucial to his presidential run. The advantage of having

Hurel along was that it suggested Macron was committed to transparency, offering rare behind-the-scenes access to a journalist. As such it was nothing new: ex-president Giscard d'Estaing had done the same with renowned filmmaker Raymond Depardon in 1974, who was himself inspired by the 1960 election film on J.F. Kennedy called *Primary*. Dismayed by the final product, Giscard d'Estaing later blocked the release of Depardon's film, *Une Partie de Campagne*, until 2002.

Hurel's largely flattering production, *Macron, la Stratégie du Météore* ('Macron, the Strategy of the Meteor'), would have no such issues when it was broadcast on one of the main channels in November just as Macron was launching his presidential bid. Macron even shared his wedding video, showing his speech as well as him and Brigitte dancing afterwards.

His decision to allow himself to be filmed repeatedly also underlined his confidence in his self-control, knowing that an unguarded comment or reaction in front of the camera could prove disastrous. He would repeat the exercise during his presidential campaign, allowing a different documentary team to follow him around which led to similar, largely flattering results.

After arriving in Amiens for the launch, Macron rehearsed his speech with Brigitte before a few hundred people arrived to take their seats in the hall. The event had been advertised on Facebook, with Macron's team then selecting the applicants who would attend individually. Brigitte, her youngest daughter Tiphaine and her husband, as well as Macron's mother sat in the front row. Despite now having leaked the news to the media to raise awareness about his announcement, Macron's newly-formed team kept journalists out of the room. The moment would be captured by his hand-picked personal cameraman, but troublesome reporters who might ask questions were not desired. They were directed to a live broadcast on the internet.

Against a simple grey screen, Macron was dressed down by his standards (suit, but no tie), and he moved around the stage with a microphone in his hand and no notes, looking like he was giving a speech at a TED Talks event. The traditional left–right split in politics had no meaning any more, Macron explained to the audience. 'The division stops us in many ways. I saw it when I was proposing a law in the parliament,' he said. On the biggest issues facing France – its policy on Europe, its response to globalisation, immigration or innovation – the main parties which had structured French political life for decades were hopelessly divided, he said.

He then introduced a video to explain his ideas and thinking. Set to guitar music and images of young multi-ethnic people, it was accompanied by a narrative explaining that 'wherever you go you hear people saying the same things: France needs to move on. We need to try new ideas to advance, to dare, and put an end to being bogged down. This isn't anything new, it's France's illness … it's time to get ourselves on the move.'

The final image flashed up the name of En Marche for the first time. 'It's a new political movement. I don't know if it's going to work,' Macron said. He looked genuinely unsure, almost sheepish and goofy at times. The whole event was low-key. There was no inspirational rhetoric or thunderous applause. It was just a man in a suit on a cheap-looking stage saying he wanted to transform the country.

He stressed again how the roots of his initiative stretched back to the humiliating day in parliament when his law had been blocked by rebels within the Socialist Party. Although it was intended to be a people's movement, Macron made clear that En Marche was intended to serve him and his agenda. 'I can see everything that I can't do, that's blocked, and this movement is [an attempt] to get past all that,' he said.

'It was neither of the left nor the right,' he explained. 'It's a bit radical, it might seem a bit crazy here tonight, but there's such energy in the country. I hear the protests and the fears. But I want the positive energy, those people who want to propose ideas, to go forward. They can join this movement and get on the move. It starts tonight and everything depends on you.'

In the city of Nantes in western France, Morgan Simon, a 30-year-old entrepreneur who ran two franchised Pizza Hut restaurants, was watching the webcast over the internet. He had never been involved in politics before, but he logged on to the movement's new website the same evening and followed the easy procedure to sign up, filling in just basic personal details. 'I already liked him,' explained Simon, a large man with a scruffy beard who usually dresses in a cap and sweatshirt. 'It was his speeches, the "Macron Law", the way he talked about trying to get France moving. I followed the launch and said to myself that something was happening.'

Back at En Marche headquarters in Paris, the team waited for the reaction. Did Macron have the charisma and public profile to rally support? Was there appetite for his message of youth, action and optimism? 'We were surprised by how quickly it took off, it was really fast,' said Guerini. 'In the hours after the announcement, we had a new person sign up every second on average. It was impressive.'

In the media, the launch was interpreted immediately as yet another sign that Macron was preparing the way for a presidential run. He hadn't mentioned Valls or Hollande by name in his speech and had offered nothing more than half-hearted backing to the government's reforms. The political positioning of En Marche as 'neither left nor right' was clearly an attempt to create a new space for Macron himself. Valls called it 'absurd' to suggest that the old left–right division was obsolete. 'That's the way our democracy works,' he said. Hollande was more supportive, saying: 'A minister who wants to start a conversation with citizens and try to spread his convictions, that's called politics.'

After the launch, Brigitte followed up with her first ever interview, which ran in *Paris Match*. The glossy still sells half a million copies every week, mixing serious news, celebrity and royal coverage with photo essays. Brigitte's interview was splashed on the front page with the headline 'Together on the road to power'. She revealed for the first time in public how the power couple had got together. Over four pages inside there were pictures of them and snaps from the family album. One featured them skiing, another showed Macron playing with their large cream-coloured dog, Figaro, at their holiday home in Le Touquet; in another, he was bottle-feeding one of Brigitte's grandchildren.

Hollande was due to go on television that evening for a major interview and was furious with his economy minister. The decision was 'stupid', Macron explained, and was because Brigitte didn't understand how the media worked. 'The idea is not to expose my family life, it's probably a mistake and not something we'll do again,' he told reporters. Between April 2016 and the election, the couple featured on the front page – each time with their assent – five times, once with Brigitte in a swimsuit.

The latter photo shoot, on the beach in Biarritz in the summer of 2016, was organised on the advice of the gravelly-voiced queen of the Paris paparazzi, Michèle Marchand, who the couple had taken on as a consultant in the spring, after being introduced to her by the tycoon Xavier Niel.

'Think about it,' was Marchand's advice to Brigitte about the swimwear pose. 'The whole of France is talking about your age gap, and you'll blow them away. Accept it, you're beautiful,' she said, according to her version of their conversation, recounted to *Vanity Fair* in a rare interview.

'Mimi', as the 70-year-old Marchand is known in her business, is a chain-smoking former mechanic and nightclub owner who works with a host of celebrities and politicians, including Sarkozy's popstar wife Carla Bruni. Able to snuff out troublesome images or arrange for paparazzi to take pictures if requested, Marchand is head of the Bestimage agency, which works hand-in-glove with France's voracious celebrity press.

In fact, her first task for the Macrons was to hunt for compromising pictures of Macron which were rumoured to be in circulation, a friend of the couple said on condition of anonymity. Brigitte confided that she was worried a paparazzo might have taken images of her husband that, through their composition, would give the false impression that he was cheating on her with a man. Speaking of her 'image management' work for the rich and famous in the April 2017 interview, Marchand confided: 'Soon I'll have more dirt under the carpet than on top of it.' But the family friend insisted that Marchand had found nothing when looking for the Macron images. 'The rumour was false,' the friend said.

The impact of the Macrons' first appearance in *Paris Match* was huge. 'As a magazine, we're still a bellwether for the country because we sell a lot through newsagents and retailers all over the country, so you can see the reaction to each edition,' the magazine's editor Olivier Royant said. 'There was a big increase in sales with the first Macron cover and I said to myself "there's something going on here". I think there was a real interest in the couple because they were different and it was an extraordinary love story. I think readers sensed that they were genuine. And for Macron, I think it was a revelation too.'

As for Macron's suggestion that the interview was a mistake by Brigitte, 'that was what he had to say in front of Hollande,' Royant added, noting that the images of the happy couple and their family life contrasted with the troubled personal life of the head of state, who was then living alone in the Élysée. Brigitte's revelations about how they had co-written the play together at school, how she had fallen under the spell of his intelligence and then seen him leave for Paris were widely picked up by celebrity and women's magazines. Some commentators in the mainstream news media scoffed at a rather blatant and hackneyed piece of publicity and pointed out how Brigitte seemed to conform to all the stereotypes of a traditional political wife. 'I have to be attentive to everything, to do everything to protect him,' she explained, while watching her phone in case Emmanuel called.

'The minister's wife understands the requirements and her mission,' a commentator at *L'Obs* magazine wrote. 'The former literature and Latin teacher, no doubt a well-read woman, has transformed into a simple foil for her husband.'

During the spring and early summer of 2016, major protests were sweeping the country. Opposition to the government's labour market reforms saw a series of huge trade union-backed demonstrations, infiltrated by anarchists and thugs who threw bottles, rocks and Molotov cocktails at the police. Around

300 officers were injured in the first few months in some of the worst clashes in recent memory and around 1,000 people were arrested, some of them with excessive force.[2] Strikes on the railways, blockades at oil refineries and a walk-out by rubbish collectors just before the start of the Euro football competition in June heaped embarrassment on France and reinforced its image internationally as an unreformable country. 'Stench of garbage looms over Euro 2016,' read a headline on CNN over a story in which the US network's Paris correspondent noted that 'many people are asking why the French won't stop whining and get to work.'

A new grassroots leftist movement had also sprung up called *Nuit Debout* ('Night on Your Feet') which saw thousands of students and young people occupy the vast Republic Square in Paris in a spontaneous nocturnal sit-in. It sparked copycat action in cities across the country, rattling Valls and Hollande. Some saw a parallel with the Occupy anti-globalisation movement that had started in the United States in 2011 or the *Indignados* protests that roiled Spain in the same year. Other French commentators speculated that it had echoes of the Paris student uprising of May 1968. Whatever the conclusion, wrote commentator Pierre Haski, it was clear that 'the French political system is hopelessly alienated from large sections of its youth.'

While the left-wing *Nuit Debout* protesters met for discussions in a haze of marijuana with no leaders and a fluid, organic structure that was self-organising, the En Marche team was also plotting how to harness the same anti-establishment, anti-elite feeling evident across French society and in other Western democracies. Britain's vote to leave the European Union in June 2016, followed by Donald Trump's victory in the US in November were part of this broad picture of disaffection. *Nuit Debout* was a sign of the anger among the young and those on the far-left, while Marine Le Pen's National Front was mobilising the embittered working classes. En Marche aimed to offer a different vision for the future that was also anti-establishment, but would appeal to middle-class voters, small business owners and professionals. Their strategy, cooked up by a slick, tight-knit core of young political operatives, was taking shape.

In the months after the launch on 7 April, tens of thousands of people signed up as members of En Marche. Each of them was then contacted by a local coordinator and invited to attend a meeting. Some of the new members were selected to start new committees in their area, meaning a network of ever-smaller groups gradually spread across the country.

But En Marche wanted to be different: it wanted to be a political organisation that proposed more than just member-ship. To help structure their plan, they contacted a consultancy based in Paris called Liegey Muller Pons (LMP) which special-ised in organising grassroots campaigns. It was headed by three Harvard-educated Frenchmen in their thirties who had travelled to the US in 2008 to volunteer for Barack Obama's campaign for the White House.

'Our experience with Obama influenced the whole company,' Guillaume Liegey explained. 'They [En Marche] knew that they didn't want to just launch a movement and do a media event. They wanted to propose something concrete to the people who were going to join.'

As well as using LMP, the En Marche team also reached out for advice from Obama's campaign strategists David Plouffe and Jim Messina. Obama himself intervened personally to send a message of support for Macron right before the election. Macron also made regular use of his network of political contacts for informal advice, consulting former British Prime Minister Tony Blair, as well Blair's closest aides Peter Mandelson and Alastair Campbell.

Working together, LMP and the En Marche inner circle conceived a plan to send their first members door-to-door across the country with a simple questionnaire, available via an application downloaded on their smart phones. It would ask people what they felt worked in France and what didn't, what they were worried about, what gave them hope. Volunteers, the first *marcheurs*, would fill in data about the location, age and profession of the respondents. The operation would be called *La Grande Marche* (The Big Walk), a giant nation-wide surveying exercise to diagnose France's problems. The intention was never to ask people what they thought Macron's policies should be. 'That would be idiotic,' says Liegey. 'If you knock on my door and ask me what France's industrial policy should be, I've got no idea.'

Rather, it would help understand voters' priorities about what they thought needed to be changed, and across all sections of society. Using LMP's expertise, En Marche volunteers were sent into specifically-targeted streets, villages or housing estates to survey a sample of people broadly representative of France as a whole, from far-right voters to Communists.

It had other important benefits. Firstly, it helped with team-building in the hundreds of committees that sprung up. It also spread the word about En Marche to voters. And it gave the team in headquarters an invaluable database of people who could be targeted with political marketing in the future.

The pizza shop owner, Morgan Simon, who had joined En Marche after listening to Macron's speech in Amiens, headed out with groups of fellow helpers around his home town of Nantes. Before long, he was asked by the regional coordinator of En Marche to follow a training session, which was based on the same methods used by Obama's team in 2008, enabling him to become a local team leader and then train other people.

'We weren't trying to sell Macron. We were really just listening,' he remembers of the weekend afternoons spent knocking on doors. 'At a human level it was interesting. There were lots of nice moments meeting people.'

In total, over the summer of 2016, En Marche volunteers knocked on around 100,000 doors. One in four people agreed to answer. Liegey compares this approach to the use of focus groups by traditional political parties, when ideas are tested on six to ten people. '*La Grande Marche* was 25,000 conversations,' he says. 'It's on another scale.'

The responses were collated and rolled into a 180-page report for the campaign team. What was the main conclusion? 'When we asked people what was wrong in France, their first response was: the politicians,' a senior member of the Macron team said, again on condition of anonymity. 'So we knew the campaign was going to be structured around that. And that was the whole reason behind our movement.'

But to stand any chance of being a serious force in the presidential race, the movement needed money. Lots of it. Its office, IT networks, external consultants and first employees now needed paying. There would be bills in the future for marketing material, venues, transport and security. The main political parties (the Socialists and the Republicans) relied on annual membership fees from activists and private donations as well as government subsidies for each of their elected lawmakers.

Although En Marche had made their registration process as easy as possible and did not make donating a condition of membership, everyone was quickly encouraged to stump up cash. At the very end of the campaign in April 2017, the organisation was inundated with small contributions, but in the summer of 2016 they were a start-up that needed capital in large quantities and quickly.

At this critical time, Macron's network of wealthy contacts that he had built up through his time at ENA, the Attali Commission, the Élysée, Rothschild and his feverish socialising at the economy ministry was essential. In the business world the first funds needed to launch a new venture are known as 'seed capital'. Around 30 people stumped up an average of $5,500 each in the first month in April, according to an internal budget document published by the *Mediapart* investigative website. The team now needed to harvest far and wide.

Cédric O and Emmanuel Miquel, two members of the inner circle, were the leaders, using their network from the HEC business school. They also teamed up with Christian Dargnat, who had been dealing with the capital's richest investors for years as head of the private investment division of French banking giant BNP Paribas. He quit his position there to go full-time with En Marche.

In a meticulously-organised operation, they asked Macron and everybody in the team to turn over contact details for people likely to sign a cheque for the maximum authorised limit of €7,500. France does not allow donations from companies. This first ring of people was then contacted and either invited to a networking breakfast, lunch or dinner, or asked if they would be interested in organising an event themselves. Naturally, the targets were rich, often in banking and finance, law, lobbying or business – the sort of people Macron and the rest of the team knew socially and professionally.

One of them was Guillaume Rambourg, the founder of an investment fund headquartered in Paris, who had arranged a meeting with Macron in 2013 when he was working at the Élysée through a mutual friend. They had talked business for an hour or so. 'I moved back to Paris in 2012 from London when there was a wave of French people leaving [France] after the election of Hollande,' he said. 'I was the other side of the Eurostar traffic. It wasn't easy for me in the French environment with finance being called the "enemy" and the 75 per cent tax. People in America thought I was a fruit loop to move back to a "Communist" country.'

Rambourg attended his first fundraising evening in July 2016, organised by a Jewish lobby group. Macron showed up and gave a speech for 45 minutes to explain his plans. The crowd was 'quite right-wing and not really on board with his programme,' Rambourg remembers. 'I don't think they raised much that night.' Rambourg considered himself left-wing but had never been active in politics. He handed over a cheque for €15,000 for himself and his wife, and offered to organise a cocktail party at his Parisian apartment.

'The format was the same: there were canapés and drinks, people arrived, talked among themselves, then [En Marche fundraiser] Christian Dargnat explained how the evening was going to be organised. Basically there was a clear intent on raising money,' Rambourg said.

The crowd was a mix of bankers, hedge fund managers or private equity investors from Rambourg's network in Paris and

London. At 9pm, Macron arrived, went round the room shaking everyone's hand and then spoke for twenty minutes. After that, the floor was opened up to questions.

'He genuinely really enjoys it [the networking] and it's something that comes naturally to him. It doesn't seem fake. He seems to really enjoy the eye contact and the handshakes,' Rambourg explained. By the end of October after several events, Rambourg had helped raise €200,000 on his own and had inspired a few others. 'Some people after my dinners did their own dinners,' he said.

This word-of-mouth momentum was vital and a pre-condition for Macron's presidential run. The movement needed to pull in thousands of members for *La Grande Marche* and have steady inflows of cash to sustain the organisation. The target was to raise €13 million by the time of the election. In addition to a bank loan of €9 million, this would give En Marche the maximum authorised war chest of €22 million to contest the election.

The French community in London was another target, because of the number of expats with prominent jobs in the City. Macron travelled there in September 2016 and attended a dinner at the home of Franco-Lebanese banker Samir Assaf, the head of HSBC's global banking and markets division who became an important fundraiser for En Marche. A separate event at the London home of an e-commerce executive raised €281,000 in one hit, according to an investigation by the *Mediapart* website. There were other trips by Macron to Geneva, Brussels and New York in December, where another top HSBC banker, Christian Deseglise, was in charge of fundraising.

'Democracy doesn't have a price but it has a cost,' Macron told reporters in New York when questioned about a cocktail party and two dinners he was attending there. 'I created a political movement and the only way I have to raise money while respecting electoral law is to raise money from people. I don't consider there is anything wrong with that.'

En Marche understandably portrayed itself as a primarily crowd-funded political organisation during campaigning. Spokespeople as well as Macron himself consistently pointed out that the median donation was around €50–60. Only 2 per cent of donations were above €5,000. Yet those biggest givers accounted for two-thirds of funds by September, according to an internal document seen by the *Libération* newspaper. When Macron's opponents called him 'the candidate of the banks' there was an element of truth to it, particularly at the start. His appeal was as a pro-business moderniser, who, having worked in it, understood the banking sector. He was also promising to cut company and wealth taxes and, once elected, would introduce a flat 30 per cent levy on financial dividends that would be a boon for the industry and anyone with an investment portfolio. Keen to avoid further restrictions on their operations imposed after the global financial crisis in 2008, financiers were also drawn to his reputation as a light-touch banking regulator.

In the early stages of fundraising, there were also risks of conflicts of interest. Macron was still at the economy ministry. *Mediapart* found at least one instance in which a donor asked for a one-to-one meeting with him, which was passed on to Macron's chief of staff in the ministry. Aware of the danger, several cheques were suspended by the team because Macron was overseeing business with the person involved, the website reported.

And some major potential donors were wary of giving to En Marche while Macron was still in the government because of

212 | THE FRENCH EXCEPTION: EMMANUEL MACRON

his association with Hollande. From March onwards there was a debate within the movement about the optimal moment for him to quit, with some like Chaker arguing for him to leave early. Macron had been tripped up by his infamous outburst on how 'the best way to buy a suit is to work' at the end of May, while *Mediapart* and *Le Canard enchaîné* newspaper revealed that he'd had to pay a fine after undervaluing his and Brigitte's holiday home in Le Touquet by €250,000 in his tax declaration. Macron saw the reports at the end of May about his tax affairs as a deliberate leak meant to damage him.

Budget Minister Christian Eckert said that he and other colleagues in cabinet had begun wondering about Macron's intentions from March 2016 when the first reports surfaced that he was preparing to launch his own political party. 'What I noticed was that his ministerial cabinet was extremely large. It had grown to around 25 people,' he said. 'And you could see that he was starting to be preoccupied with other things.'

'We said to ourselves that he was going to leave, that he'd start his own thing, but to be honest none of us could believe it. It seemed so far-fetched that it seemed impossible,' he said.

Staying in the government also gave Macron visibility as he worked on expanding En Marche and it fuelled a government soap-opera of jealousy and attacks by his colleagues which kept him in the headlines. 'In a government team, there's the coach who is the head of state and there's the captain who is the prime minister,' said Defence Minister Jean-Yves Le Drian. 'And the best player, if he plays on his own, doesn't score. So I would like Emmanuel Macron to play for the team.'

Macron decided he would leave in mid-July after a speech organised at the art deco Maison de la Mutualité theatre hall in

Left-Bank Paris, a short walk from his old school Henri IV and Sciences Po. It has long been used for important political gatherings and Emelien wanted to put on a major event to demonstrate the groundswell of support for En Marche. 'Everyone was saying the membership figures were made up, that people were just clicking on the website. But we knew what was happening, people were signing the charter and leaving their contact details,' Guerini said. 'This meeting was ultra-important, a founding moment for us.'

Supporters quickly packed out the 3,000-capacity venue and hundreds more were left outside, where not everyone was a fan. 'The bourgeois, the bankers, it's this way,' shouted one of a few hundred protesters, pointing to the entrance.

With Socialist Party figures like the mayor of Lyon Gérard Collomb and MP Richard Ferrand in the front row – despite Hollande's request not to include politicians in En Marche – Macron declared that France was 'worn down by broken promises'.

'From tonight, we need to be what we are: that's the movement of hope,' he announced to cheers. It was a show of force and a blatant challenge to Valls and Hollande who took no time in criticising him.

Hollande's tolerance and indulgence of Macron over so many months was now at an end. The veteran politician, so adept at political games in his party, spotted the treachery too late, like Julius Caesar failing to see the danger of his murderer Brutus. 'He just thought that he would be able to manipulate him like he always did with other people,' believes Aquilino Morelle, the embittered former speechwriter from the Élysée. 'He thought Emmanuel would do what he told him to.'

Macron has always denied betraying the President, who plucked him from obscurity to appoint him as minister in 2014. 'What is my relationship with François Hollande?', he said during campaigning. 'It's not one in which I have an obligation. We're not in a feudal system.'[3] In other words, politics is just a succession of treacherous acts in the pursuit of power. 'Twas ever thus.

But before Macron could resign, France was plunged into mourning again by the third major terror attack in a year and a half. On the night of 14 July 2016, France's national day, a 31-year-old Tunisian drove a delivery truck into crowds of families gathered to watch a fireworks display on the famed beachfront promenade of the southern city of Nice. Eighty-six people died, around a third of them Muslims, in a killing spree that left bodies spread over nearly two kilometres along the road. The driver was a self-radicalised, drug-taking extremist with a history of domestic violence and assault. 'After the 14 July attacks I couldn't leave the government with any dignity,' Macron explained later.[4]

His final month in office was overshadowed by a bitter and divisive row about the burkini, the full-body swimming suit worn by a tiny number of ultra-conservative Muslim women. It was sparked when the mayor of Cannes, a Riviera resort near Nice, banned any beachwear that displayed 'religious affiliation' on 11 August on the grounds that it could spark public order problems. Another 30 towns announced similar restrictions in the next fortnight, with one mayor citing 'hygiene reasons' as justification. The issue was further inflamed when a photographer captured pictures that appeared to show police surrounding a woman in a headscarf and a long-sleeved top to enforce the ban on a beach in Nice.

Prime Minister Manuel Valls came out in support of the burkini ban, arguing for an activist interpretation of France's secular laws that would see the state battle to free Muslim women from the oppression of their religion. The burkini was 'the expression of a political project, an alternative society, based notably on the enslavement of women,' Valls said. The ban was later overturned by France's top court on 26 August.

Macron's views on secularism are different to Valls' and even to those of his own wife Brigitte, who favours extending an existing ban on religious symbols in French schools to universities. Macron urged France to combat the burkini politically and ideologically, but he argued that the state must stick to the original sense of its landmark 1905 law separating the church from the state: that religious groups keep out of the public sphere, while the state protects individuals' right to believe – or not – in private. 'We need to protect individual liberties, public order, but above all we need to ensure the state responds in the right way,' he said afterwards, warning that the Muslim community risked feeling 'excluded because of their faith and our reaction'.[5]

After weeks of rumours, the day of his departure was finally set for 30 August, leaked to the media in advance for the morning news bulletins. Macron convened his cabinet at the economy ministry, shaking each of the men by hand and exchanging kisses with the women. He thanked them for their tireless work in a scene captured by his trailing camera crew, which also confirmed the role Brigitte had been playing behind the scenes. 'Brigitte wanted to join me in thanking you because she has been part of the life of the cabinet too,' Macron said with her sitting by his side. 'Thanks for making a space for me,' she said, exchanging smiles with the team. Macron acknowledged it was 'unusual' for a minister's wife to have such a role, 'but it was important for us,' he said, turning to look his wife in the eyes.

In his resignation speech, carried live on the news channels, Macron declared that he had 'seen at first hand the limits of our political system' and said he needed to devote himself to his own movement to 'transform' France. He acknowledged France's paralysing sense of self-doubt and new fears about terrorism, while criticising politicians for putting their own interests above those of the country. 'I want to start a new stage in my combat today, to build something that will serve only the public interest,' he said. He set off in a ministerial boat along the Seine for the Élysée Palace, to hand over his resignation. Television cameras followed his progress up the river towards the presidential palace where the head of state was politically wounded but also deeply hurt personally.

'I said to him "firstly it's disloyal to me and above all you'll finish with 7, 8, maybe 10 per cent",' Hollande recalls of the meeting. 'He just replied to me "we'll see".'[6] It was a bitter, unpleasant moment but Macron was now free from the shadow of his former mentor, six years after he first started working for Hollande on his election programme and almost two years to the day since he'd entered the economy ministry in such chaotic and unforeseen circumstances. 'I've always kept politics and personal relations separate,' Macron later told the author Philippe Besson coldly, saying the exchange with Hollande had been 'factual'.

CHAPTER 12

The Planets Align

IMMEDIATELY AFTER MACRON STEPPED DOWN AS MINIS-
ter, the level of funds flowing into En Marche exploded.
Since April, they had averaged about €240,000 per month. In
September, the party raised four times that amount at €900,000.[1]
A ticker on the movement's website showing the number of
people who had signed up as members hit 80,000, compared
with 13,000 in the month after the launch. 'We could feel the
momentum, we could see that members were increasing, that
there was a real interest in taking part,' said one of the top members of the team who asked not to be named.

The group had now outgrown its bunker on the Rue des
Plantes in southern Paris. Over the summer, some days there had
been 15–20 people, many of them permanent volunteers in their
twenties, crammed into about 60 square metres of badly ventilated
space. People would arrive in work clothes and then strip down
to t-shirts, shorts and flip-flops while working on their laptops.
Realising they needed more space, they rented a bigger office
on the fourteenth floor of the Montparnasse Tower in southern

Paris with panoramic views over the city and the Eiffel Tower. The organisation also bulked up: Benjamin Griveaux quit his job doing communications for a property developer to go full-time with En Marche, earning a third of his previous salary. Sibeth Ndiaye, who was a media advisor for Macron at the economy ministry (and the daughter of a well-connected Senegalese politician), also left her job to help run communications for En Marche in September. With her dreadlocks and trainers, Ndiaye would become an almost permanent presence at Macron's side, constantly photographed behind him during his public appearances. 'I joined without necessarily thinking that we were going to win, but with the real conviction that we could change the political landscape,' she said in an interview. Other newcomers included Sylvain Fort, who joined as head of communications.

As well as addressing what were still fairly small meetings across the country, Macron was also trying to finish off his pre-election book, a tradition and necessity for all serious French politicians, which he had sold to the XO publishing house. The book sold 150,000 copies between November and the end of May 2017, a measure both of interest in Macron and in politics generally among French voters. In 2016, royalty statements showed that he had earned €270,000 from sales of the book that year. The country's politicians are a prolific source of books. Ex-president Nicolas Sarkozy managed two alone in 2016: a political memoir *La France Pour la Vie* ('France for Life') which sold around 150,000 copies followed by his election book *Tout pour la France* ('Everything for France'). Justice Minister Christiane Taubira turned her government experience into a book that sold 160,000 copies in the same year.

Macron's first novels, written as a schoolboy, had never been published, but he had continued to write regularly throughout his life and Brigitte is the guardian of numerous unpublished manuscripts. For his first publishing deal, he pored over the language, constantly modifying chapters and declaring himself unhappy with the writing. 'It was a difficult birth, let's put it that way,' remembers his friend Marc Ferracci, who followed the tortuous progress and offered advice.

The book is elegantly written during the first few chapters as it describes his childhood in Amiens and relationships with his grandmother and Brigitte. It then moves into his political vision, explaining why he believed voters had lost faith in their leaders, why France needed to be more welcoming for entrepreneurs or why the state needed to cut its spending.

He initially locked himself away over the summer of 2016 on the Île de Ré off France's western coast at the home of actor Fabrice Luchini before finishing it off in Le Touquet, often at weekends and in the evenings.

As he worked on *Révolution*, his route to victory in the election in 2017 still looked incredibly narrow. A poll at the end of September showed that Macron could win 14–15 per cent of the vote if the first round of the presidential election (scheduled for 23 April the following year) was held immediately. This gave him about the same share as Hollande, who had still not made his mind up as to whether he would seek re-election and was forecast to win 12–16 per cent.[2]

If the polls were correct, this would mean both of them being eliminated: exactly what Hollande had forecast when Macron had come to deliver his resignation letter. The poll showed the far-right leader Marine Le Pen topping the first round with 27–28 per cent of votes.

Le Pen was the daughter of the French far-right patriarch and international pariah Jean-Marie Le Pen, an anti-Semitic former army paratrooper. The ex-lawyer had made her first national television appearance in 2002 defending her father when he made it through to the second round of the presidential election of that year. In the assessment of her own mother, who left Jean-Marie in 1984, Marine and her sisters had been 'brought up in complete and utter racism.'[3]

Since taking over the party in 2011, Marine had spent five years reworking its programme and trying to clean up its image. Out went her father's free-market economics in favour of a left-wing platform committed to increased public spending, nationalisations and protectionist measures to help French workers. This explained in part the National Front's expansion beyond its historic base in southern France into the former Communist bastions of the rustbelt north-east. The core appeal of the party remained its anti-immigration platform, its hard line on crime (including backing for the death penalty) and its promise to protect 'French culture'.

In public, she had also taken a zero-tolerance approach to the most obvious acts of racism and anti-Semitism within the party, expelling members including her own father in 2015 when he repeated his view that the gas chambers of the Second World War were a 'detail of history'. This helped make the party more socially acceptable, while her vocal defence of women and gay rights in the face of rising Islamism broadened her appeal. Unfortunately for her, a prosecution for hate speech stemming from remarks she had made in 2010 (in which she compared Muslims praying in the street to the sight of occupying Nazi forces) was a reminder of her own incendiary rhetoric in the past as the case ground its way through the courts.

In November, she unveiled her campaign logo mixing a rose, which was associated with the Socialist Party, and the blue colour of the Republicans. 'Marine, in the name of the people,' read her slogan, making no mention of the party or her still-toxic surname. She'd also rented a new campaign office less than two kilometres from the Élysée Palace, 'which will make the move easier in May,' as one of her advisors joked.

Political analysts, media commentators and pollsters all still expected her opponent in the second-round run-off election to be Alain Juppé. He was then forecast to easily beat the far-right candidate and become president. In Britain, pollsters and most political experts had miscalled the results for the June referendum, forecasting that the country would opt to stay in the European Union. At least the French election looked fairly predictable.

Juppé was a former prime minister who had polled as France's most popular politician for much of the last two years. He was a moderate right-winger from the Republicans party and a well-respected mayor of the city of Bordeaux, which he had helped transform over two decades. He was known for having a razor-sharp intellect allied with a sometimes cutting and arrogant personality. At 71 years old, he was the perfect illustration of how French politics appeared to be a constant exercise in recycling the same faces at different elections. A conviction in 2004 over party financing dating back to his time working under the former president Jacques Chirac at Paris city hall in the 1990s looked to have buried his career. 'There are always possibilities for resurrection,' he said afterwards, and in 2011, he was back as foreign minister under President Sarkozy.

For the first time, the Republicans party had decided to organise an American-style primary to choose its candidate on

20 and 27 November. The vote was open to anyone who was prepared to pay a small fee and would signal the start of the 2017 presidential season. As well as helping raise awareness about the Republicans, it would also bring in desperately needed money for the heavily-indebted party.

Juppé was a candidate, as was the then chairman of the Republicans party, ex-president Nicolas Sarkozy, who was back gunning for his revenge on Hollande despite a series of corruption cases dating from his time in power. The five-foot-five-inch leader, who wore leather shoes with stacked heels to compensate for his small frame, was still as twitchy and hyperactive as ever and ready to stir up the vexed issue of French national identity in the wake of the recent terror attacks. At the end of September Sarkozy, himself a mix of Hungarian, French and Greek Jewish blood, said that 'we will no longer accept a system of integration [of foreigners] that no longer works, we will demand assimilation. As soon as you become French, your ancestors become the Gauls.' The point, simplified to the point of ridicule, was that immigrants should abandon their culture and adopt France's. He had also spoken out about the 'tyranny of minorities' – meaning Muslims in all but name. The reference to the Gauls led many scurrying for the history books as well as a series of jokes about 'Sarkozix', a reference to the comic book tales of Asterix which are set in a village of Gauls in 50 BC at the time of the Roman invasion.

Juppé was clearly the most dangerous opponent for Macron, as he would attract many of the moderate centre-right voters who En Marche was targeting. Juppé's economic programme – cuts to public spending and labour market reform – was coupled with a promise to take into account France's diversity and develop a 'happy identity'. He had a record of reaching out to the Muslim community in Bordeaux, which would be used against him during the campaign.

Other contenders included the former Republicans party chairman Jean-François Copé, a bitter rival of Sarkozy's, whose marginal chances of victory evaporated at the end of October after his gaffe about the price of a pain au chocolat. 'I've no idea … It'd be around ten to fifteen *centimes*,' he said during a morning radio interview, leaving millions of French people listening in over breakfast laughing into their pastries. The real price was around a euro and the story had the unfortunate effect of focusing attention on other blunders by out-of-touch politicians. Another of the right-wing candidates, the moderate Nathalie Kosciusko-Morizet who had served as a minister and spokeswoman under Sarkozy's presidency, had been tripped up several years before when asked about the price of a metro ticket in Paris.

The third-placed man of the race, far behind Sarkozy and Juppé in the polls at the end of October, was the former prime minister François Fillon, a devout Catholic who had been travelling the country for the last two years quietly drumming up support. He was keen to stress his squeaky-clean image compared to those of the scandal-tainted Sarkozy and Juppé.

Macron faced a dilemma: the media space at the time was saturated by the right-wing primary and particularly the continued incendiary comments of Nicolas Sarkozy, who was campaigning as a hard-right candidate looking to attract many National Front voters. At a campaign stop in the wealthy Paris suburb of Neuilly-sur-Seine in early November, the ex-president had weighed in on the issue of school meals, where Jewish and Muslim groups had long asked that the rigid one-dish state school menu be adapted for pupils who did not want to eat pork for religious reasons (the diets of less vocal vegetarians are similarly overlooked). At issue was the broader issue of how much the state should try to accommodate cultural preferences, which Sarkozy dealt with in characteristic style: 'If at the canteen there's a slice of ham and chips, well, the kid should take a double portion of chips!' Sarkozy said to applause. 'This is the Republic! It's the same menu and the same rules for everyone!'

The US presidential election on 8 November also detonated at this time, sending shockwaves through Western democracies. Donald Trump's victory in defiance of most of the American Republican Party, and against the predictions of the best pollsters and most experienced media pundits, appeared to herald a new epoch. The Brexit vote in June had laid bare the strains visible in Western democracies for decades over mass migration, job losses in industrial areas and worries about loss of sovereignty in an increasingly inter-connected world. Trump's triumph on an anti-globalisation platform and a frequently racist campaign against immigrants and minority groups brought an unstable and right-wing nationalist to the commands of the world's superpower in a seismic shift. As old certainties about the 'inevitable' advance of the liberal West faded, media organisations and pundits in France began to reassess their own assumptions about what had so far seemed a boringly predictable election. Could French opinion polls be trusted? Was Juppé still on track for victory? And was France's two-round voting system, with its requirement that any winner get more than 50 per cent of the vote, still an insurmountable firewall against populists? Far-right leader Le Pen said that Trump had 'made possible what had previously been presented as impossible.'

Coming elections in small EU member states suddenly took on renewed importance as experts and leaders wondered how high the rising tide of nationalism would reach. Austria was to hold a presidential election in December 2016 in which the far-right leader Norbert Hofer was a frontrunner. The Netherlands would have parliamentary polls in March 2017 where the party of the openly Islamophobic populist Geert Wilders was forecast to win the largest number of seats. After these votes would come the big one: France in April and May 2017.

On 16 November 2016, four days before the first round of the Republicans party held their primary, Macron confirmed publicly what everyone had known for months: he was going to run for president, irrespective of whether Hollande decided to be a candidate himself. He and his team were satisfied that the funding and the grassroots momentum were sufficient to justify the risk, but even his most ardent supporters doubted his chances. 'We've got about a 20–30 per cent chance of winning,' Ismaël Emelien told a visitor to headquarters at around this time.

The announcement of Macron's candidacy was made at a youth training centre in Bobigny, a deprived, multi-ethnic suburb north of Paris where he spoke against a conventional blue screen with the French and European flags behind him. The declaration was timed to interfere with the primary and to try to draw the spotlight away from Juppé and Sarkozy.

'I hear some people say that our country is in decline, that the worst is to come, that our civilisation is losing ground. And they propose withdrawal, civil war or the old recipes of the last century,' he began in comments clearly directed at Le Pen. He then took aim at the candidates for the right – 'the same faces, the same men, for so many years' – and the 'vacuity' of the old two-party political system which he called 'the biggest obstacle to the transformation of the country.' France, he said, 'has the strength, the destiny and the desire to move forward because it has a history and a people committed to that. France has always been a driver of progress.'

The Republicans primary four days later sprung the first of many surprises on France's pundits. Over the course of three dense and lengthy debates, the ex-Prime Minister François Fillon had slowly emerged as an alternative candidate with his seemingly unflappable temperament and extremely conservative programme. Driven by a desire to rectify what he saw as his generation's biggest failure – France's huge public debt – the 62 year old said proudly that he was planning to 'tear the house down.' The admirer of the former British Prime Minister Margaret Thatcher proposed cutting 500,000 civil servants' jobs, slashing public spending by €100 billion and raising the retirement age to 65 from 62. Working hours would be raised from 35 to 39 hours and basic doctor visits would also be paid for by private health insurance, not the social security system. Boosting his credentials among grassroots right-wingers, Fillon proposed cutting immigration to 'a strict minimum'. He also had conservative views on the family and gay adoption, and had written a book called *Beating Islamic Totalitarianism*, which sold 50,000 copies in 2016.

Sarkozy meanwhile had been entangled in yet more legal problems. Ziad Takieddine, a Lebanese businessman, gave an interview in which he claimed that he had delivered three suitcases of cash containing €5 million to the right-winger in 2007 from the late Libyan dictator Muammar Gaddafi. 'What an indignity!' Sarkozy said angrily as he denied the claims during the third and final televised debate. (His failed 2012 re-election campaign, notable for its epic US-style stadium rallies, had been financed in part by using fraudulent billing to avoid campaign financing restrictions.)

Fillon tried to soften what he admitted was his own 'boring' image with an appearance on a hit new political interview show called *Ambition Intime* ('Intimate Ambition') presented by a flirty ex-model, Karine Le Marchand, who posed gentle personal questions about his love of cooking, his nerves in parliament and even his bushy eyebrows. Satirist Anne Roumanoff joked that seeing Le Marchand interview a politician was like 'watching a couple who have just met on Tinder.' But Fillon was in no doubt about its impact. 'If we judge it by the number of reactions, it was massive,' he told *Le Parisien* newspaper. Despite the importance of grassroots campaigning and the impact of social media, the old-fashioned medium of television proved to be the most influential throughout the 2017 election.

Over the summer, polls had shown Fillon winning under 10 per cent in the primary. In the run-up to the first vote on 20 November, surveys picked up a sharp rise in support for him but still showed him finishing behind Juppé and Sarkozy. He ended up by beating both of them by a huge margin, finishing top with 44 per cent of the vote ahead of Juppé on 28 per cent. Juppé contemplated pulling out of the second round on the same evening, but vowed to fight on.

The results appeared to show that French polls suffered from the same problems as the American or British ones. More importantly, from Macron's perspective, the vote looked to have eliminated his most dangerous rival, Juppé. Republicans party activists had opted for someone popular with the base, but not necessarily with the wider public.

Juppé fought on in the second round of the primary, denouncing Fillon's programme as economically 'brutal' and saying his opponent had an 'extremely traditionalist and even retrograde vision on the role of women, the family and on marriage.' But Juppé suddenly looked all of his 71 years. As his ally and campaign strategist Gilles Boyer conceded, 'Juppé-mania' had faded. He had been 'too high, too early' and had seen his support gradually crumble.

Fillon had the wind in his sails as he appeared on 25 November at a final rally of his supporters at a huge conference centre in southern Paris. The flag-waving crowd of several thousand was overwhelmingly white, elderly, middle class and conservative. Fillon arrived to the sound of ear-splitting techno music, forcing many supporters to adjust their hearing aids. He presented himself as the underdog who had proved the doubters and naysayers wrong. There was some tough talk on law and order – 'a juvenile delinquent is not a young person who's having an identity crisis, they're a delinquent' – and he dismissed the idea of 'multiculturalism' in France. The biggest cheers were revealing of the main preoccupations of those present in the giant hangar-like space on a chilly Friday night. Muslims, like Catholics and Jews before them, needed to stop challenging the rules of the secular Republic and adapt, he said to shouts of support. 'When you enter someone else's house you do not take over,' he boomed.

Among the crowd, retired finance director Jean-Claude Hegy was impressed. 'His ideas on immigration are close to the National Front, but his economic programme is clearly superior,' the 65 year old said. Juppé himself crashed out in the vote that weekend, winning only 33 per cent. Fillon became the immediate favourite to become president and the man to take on the leader of the far-right. As Juppé later noted, Fillon had 'an open road in front of him.'

Fillon's victory was seen as a huge opportunity in the En Marche headquarters. The team moved for a second and final time at the end of November, leaving behind the Montparnasse skyscraper after only a few months to take over three floors of a bigger office in the 15th district of Paris. It was soon filled with new staff and volunteers, with beds provided in quiet rooms for those who needed to stay overnight. There were also yoga classes for the young and trendy staff of France's 'political start-up'. The top floor – the sixth – was reserved for the key advisors and Macron, whose own office featured some of the giant pictures of him which were plastered throughout the building.

Fillon's breakthrough 'demonstrated in a very clear way what Emmanuel Macron had theorised: that the primaries would favour marginal candidates, rendering the traditional parties more and more extreme,' Macron's spokeswoman Ndiaye remembered. 'That would mean space being left for a progressive force in the centre,' she added. Having joined En Marche not being sure whether Macron could win, she began to seriously consider the possibility.

Fillon's result was the first of many surprises of the campaign and was the earliest sign that the election would be like no other. It was also welcomed in Moscow. In the Kremlin, President Vladimir Putin had hailed Fillon as a 'great professional' and 'very principled person' during the campaign. The two men had got to know each other when they had overlapped as prime ministers from 2008 to 2012.

Fillon was consistently supportive of Putin and had condemned the EU and US sanctions imposed on Russia after its invasion of Ukraine in 2014. 'The question is: must we continue to provoke the Russians, refusing dialogue with them and pushing them to be more and more violent, aggressive and less and less European?', Fillon said in October.

In 2016, with the West looking weaker than ever, everything seemed to be going Putin's way: his intervention in the Syrian civil war to prop up Bashar al-Assad had demonstrated Russian firepower and influence in the Middle East while sidelining the US, which had baulked at intervening under President Obama. Brexit had seriously weakened the European Union, an outcome Putin had been seeking for years through his support for various Eurosceptic groups; and Trump's victory had put an openly friendly figure in the White House. In France, the predicted match up between Fillon and Le Pen in the final round of the election would be win-win for Putin: a competition between two ardent Russophiles.

But despite all the confidence about Fillon's prospects, he and his programme had obvious flaws. Not only did his association with Thatcher terrify France's trade unions and left-leaning voters, his budget-slashing economic programme would likely lead to a severe downturn in domestic demand at a time when the economy was struggling. His social views and unabashed Christian identity also looked out of step with most of the country.

A further vital piece of the election puzzle also fell into place before the end of the year. Hollande had been dithering about whether to run for re-election. If he wanted to, he would have to stand as a candidate in the Socialist Party primary which was scheduled for January of 2017. He'd inevitably face some of his left-wing tormentors like the former ministers

Arnaud Montebourg and Benoît Hamon, who would delight in attacking his record. In addition, his approval ratings were catastrophic.

Hollande's hand was finally forced by one of his weaknesses (privately viewed as a quality by many journalists), namely his love for chatting with the political press pack and sharing gossip. He had found time to sit down for more than 60 interviews during his presidency with *Le Monde* journalists Gérard Davet and Fabrice Lhomme, sometimes at the Élysée or over dinner at their homes. They turned the material into a 660-page book published at the end of 2016 called *A President Shouldn't Say That* …. Hollande had apparently expected it to be published after his time in office.

There were touching revelations in the book, about how he missed his old family life and often felt like a 'ghost' in the Élysée Palace. But he also criticised, among others, judges, some of his own ministers, French footballers ('guys from housing estates without any values') and immigrants ('we teach them to speak French and then another group arrives and we have to start all over again'). One Socialist MP compared its impact to a 'fragmentation bomb'. His approval ratings toppled into the abyss: only 4 per cent of people were satisfied with his presidency.

On 1 December, under pressure from Prime Minister Valls to step aside, Hollande addressed the nation to state his intentions. Keeping viewers guessing, he first reeled off his accomplishments: keeping the country together in the face of terrorism, his belated economic reforms which he promised would eventually yield new jobs. 'I've served for four and half years with honesty,' he said. But a presidential run risked doing more harm than good to the left, he eventually conceded. 'I have decided not to be a candidate in the election,' Hollande declared. He was the first leader of France since the start of the presidential system in 1958 to choose not to defend his record.

Macron had been telling friends since the summer that he thought Hollande would be unable to run for re-election. And the fact that the final straw had been an egregious act of self-harm caused by his overly cosy relationship with journalists was not a surprise either. 'He [Macron] used to be appalled while he was a minister at how Hollande was on Twitter or sending messages all day,' Macron's philosopher friend Olivier Mongin remembered. 'He didn't understand why he needed to be reassured by journalists.' Hollande's supporters hailed his decision to stand aside as an act of 'dignity'.

For En Marche, it was another planet which had aligned. The Republicans had lurched to the right. Now Hollande was out of the way. Before the end of the year, they planned to put on a show of force in Paris with another big rally to demonstrate that their supporters were real, amid continuing attacks in the media that membership numbers – now up to 120,000 – were fake or exaggerated. The team booked a 15,000-capacity venue at the Porte de Versailles conference centre in southern Paris and watched as people signed up to attend via the website or on Facebook. 'We could see it was going to be big,' one member of the team remembered during an interview.

The conference hall was packed on the night and shouts of 'Macron! President!' reverberated around it before he arrived on stage. He delivered a long speech of nearly two hours filled with vague policy promises, pledging to be the 'candidate of work' and the 'candidate of justice', adding that 'France needed to find its taste for risk again.' The speech did nothing to answer his critics, who were by now hammering him as a man with no programme and a confusing 'neither right nor left' identity.

But the night would be remembered for its final scenes. As he basked in the cheers and adulation of the biggest crowd he'd ever addressed, Macron drew his speech to a close screaming until his voice cracked: 'What I want! … is that you! … everywhere! … go out! … and make us win! … because it's our project! … *Vive la République*! *Vive la France*!'

Having delivered the final words, he threw his arms aloft and stared up at the heavens, messianic in form. In a recording of the final scenes, watched millions of times on television and online, a woman sitting behind him with dark hair and a bright yellow jumper turns to a friend and looks slightly embarrassed for him.

Backstage, Brigitte was waiting. 'I gave so much,' an exhausted-looking Macron told her. 'The room gave me so much energy.'

'It was fantastic,' she told him.[4]

On the internet, images of the climax of his speech began spreading like wildfire on social media. 'When you're completely wasted at the end of the night and you really think you're the king of the world,' commented comedian @Superzappeur to his tens of thousands of followers.

Was this a 'Howard Dean scream' moment? Dean had famously tried to clinch the nomination for the Democratic Party in 2004 when he got carried away in front of supporters in Iowa and let out the most famous 'Yaaaaooowww!' in US politics. The mockery of his high-pitched shriek was said to have doomed his campaign.

Laurence David-Moalic, a 57-year-old civil servant from Amiens, was sitting high up in the stands as Macron began screeching. She watched, slightly baffled, as he got carried away but put it down to a beginner's mistake. 'He's human. He has his weaknesses, we're not robots and thank goodness,' she said.

Ludovic Chaker, the head of operations at En Marche, said part of the problem was that they hadn't soundproofed the room properly and there were no feedback speakers for Macron on the stage as he spoke. 'Everyone was shouting so much you couldn't hear anything. I was standing five metres away from Emmanuel. At the end in the fervour of the moment, he shouted. But it created such a buzz afterwards I don't think it was a bad thing and he learnt to control his voice,' he said.

Macron, speaking at the end of the campaign, said he'd found the reactions on social media amusing. 'They helped spread the message and it reached people who hadn't watched the meeting or listened before,' he said.[5] But in truth, the one-time amateur actor had been anxious about his delivery since the start of campaigning. He admitted to his public speaking coach, the former opera singer Jean-Philippe Lafont, that up until then he had been lowering his voice on purpose to make himself sound older.[6]

Macron's chief of staff Sophie Ferracci, wife of his best friend from his Paris student days Marc Ferracci, revealed how the events of the end of 2016 had changed her view of the En Marche campaign's prospects. 'From around December, we started thinking that it's possible we might win,' she said. There was a lag, however, between the rising optimism within the movement and how most observers saw the election. As he turned 39 at the end of the year, Macron was still a rank outsider, an extremely young, inexperienced ex-economy minister and banker standing in his first election at the head of a party that was only nine months old. At the turn of the year, British bookmakers were offering odds of 7/1 or 6/1 on him becoming president. The huge rally in Paris had certainly made the sceptics and his rivals sit up and take notice, but the momentum behind En Marche still hadn't pierced the national conscience.

CHAPTER 13

A Path to Victory

OUTSIDE OF A SPORTS CENTRE IN THE CITY OF QUIMPER at around 8pm in mid-January 2017, fine rain was drifting down gently, visible in the bright overhead lights which illuminated a striking scene below. Huddled underneath were hundreds of people who had formed a snaking line that started at the doors of the venue, went down past the building and finished in the car park 150 metres away. 'We have a saying around here: "it only rains on idiots",' joked Jean Yvard as he turned his collar up and hunched his shoulders in the cold. It's what the locals say to tourists if they complain about the weather, which is notoriously wet and windy in this exposed corner of north-west France near the Atlantic Ocean. Tonight, the 'idiots' were the locals who were standing in the drizzle for a chance to see Emmanuel Macron.

'I wanted to come because I think he's a sort of social phenomenon. Something's happening. I don't know what yet, but I'll find out tonight,' Yvard, a 53-year-old entrepreneur who owns a metal business, explained. 'What he's offering is still not totally known. But it's his attitude, the personality, that's interesting. There's something modern and fresh. And I've never voted left-wing in my life!'

His friend Frank Lauferon, 45, was more sceptical. He admitted to being dragged along by Jean and didn't think much of Macron's 'neither left, nor right' rhetoric. The priority for the country should be making it easier for companies like Lauferon's boat-maintenance firm to do business whilst getting the public finances under control. He, too, usually voted for the right: 'The problem is that everyone says that Fillon is like Margaret Thatcher but Thatcher won't work in France,' he said.

'Thatcher in France? There'd be a revolution!' said his friend Jean.

Further ahead near the front of the queue stood 63-year-old retiree Dominique Surbled who said she had been waiting for an hour. 'I'm here because I heard that the crowds are big everywhere. I was curious. There's a sort of Macron-mania, but I still can't work out what he really stands for,' she said.

This feeling was expressed over and again to varying degrees by people in the queue. The crowd was a mix of ages, mostly middle class and with noticeably large numbers of small business owners. Many liked that he seemed to understand and care about helping companies to create jobs. Others were drawn by his sense of optimism, as the only candidate in the race who seemed to offer the depressed country an upbeat vision for its future. Some simply liked what he represented: a new face in a fossilised political system where the same characters seemed to appear for election after election. Marine Gonidou, a 23-year-old shop assistant, summed up Macron's appeal as 'youth, dynamism and freshness.'

It was one thing to draw big crowds in Paris, where Macron was expected to do well among the professional classes of the capital, it was another to draw thousands of people on a rainy mid-week day in January in Quimper (population: 60,000). He'd done the same thing ten days earlier in Clermont-Ferrand, a town in central France.

Before Yvard and Laferon could get to the doors, security guards announced that the venue was full and pulled metal railings across the entrance, leaving around 500 people stranded outside.

Bickering and arguments followed. Then out of the gloom in front of the sports centre, Macron appeared, microphone in hand, with an aide carrying a speaker. 'I wanted to come to apologise in person,' he said. 'The venue's full, we can't let anyone else in.'

He'd spent the day visiting farms in the area, eating home-made cake washed down with a glass of champagne while chatting to local dairy producers about their problems. He'd pledged to help protect them from price fluctuations and the power of supermarkets, which had destroyed their profit margins. Later he'd inspected a cow shed, squelching through the mud in his shiny leather shoes with a gaggle of television cameras in tow.

There'd been another stop at a local travel agent where local business people had been invited. 'France is ready to vote for pretty much anyone to change things,' said local accountant Patrick Moneger, whose firm in the nearby city of Brest employed 100 people. As a successful local businessman in his late 60s, he was an unlikely anti-elite rebel. But he too was at his wits' end. 'I'm like them. We're all fed up with seeing the same people,' he said.

Inside the venue in Quimper, polite helpers in white En Marche t-shirts pointed people towards the chairs. The sports centre's capacity was around 2,000 and once the seats were full, several hundred people stood on the sides. It was strikingly low-key. There was almost no music, no special lighting nor inspiring warm-up acts to get the audience pumped up. Unlike Le Pen or Fillon rallies, there were barely any flags, other than a single tricolore next to the European flag on the stage.

Macron delivered a 90-minute speech that began with a lengthy tribute to the surrounding Brittany region and to Quimper, which he pointed out stood at the confluence of the rivers Le Steir and L'Odet – a metaphor for his own attempts to merge the left and right. The audience clapped politely at times and there were occasional cheers – particularly for his plans to cut taxes on small businesses – but there was none of the fervour of his giant meeting in Paris in December.

Although he was always excellent one-to-one with voters and came alive in question and answer sessions, Macron often seemed slightly wooden while delivering his stump speeches in the early months of campaigning. There were literary references and lines of poetry mixed up with his diagnosis of France's problems. 'We're the only ones to defend the European Union and we do it with pride,' he told the Quimper audience. His speech held their attention without ever firing up the crowd.

Damon Mayaffre, an academic who specialises in political communication, said part of Macron's problem in connecting with audiences was the repetition of abstract nouns during his speeches such as 'transformation', 'innovation', 'reform' or 'hope'. 'When you attend a Macron rally, you hear all these words but at the end you have a sense of an ideological void,' he said.

But heading home afterwards, the local shopkeeper and life-long Socialist voter Nadine Griffon was impressed. She said she hadn't been as excited about voting since François Mitterrand's breakthrough in 1981 (enthusiasm that quickly turned to disappointment, she said). '[Macron] makes us dream a bit and, hey, we all need to dream a bit, especially when you see what's happening in the United States,' the 56 year old explained.

In the days after the Quimper meeting, reports of the over-flowing rallies saw the foreign media suddenly latch on for the first time to the Macron dynamic. The *Financial Times*, the *Guardian* and the *Economist*, as well as the international news agencies *Reuters*, *AFP* and *Bloomberg* all published reports in quick succession about his campaign and his rising approval figures. 'I noticed from the start of January that we had real momentum on the ground,' Macron remembers. 'The rallies in January were one of the drivers of our campaign. I could see that the programme from the right [meaning Fillon] was very radical. And at that point, I became convinced that I could represent something central that was gradually getting through to the general public.'[1]

The programme from the left was still unknown. The Socialist Party's primary was scheduled for the end of January. 'They'll pick Valls, surely,' Macron's chief of staff Sophie Ferracci said in comments made on one of the farms near Quimper, referring to the former prime minister who had stepped down at the beginning of December to launch his campaign.

But Valls was struggling. As a centre-left moderate he'd alienated large parts of the party's left-wing base during his time in office with his support for Hollande's economic reforms and his use of the '49.3' mechanism to force legislation through parliament. He had also taken a hard line on Islam, favouring the (overturned) ban on the burkini swimsuit and proposing outlawing veils in universities in the name of women's rights. Above all, there was no escaping his association with the deeply unpopular government of Hollande – unlike Macron who had skipped out six months earlier.

Valls was slapped by a protestor, and another threw a bag of flour over him. The *Politico* website said he was campaigning with 'all the *joie de vivre* of someone who just ran a marathon in shoes that are one size too small.'

Having been the clear favourite in December and early January, Valls had since lost ground to the left-wing former Industry Minister Arnaud Montebourg. And ex-Education Minister Benoît Hamon – the leader of the rebellion against 'Macron's Law' – emerged as a surprise challenger for the Socialist nomination in the run up to the first round of voting on 22 January.

Hamon, 49 and a career politician, was proposing a futuristic programme aimed at tackling what he saw as the looming crisis in the workplace due to robotisation and artificial intelligence. He proposed paying everyone a basic state income, beginning with the young and the jobless poor, that would eventually reach €750 per person per month. 'I expect that the digital revolution is going to make work increasingly rare ... and we need to prepare for that,' he explained.

The idea of basic or universal income – giving everyone a handout every month – had been gaining traction as an idea worldwide. Finland had begun a two-year experiment paying 2,000 unemployed workers a monthly stipend. The practice had high-profile supporters including the American business luminary Elon Musk, the head of electric vehicle group Tesla, and the renowned left-leaning French economist Thomas Piketty, whose book on the distribution of wealth over the last 250 years had been a runaway bestseller in 2013.

However, universal basic income was also eye-wateringly expensive. Researchers at the OFCE think-tank at Sciences Po university in Paris estimated Hamon's proposal would cost as much as €480 billion annually – ten times France's defence budget. 'It's almost a new sort of societal model he is imagining, post-capitalist,' Mathieu Plane, an economist at the OFCE, commented.

Valls called Hamon a 'dreamer' but the idea sparked a larger debate about the future of work which made Hamon seem original and inventive. He also had solid green credentials and planned to legalise cannabis, which went down well with left-wing activists.

Finding little traction with his own programme, Valls did his best to paint Hamon as being soft on the spread of Islamic fundamentalism. It was an argument that had been used effectively against Alain Juppé in the right-wing primary, who had faced the same accusations from Sarkozy and Fillon. Hamon, an MP for an area outside of Paris from where several young men had left to join the Islamic State group, was 'ambiguous' on the question, Valls said.

Valls' attacks had little impact on Socialist voters. Like the right-wing primary before, the result did not go to script. Hamon finished top in the first round with 37 per cent, ahead of Valls on 32 per cent. In the second round a week later, Hamon crushed his rival with 59 per cent of votes.

Valls joined ex-Prime Minister Juppé, former president Sarkozy and outgoing president Hollande on the political scrapheap, the latest victim of what became known as the spirit of *dégagisme* – the urge by French voters to chuck out their political leaders. For Macron, the result could scarcely have been better and again confirmed what he had bet on: the Socialists had opted for a left-winger with a fantasy economic programme, leaving the centre ground wide open.

'Hamon had a good campaign but I doubt very much that he'll be able to unite the Socialist Party behind him,' Alain Duhamel, a veteran journalist and observer of French politics, said the morning after on RTL radio. 'Benoît Hamon has won, but the most likely beneficiary will be Emmanuel Macron.' He was right on both fronts.

The bigger gift for Macron, and the campaign's biggest bombshell, dropped on the evening of Tuesday 24 January. Like so many of France's political scandals in the past, it appeared in the pages of *Le Canard enchaîné*, the country's best-known satirical newspaper with its distinctive red, white and black colour scheme and cheap newsprint. Its weekly dose of news, political intrigue, biting commentary and jokes is read avidly in parliament and bought by around 400,000 people every week. More than 100 years old, it was founded to counter government propaganda in the First World War, and, proudly unfashionable, it refuses to publish its stories on its website, leading politicians to send aides around to its offices on Tuesday nights when the first editions appear in order to be prepared in advance to fight any allegations. Being featured on its front page can be deadly: the former President Valéry Giscard d'Estaing's reputation never completely recovered after the paper revealed in 1979 that he had accepted diamonds from the murderous, blood-soaked Central African dictator Jean-Bédel Bokassa. In

2005, Economy Minister Hervé Gaymard's promising career came to a halt after the paper reported that he was living in a 600-square-metre apartment at a cost to the state of €14,000 a month. More recently, it had been behind the news that François Hollande's hairdresser was paid nearly €10,000 a month at the Élysée.

Le Canard enchaîné thrives on investigations, often kicked off by a call or tip from a contact looking to dish some dirt on a rival. It had been digging into the finances of François Fillon, the Republicans party's candidate and current favourite to win the presidency, on the basis of asset declarations made to electoral authorities in the past. Its initial interest was in a private consultancy that had been set up by Fillon called 2F Conseil at the end of his five-year term as prime minister which – the paper reported in November – had paid him more than €750,000 between 2012 and 2015. *Le Canard* also revealed how he collected luxury watches worth up to €15,000.

But the exposé in the 24 January edition of the paper was to have the biggest impact, under a typical *Canard* headline which included a play on words: '*Pour Fillon, Penelope est un bon filon.*' (For Fillon, Penelope is a Money-Spinner.) Citing payslips, it reported that Fillon's British-born wife Penelope had been paid around €600,000 in pre-tax salaries over a decade for her apparent work as a parliamentary aide to her husband. Employing a spouse as an assistant was not illegal in France, unlike in Germany or at the EU parliament. But the *Canard* had been unable to find any witnesses to her work and his colleagues and political journalists had always assumed she was a housewife, busy raising the couple's five children and exercising their horses at their 12th-century manor house in central France.

She was also reported to have been paid around €5,000 a month between May 2012 and December 2013 by the current affairs periodical *La Revue des Deux Mondes*, owned by a billionaire friend of the couple, Marc Ladreit de Lacharrière. But the director of the monthly, Michel Crépu, was quoted as saying 'I have never met Penelope Fillon and I have never seen her in the offices of the *Review*.'

The potential impact of these revelations was huge. Despite Macron's recent gains, Fillon was still the frontrunner in the polls and was widely assumed to be on course for victory. But the claims struck at the foundations of his candidacy. He had presented himself as 'Mr Clean', famously saying during the primary that Sarkozy's legal problems made him an illegitimate candidate, and highlighting his own blemish-free record in nearly 40 years in politics. He was also promising to cut 500,000 civil service jobs in his war on public spending and benefits scroungers. In light of the paper's revelations, old tweets were dug up in which he'd written how 'the president and his ministers must be beyond reproach' while railing against 'the social injustice of those who work hard for not much and those who don't work and receive public money.' Inevitably, the scandal was dubbed #Penelopegate, and it led news bulletins that evening and began trending immediately on social media.

Fillon's camp was in crisis. A spokesman was sent out to brief the media, confirming that Fillon had indeed employed his wife (to the surprise of his colleagues). 'It is common for the spouses of MPs to work with them,' Thierry Solère told reporters. He was correct: around a fifth of the 577 parliamentarians in the national assembly were estimated to employ a family member. The problem was that no one had any memory of having seen

Penelope working to justify her salary, which reached more than €10,000 pre-tax some months.

The next day, the national financial prosecutor's office opened a preliminary investigation into the potential misuse of public money, the trafficking of influence and conspiracy. Fillon was at a scheduled campaign stop in Bordeaux visiting an aerospace factory and a wine museum alongside his former rival Alain Juppé when he learned of this via the media. 'I see the mud-slinging season has begun,' he said in his first reaction. 'I'm outraged by the contempt and misogyny of this article. Because she's my wife she isn't allowed to work? Imagine if a male politician said that a woman was only good for making jam, as this article claims? The feminists would go crazy.' He later welcomed the fact that an investigation had been opened so quickly, which he said would 'end this campaign of lies.'

Facing pressure to explain himself, Fillon agreed to go on the Thursday night prime-time evening interview slot on the TF1 channel, 48 hours after the first story appeared. His advisors would later admit they had been too slow to react. Fillon said he was thick-skinned enough to resist the pressure, which he claimed was designed to destroy his presidential candidacy. 'There's not the slightest doubt: my wife worked for me for years as my parliamentary assistant,' he said, listing her tasks as managing mail, attending meetings with him or meeting people on his behalf.

He then dropped two major announcements: he revealed that two of his children, both lawyers, had also worked for him as assistants while he was a senator from 2005 to 2007, to advise on legal issues. And he set a clear condition for his withdrawal: 'The only thing that would stop me being a candidate is if my honour was called into question, if I was charged.'

The revelation about his children immediately boomeranged when it emerged that neither of them were qualified at the time they were helping their father. But setting out a clear red line on whether he would withdraw had the merit of buying him some time with the party and potential rivals. He pointed to his right to the presumption of innocence and continued to paint the revelations as a politically motivated attack on his family.

'It's not a good sign for Mr Fillon when some of his friends are starting to ask who is going to replace him,' Marine Le Pen said on the Friday night. Among Republicans, party elders were terrified and stunned – no one had been aware that Penelope was his assistant. It was noticeable how few senior figures were willing to go out in public during the first week of the crisis to defend him.

Macron deliberately steered clear of the scandal, saying that Fillon was innocent until proven guilty and that the justice system must be allowed to determine if there was any wrongdoing. 'He asked everyone in the team to be very careful about what they said,' communications chief Sibeth Ndiaye recalled. 'His view was that a would-be president of the Republic shouldn't be seen to jump on the bandwagon on the basis of a news report.'

The following Tuesday evening, a larger than usual gaggle of parliamentary aides arrived at the offices of *Le Canard* amid rumours that the newspaper was preparing fresh revelations. Its edition of the previous week had sold out nation-wide and a bigger print-run had been ordered for the follow up. 'The bill shoots higher: another €330,000 for Penelope and €84,000 for the children,' it announced. The paper's reporters had some-how accessed more payslips showing that Penelope had been employed in three distinct periods between 1988 and 2013 with a total pre-tax salary of €831,440. She'd also been paid €100,000 by Fillon's friend's magazine, *La Revue des Deux Mondes*, while their children had earned €84,000 between 2005 and 2007 from parliamentary expenses, with part of their salaries transferred to their parents. A total of around €1 million pre-tax. Earlier in the day investigators leading the judicial investigation had raided Fillon's office in parliament and were seen leaving with boxes of documents.

'To my knowledge, never under the Fifth Republic has a situation like this ever occurred. Never has an operation of this scale and professionalism been mounted to try to eliminate a candidate three months before the presidential election,' Fillon said the same day.

Throughout Penelopegate, Fillon would stick to this defence in increasingly aggressive terms: it was a conspiracy cooked up by the mainstream media with the connivance of the government and a justice system that even critics conceded had been known to be subject to political pressure. He would also seek the public's sympathy for the intrusion into his nearly 40-year marriage, which had been a key part of his personal appeal to conservative voters. It was a successful argument for his core supporters, who angrily repeated the claims, particularly about the media's role, right up to election day. His support never fell below 17–18 per cent in the polls despite all the revelations. But there was a sizeable slice of the electorate – around 5–10 per cent judging by the polls – who were not convinced by his protestations.

The problem in the court of public opinion was the lack of evidence to back him up. Penelope appeared at a major rally in Paris a few days after the first revelations where she received a standing ovation and the crowd chanted her name. But the chemistry between the couple as they sat on the front row looked terrible. She was tense and awkward – understandable given the attention – and barely responded when Fillon took her hand in his. 'If someone wants to attack me, attack me while looking me straight in the eyes. But leave my wife out of politics!' Fillon said later from the stage.

Journalists raked through parliament and his constituency in the Sarthe region of central France near Le Mans, home to the 24-hour car race, without finding people who would testify to Penelope's work. She didn't have a security pass for the parliament building nor a parliamentary email address.

Fillon's media team might have produced a dossier of emails, letters or speeches containing her contributions to remove all doubt – but they didn't. Only two articles could be found in *La Revue des Deux Mondes* bearing her byline, which appeared to have earned her a pre-tax salary of €100,000. An impoverished contributor to the magazine, in contrast, recalled how she had been paid around €75 for translating a 750-word article for the publication in 2009.[2]

But the couple were damned more than anything by their own words.

The Fillons had met in their mid-20s while Penelope, originally from Abergavenny in Wales, was studying at the Sorbonne university in Paris when her future husband was a young parliamentary assistant. They were married in the Welsh village of Llanover in 1980 at a ceremony where Fillon's dad – 'who hated the English for historical reasons', according to Fillon – struggled to communicate with the bride's father who held similar feelings for the French.[3] (Fillon's younger brother would go on to marry Penelope's sister, Jane, a few years later.)

The couple had their first of five children a few years into their marriage as Fillon's political career took off. He became the youngest MP in parliament after elections in 1981 at the age of 27. By his own admission, he moved almost permanently to Paris, coming back to visit the family at weekends in his rural constituency. 'I didn't have much time to see the first four children grow up because I was an MP,' he told the *Ambition Intime* interview programme which had helped him win the primary back in November 2016. 'It was 24/7, so basically they were raised by their mother.'

Penelope herself had always hidden from the limelight and kept a distance from politics, even when Fillon was named as prime minister in 2007 by then president Nicolas Sarkozy. In the same year, she gave an interview to the Paris correspondent of the *Sunday Telegraph*, appearing shy and self-effacing. 'I'm just a country peasant, this is not my natural habitat,' she said.

A video of the interview was unearthed by French television show *Envoyé Special* and broadcast in February in which she seemed sad and fragile as she talked about how her 'children always think of me just as their mother'. She'd signed up for an English literature course, thinking 'it would get me going again.' Asked directly in this interview if she had helped Fillon in his career, she said she'd been to rallies and done leafleting during campaigning, but 'I've never been his assistant or anything like that.' The phrase was rewound and played twice on the *Envoyé Special* report to emphasise the point.

Another of her rare interviews was found, this time to a local newspaper *Le Bien Public* during Fillon's primary campaign in 2016. 'Until now, I have never been involved in my husband's political life,' she was quoted as saying.

A poll taken on 26–27 January, a few days after the first revelations about Fillon were published in *Le Canard enchaîné*, showed an immediate effect on voting intentions.[4] Marine Le Pen was now out ahead, credited with 26 per cent, while Fillon had slipped back to 21 per cent with Macron close behind on 20 per cent. 'I can't vote for Fillon now, it's finished,' said Carole, a 58-year-old IT professional who had always voted for the right in her wealthy area of the southern city of Marseille. 'Even if his ideas are good, I'm disappointed by his lack of awareness. You can't ask people to draw in the purse strings when you know that you're in a position like his.'

In another poll taken in the final days of January, the impact was dramatic: Macron was now in second place with 23 per cent. It was the first time he had been shown as qualifying for the second round. 'The most legitimate candidate, François Fillon, chosen just two months ago in the primary, risks exploding mid-flight,' warned journalist Cécile Cornudet in the *Les Echos* business newspaper. 'From now on, everything seems possible, including a victory for Marine Le Pen … no one is laughing any more at Emmanuel Macron, unknown only two years ago.'

Fortunately for the En Marche team, they had been planning a major rally in the western city of Lyon for the following weekend which they had intended to be another show of force. They'd booked an 8,000-capacity sports centre on Saturday, the day before Marine Le Pen was due to address her supporters in the same city. Shadowing her moves had become a tactic of the Macron's campaign, meaning he would regularly pop up in the same area as her. Le Pen's schedule was usually announced a week in advance, while Macron would inform the media of his plans sometimes only the night before. The En Marche campaign deliberately planned at the last minute, allowing Macron to be nimble.

'One of our ideas was that there was no reason we should leave her the slightest area,' one of his top advisors explained. This meant campaigning near her or in National Front strongholds, as well as challenging her attempts to cast herself as the only defender of France. 'We decided that patriotism was actually on our side. Le Pen wasn't patriotic, she was nationalistic. We decided we should talk about the flag, our values and the pride we felt at being French too.' It was all part of Macron's strategy of 'triangulation', an idea first used by US President Bill Clinton in the 1990s, which saw him steal some of the language and ideas from his right-wing opponents to shield himself from attacks.

'I knew if I succeeded with my plans to redraw politics that my offer would be centrist – progressive, pro-European, patriotic – and the polar opposite was the National Front,' Macron said as he reflected at the end of campaigning. 'It drove me on.'

The competing rallies in Lyon were now a match up between the two leading candidates. The elegant city, split by the Rhône and the Saône rivers, was awash with the new political forces shaping the election. The Communist-backed Eurosceptic leader Jean-Luc Mélenchon was also in town: he held a rally of his new *France Insoumise* (France Unbowed) movement which was drawing many of the young anti-globalisation protesters who had taken part in the nocturnal sit-ins around France in the summer of 2016 called *Nuits Debout*. Using social media to great effect and his own strong personality, Mélenchon amassed 450,000 members during the presidential election and was hugely popular among students. He was anti-trade, pro-environment and committed to massive increases in state spending, particularly via social programmes for the poor. Among many radical measures, he proposed a 90 per cent tax on any income above €400,000 a year.

At the Macron rally, thousands were again left outside where he performed his now familiar stunt of appearing in front of them to apologise for the lack of space. 'You can say "I was there",' Macron told the disappointed crowd as a consolation. Operations manager Ludovic Chaker later admitted to booking smaller-than-necessary venues on purpose, because the crowd overflow helped build the buzz around Macron's campaign.

Inside, the stage was set up like a boxing ring in the middle of the banked rows of seats. Chaker had planned for Macron to roam around the stage while speaking, which was usually when he was at his most persuasive. In the end, Macron decided to speak from a lectern, which froze him in one spot and according to Chaker 'ruined the scenography.' The speech was 'pretty bad' in the team's assessment, he said, but media coverage focused on the enthusiasm of the crowd and the number of people outside.

Macron attacked Le Pen in his speech, saying that she 'did not speak in the name of the people, but in the name of the embittered.' He also unveiled plans for 10,000 new recruits to security forces and the reintroduction of community policing, which had been scrapped during Sarkozy's and Fillon's time in office. Many experts pointed out that the lack of local policing meant security forces were missing out on local community intelligence, which was particularly important given the threat of Islamic extremism. Rather than being embedded in local communities, in many rough areas of the country the police were seen by locals as simply repressive law enforcers, and were resented as being violent and rude when they appeared. The week before the Lyon rallies a routine identity check in a northern Paris suburb had degenerated into violence. A 22-year-old local community worker with no criminal record was left with severe anal injuries caused by a policeman's baton, sparking nights of rioting and a new cycle of anti-police hatred.

On the same day, Le Pen unveiled her manifesto, which was a list of 144 commitments. They included returning to a national currency instead of the euro and pulling out of the Schengen agreement which allowed Europeans to cross national frontiers without showing their passports. She also pledged to organise an in–out referendum on the EU. Her domestic priorities included promises to lower the retirement age, increase defence spending, build 40,000 prison places and impose a tax of 35 per cent on the imports of any products manufactured by a company which had shifted production overseas. The cost of her increased spending commitments alone were budgeted at an addition €85 billion by the Business Institute think-tank, whereas the economic costs of pulling France out of the euro and returning to the franc were almost incalculable.

Her speech on the Sunday in Lyon was a return to far-right basics. At the entrance to the conference centre were stands run by far-right activists pointing out how migrants were apparently treated better than French people. To shouts of 'This is our home!' from the crowd, she warned that two 'totalitarianisms' threatened to swamp France. 'One in the name of global finance: the ideology of trade above all else; the other in the name of radical Islam: the ideology of religion above all else.'

Le Pen also raised what would become a theme of the next three months: the battle between the National Front and En Marche was between her 'patriots' and Macron's 'globalists'. It was straight out of Donald Trump's playbook in which he had rallied white working-class Americans in Rust Belt, suburban or rural areas who saw themselves as being the victims of a system of open trade and mass migration devised by the urban elite represented by Hillary Clinton.

Macron boldly drew attention in Lyon to his different view of French culture in a remark that was repeated endlessly by Le Pen and Fillon. It was a sophisticated argument that was risky in the middle of an election campaign. 'There isn't a French culture. There is a culture in France. It's diverse and multi-faceted,' he said. He would later expand on his thinking by comparing the country's character to a river into which different tributaries flowed, changing its composition over time. 'It's not something stuck in time,' he insisted. Marine Le Pen and Fillon accused him of denying the existence of French culture. 'France isn't a soulless international hotel where anonymous individuals and foreign communities come to live side by side,' Fillon said.

Macron's own culture is as French as Roquefort cheese and has been since childhood: his inner political team and friends are almost all from traditional French backgrounds, while his tastes in literature and music are monotonously Gallic. He wasn't rejecting the idea of French culture; what he was rejecting was the idea of French cultural chauvinism, which is a source of resentment among many ethnic minorities who feel pressured to either surrender their own mixed identities to be accepted or compelled to live a life on the outside.

Despite the controversy and persistent attacks from the right and far-right, Macron maintained his position in second place behind Le Pen for the next fortnight as the focus remained on whether Fillon could keep up his defiance and maintain his candidacy. 'A month ago, we looked like we couldn't lose. Now we're asking ourselves if we'll even make the run-off,' one Republicans MP lamented.[5]

CHAPTER 14

Rumours and Russians

AS MACRON'S CHANCES INCREASED THROUGHOUT January and early February, so too did speculation about his sexuality. Ever since he had been named economy minister in 2014, his unusual marriage had led to rumours that Brigitte was a cover for a hidden gay life. 'When he became economy minister, the very first call I had from a journalist was about that. The same night,' his communications advisor Sibeth Ndiaye remembered. 'And it was about Mathieu Gallet.'

Gallet was dapper, chiselled and the youngest ever head of *Radio France*, the state radio giant. At just 40, he was from the same generation as Macron and shared his taste in fine tailoring. Rumours about them having an illicit relationship had repeatedly done the rounds over the previous two years, but they reached fever pitch in early 2017.

During Parisian dinner parties, conversations about politics inevitably focused on Macron's sexuality and marriage. Journalists swapped the same gossip in a giant game of Chinese whispers usually sourced to the 'friend of a friend': of apparent sightings in gay clubs or of allegedly compromising paparazzi photos of Macron that one of the celebrity magazines was preparing to publish. Innocent sightings of him having dinner alone with another man would be enough to spark a fresh flurry of speculation. And the rumour mill was fed maliciously by Macron's opponents: the Russian state news agency Sputnik ran a story about him being backed by a 'gay lobby', fake emails were being forwarded among people warning that he was a closet homosexual, while Nicolas Sarkozy, who had described Macron as 'a bit male, a bit female' in May 2016, fuelled speculation during off-the-record briefings with journalists. So too did Sarkozy's friend, the gay banker and business advisor Philippe Villin, who energetically pushed suggestions that Macron's marriage was 'fake' over lunches with reporters.

At the start of February, Pamela Druckerman, the Paris-based author of a bestselling book on parenting called *French Children Don't Throw Food*, wrote an article for *The New York Times* about the Macron couple. She concluded with a warning about the doubts overshadowing the Macron couple and the fears, discussed privately among many moderates, that the outing of Macron would sink his burgeoning campaign.

'The French pride themselves on not moralizing,' Druckerman wrote. 'The one requirement is that a politician's love life should be sincere ... At issue isn't [Macron's] sexuality; it's his authenticity. The implication is that if his love story isn't real, his plans for the country lack substance, too.'

At around the same time, in late January, communications advisor Ndiaye went to her hairdresser's in the 9th district of Paris to get her dreadlocks re-done. It was a regular working class salon, catering to African-origin clients wanting straightening or braids. Ndiaye had never mentioned her job during the small talk of previous visits. And when her boss flashed up on a muted television screen playing on one of the walls, the salon began to discuss his prospects amid the whirl of hairdryers.

'I overheard my hairdresser talking to her colleagues and she says "He's good this Macron guy, but everyone knows he's gay. I like him but France will never elect a homosexual". I listened and smiled to myself. It also made me think,' Ndiaye remembered. As soon as she left, she sent a text message to Macron to tell him.

She and Macron laughed about it together back at campaign headquarters, but there was also a serious implication. 'What was worrying was the fact that this was my hairdresser, who is not at all connected to the political world, who doesn't watch much television and who is from a modest background,' Ndiaye said. 'Up until then, we had an idea in our heads that this was something circulating in the political-media circles of Paris. It was a revelation for him.'

In November during an interview with the *Mediapart* website, Macron had already been asked about the rumours, but his comment that 'I care more than anything else about my family and my married life' went largely unnoticed. In early 2017, Brigitte too was becoming increasingly hurt and appalled that she had to constantly justify her marriage to strangers while on the campaign trail. 'You don't understand. The rumour is everywhere. I can't travel outside of Paris without someone asking me the question,' she told a friend.[1]

Macron decided to address the issue head-on during a campaign stop in Paris on 7 February that made headlines in France and abroad.

'Those who want to spread the idea that I am a fake, that I have hidden lives or something else, first of all, it's unpleasant for Brigitte,' he said. 'She shares my whole life from morning till night and she wonders on a basic level how I could physically do anything,' he added.

'If over dinners in the city, if on forwarded emails, you're told that I have a double life with Mathieu Gallet or anyone else, it's my hologram that suddenly escaped, but it can't be me!' he joked, drawing laughter from the crowd.

On the sidelines, Ndiaye and advisor Benjamin Griveaux initially grimaced, then looked relieved. They had no idea Macron was going to slip the comments into his speech. He'd taken the decision without discussing it with them.

'I decided to handle it with humour because it's the best way to deal with rumours,' Macron said afterwards. The rumours had been 'unsettling' for him and his family, he said.[2]

He went on further to defuse the problem in several interviews with gay media outlets, including *Têtu*, in which he lambasted the misogyny of the rumour-mongers and the prejudices of people who were unable or unwilling to believe a marriage between a younger man and an older woman could be real.

With the gay issue deftly handled and Fillon facing an avalanche of bad publicity, Macron's prospects looked brighter than ever throughout early February until he blundered while overseas. On a trip to Algeria on 15 February intended to bolster his credentials on foreign policy, he was asked about France's bloody history of colonisation in the country, which had been invaded in 1830 and held in the teeth of repeated uprisings until 1962 when President de Gaulle finally ceded it its independence. A bloody colonialist war involving torture and mass killings had left hundreds of thousands dead. 'I think it's unacceptable to glorify colonisation. Some people tried to do that in France a little over ten years ago,' Macron told a journalist from the Echorouk TV station, alluding to an attempt by right-wing lawmakers to pass a law in 2005 forcing school teachers to teach the 'positive values' of colonialism.

'I have always condemned colonialism as a barbarity ... Colonisation is part of French history. It's a crime, a crime against humanity,' Macron added.

A crime against humanity? Macron was damning the millions of French settlers who had lived or were born in Algeria, as well as hundreds of thousands of French soldiers and pro-French Algerian fighters who had fought there to keep the territory under Paris' control for 130 years. 'The trip had gone brilliantly, we were really well received over there,' Macron's diplomatic advisor Aurélien Lechevallier remembers. 'And he made that comment right at the end of the interview. It was a few words. You really had to go looking for it.' The National Front and the Republicans had certainly gone looking and didn't miss this obvious opportunity. 'This hatred of our history, this permanent repentance, is unworthy of a presidential candidate,' Fillon said.

Macron had gone further than he intended to and he had also contradicted what he'd said previously, giving the impression that he was prepared to flip-flop on issues depending on the person in front of him. In an interview with *Le Point* in November he had acknowledged there had been torture in Algeria but 'also the emergence of a state, wealth and the middle classes ... it's the reality of colonisation. There was both civilisation and barbarity.'

A second interview shortly afterwards touched off another media storm when he said that the government had 'humiliated' the country's conservative Catholics who had opposed the gay marriage law pushed through by Hollande in 2013, seen by supporters as one of the president's main social accomplishments. Macron had defended the law and publicly held progressive views on gay rights. But the comments played into the narrative now being pushed aggressively by his rivals that Macron was neither right, nor left, nor of any real substance. After his comments that there wasn't 'a French culture', he was quoted in April by the right-wing magazine *Causeur* as saying that France 'wasn't and would never be a multicultural nation.'

The charitable view was that he held highly nuanced views on these difficult subjects: it was possible to believe that the government had humiliated the country's Catholics by failing to acknowledge their difficulty in accepting gay marriage, while still being in favour of the law. It was also possible to believe that French culture was mixed and heterogeneous while rejecting 'multiculturalism' as a model (adopted by Canada or Britain), in which ethnic groups are free to retain their original culture and live in their communities. 'I am against multiculturalism, but for integration which is not assimilation,' Macron later said in an interview on France 2. This was a clearer statement of his beliefs, but was still unlikely to enlighten most voters.

The more critical take on Macron's pronouncements was that on many issues he gave answers that sounded professorial, long-winded or waffly. More cynically, he seemed to say one thing that appealed to left-wing voters and then another to clarify his views afterwards that resonated with right-wingers, or vice versa. In the heat of an election campaign, the charge that he was a flip-flopper was starting to stick and he was also taking fire for having still not produced a programme. Polls suddenly showed his narrow lead over Fillon evaporate and the right-winger was back ahead of him in a survey of 21 February, despite all of his legal problems.[3] Macron desperately needed a way to recapture his momentum.

The team were also growing concerned that they had powerful enemies acting against them overseas. During February, when Macron emerged as the unexpected frontrunner, the En Marche website and its servers were hit by hundreds of cyberattacks every day targeting their databases and emails. Coverage of him in the state-run Russian media had also turned increasingly critical. The Russian news agency Sputnik published an English-language story with the headline 'Ex-French Economy Minister Macron Could Be "US Agent" Lobbying Banks' Interests', quoting a single French source – the right-wing lawmaker Nicolas Dhuicq. 'There is a very wealthy gay lobby behind him,' Dhuicq said in an article that was long on innuendo and short on evidence. It was an obvious and egregious smear, providing no justification for why Dhuicq was a credible source for the allegations. Critical articles were systematically retweeted by accounts in France to spread the message and were picked up by far-right sites in France and abroad.

The cyberattacks and critical conspiratorial 'news' stories had all the hallmarks of being from the Russian playbook used against Hillary Clinton in the US election the year before in action that US intelligence agencies believed was personally authorised by Putin. The French election had previously looked like shaping up very nicely for the Kremlin with Fillon and Le Pen in the second round.

Macron's pro-European stance and his willingness to stand up to its powerful neighbour in the east were an obvious threat to Russia. Julian Assange, the head of Wikileaks whose organisation had been used to release hacked emails against Clinton, and whose actions frequently benefit the Kremlin, gave an interview to Russian newspaper *Izvestia* saying he had 'interesting information' on Macron without providing details.

En Marche had begun receiving their first phishing emails in December. This tactic sees hackers register a web domain name similar to the organisation they are trying to compromise. In the case of En Marche, it could be www.ennarche.fr, for example. The hackers then send emails purporting to be from someone inside the organisation, asking staff to download a piece of software or enter their log in details. Doing either means the hackers can access the IT networks. Phishing was used to infiltrate the Democratic National Committee in the US.

In January, En Marche had taken on the self-proclaimed geek and computer expert Mounir Mahjoubi to manage its digital advertising and IT security. The 32 year old, born to working-class Moroccan parents in eastern Paris, had made a name for himself as a government advisor and e-commerce entrepreneur who had set up an online network for sourcing local food. He was taken on mostly to handle En Marche's online communications, but instead found himself on the front line working with French intelligence services in trying to stop hackers compromising the election.

With a small in-house digital team that numbered only eighteen at its height, resources were extremely tight. Part of the response was educating staff about the risks they faced and enforcing strict rules that required everyone to regularly change their passwords. Logistics head Ludovic Chaker also helped to spread the message. 'I had done some training and explained to everyone that we should consider email as an open[ly accessible] resource.'

Mahjoubi also oversaw other measures such as setting up fake email accounts filled with fake content. It meant that if the movement's networks were ever compromised, the hackers would have to sift through enormous quantities of made up information that would cast doubt on the credibility of their leaks.

The core political team, including Macron, had also been using the messaging service Telegram instead of email since the beginning of the campaign to share the most sensitive information about their tactics or financing. The encrypted phone app is still considered beyond the reach of intelligence services – making it popular with jihadists in Syria and Iraq.

In mid-February, En Marche decided to go public with their concerns in a bid to shine unwelcome light on their saboteurs and scare off Moscow. The secretary general of the movement, Richard Ferrand, wrote an article in *Le Monde* denouncing the 'intervention of a foreign state determined to destabilise our election.' The message was repeated by En Marche spokesmen, while the French government issued an equally frank warning the following day.

'We will not accept any interference whatsoever in our electoral process, whether by Russia or any other state,' French Foreign Minister Jean-Marc Ayrault told parliament. 'After what happened in the United States, it is our responsibility to take all steps necessary to ensure that the integrity of our democratic process is fully respected.' The Kremlin issued a statement denying any responsibility.

After this distraction and the controversies in February over French culture, colonialism and whether French Catholics had been 'humiliated' by gay marriage, Macron needed to refocus voter attention on his core messages on business, Europe and his aim of overhauling French politics. Fortunately he had a card up his sleeve.

He'd been in talks over the month with the fellow centrist François Bayrou, a three-time candidate for the presidency who in 2007 had won 18.6 per cent in the first round of the election. The head of his own party, MoDem, which was strong in south-west France, Bayrou had still not declared whether he would have another tilt at the presidency in 2017. His political positioning was almost identical to Macron's. 'It was my space which I had cleared, ploughed and watered for many years, then Macron set up there,' Bayrou said.[4]

But to extend his own metaphor, Bayrou was a reliable and slightly battered old tractor while Macron was a shiny new combine harvester with a Wi-Fi connection. Bayrou had almost no chance of making it through to the final round and was unsure if he could raise the financing or sponsors needed to mount another challenge. The two men patched up a deal.

Macron informed his team on the sixth floor of his headquarters in their morning planning meeting, in a moment captured by the documentary team that had been authorised to film behind the scenes. 'Bayrou is going to announce that he's not running and he'll propose an alliance with us so that the centrist family can flourish etcetera, which is his aim,' he said. 'It can't come out before 4:30pm, so watch out. Don't tweet or SMS anyone, kids,' he added, looking around the room.

Behind closed doors Macron referred to his team as 'kids' throughout the campaign. Many of his aides were strikingly young, particularly the 27-year-old speech writer Quentin Lafay, or his closest advisor, Ismaël Emelien, who was 29. The term 'kids' speaks volumes about the power relationships within En Marche.

Despite his love of horizontal organisations and start-up culture, Macron's movement was a highly centralised organisation built around him. He inspired complete devotion and often took the big decisions alone, after consulting Brigitte. Despite the 'kids' often being around the same age as him, there was no doubt who the boss was.

After announcing the deal with Bayrou, Macron turned to Emelien and scolded him for looking at his phone in the manner of an irritated parent speaking to a teenager. 'I'm speaking and you're doing something else,' Macron snapped in front of everyone.

'OK, but there's stuff happening,' Emelien replied.

'This is sufficiently important for us to take five minutes,' Macron shot back at him intemperately.[5]

As agreed, Bayrou made his announcement in the afternoon and he and Macron later held a press conference in a swanky bar and restaurant near the Trocadero complex opposite the Eiffel Tower. Beforehand, they sat down for a chat one-to-one at a table, a conversation again recorded by the documentary team.

'I said it before, I'm here to help. I've taken a big risk but I'm used to taking them,' Bayrou said. 'It's a strange thing being president of the republic,' he said disbelievingly. 'You're not really old enough, but hey, it's not important.' It was both an admission of his own incomprehension about a campaign that was defying all the rules, and the passing of a flame from one generation to another. Bayrou insisted that the only condition for his support was that Macron should pass a new law to raise ethical standards in public life and prevent conflicts of interest if he were elected – something Macron was happy to agree to and to publicise amid Fillon's woes.

Bayrou's support gave Macron a solidity and experience he lacked. It also cleared the final potential obstruction away from the centre ground. Macron's polling numbers jumped five to six points into the mid-twenties in the aftermath of the announcement, putting clear water between him and Fillon. 'After a week full of controversy, Emmanuel Macron has found a way to relaunch his campaign which was starting to stagnate,' said an editorial in *Libération* newspaper.

Macron's old confidant and supporter Alain Minc saw it as further evidence of his ability to find a way to rebound. 'He'll make mistakes. I've no doubt about it. The comments on colonialism were stupid. But he's like a cat: you throw him out of the window and he'll land on his feet.'

CHAPTER 15

A Vision for France

DODGING RAIN SHOWERS OUTSIDE THE RAILWAY STATION in the city of Le Mans on a dank grey day in early March of 2017, Aurélie Perot and fellow En Marche activist Pascale Fontenel were handing out flyers to passers-by. Perot, a right-leaning former teacher and local councillor, had joined up after reading Macron's book. 'I feel like he's got a very modern vision of France. We might finally enter into the 21st century,' explained the 45 year old.

Fontenel, 54 and the owner of a local taxi firm, said she'd always voted for the Socialists but liked Macron's ideas 'that went beyond the traditional divisions of French politics.'

They'd both spent weekends and evenings knocking on doors and handing out flyers at local markets. And they'd both noticed that people were increasingly asking about Macron's programme, and more precisely why there still wasn't one.

'They're saying "yeah he seems nice but we're waiting",' Fontenel explained.

'We tell them there is a programme. But the other parties have had primaries which gave their candidates a chance to talk about their policies. This week will be like our primary,' explained Perot.

Macron had finally set a date for the grand unveiling, just eight weeks before the first round of the presidential election on 23 April. He'd repeatedly said that he didn't believe in the idea of a programme or a succession of promises that in the past had been ignored by the winning candidate once he took power. He'd dripped out his proposals at his rallies. But voters still expected something written down, a contract with the nation, even if it was modified beyond recognition further down the track.

The man charged with pulling a Macron manifesto together in a hurry was Jean Pisani-Ferry. The 65 year old was the founder of Brussels-based think-tank the Bruegel Institute and had known Macron since late 2010 when they'd worked together on François Hollande's economic programme when he began his run for president.

Pisani-Ferry had come to the conclusion that it was a momentous time for France: 'Trump and Brexit were both a shock to me,' he explained. 'I said to myself that this wasn't just any old election. We were in extraordinary times and I didn't want to be sitting on the sidelines, I wanted to get involved.'

He resigned his job as head of a policy advisory body in the prime minister's office in January and offered his services to Macron, taking on the task of pulling together a detailed programme that also needed to be costed. As well as a basic framework of ideas from Macron, there were also hundreds of policy propositions from local En Marche committees around the country, which had been encouraged to propose solutions to France's problems. Furthermore, working groups headed by hand-picked experts had submitted their proposals in areas such as health, education, security, agriculture or foreign policy. 'We're a small team,' Pisani-Ferry said from his office on the top floor of En Marche headquarters. 'I've worked a lot in my life but never this much. It's completely insane.'

The election, he argued, was shaping up as 'the opposition between open and closed,' reprising in different words the same argument that Le Pen had made: that voters had a choice between nationalists and globalists. The split was also between modern and conservative, Pisani-Ferry explained. The appeal of Le Pen, Trump and Brexit was explained by a 'backwards desire to see the return of the idealised France of the past, an idealised former America or former Britain in which we return to an age before the digital revolution, before the rise of emerging market countries, before globalisation.'

In his speeches and the founding charter of En Marche, Macron had made clear that he favoured being open to international trade, open to (controlled) migration and refugees, and open to new technology and innovation. In each area, he saw a response needed both at the French level and the European one. Pisani-Ferry said that at its core the En Marche manifesto was driven with a view to stimulating job creation in France but also addressing the desire for 'protection' and 'equality' in a globalised world. Achieving these goals simultaneously would require a radical overhaul of the EU as well as the French economy and its social security system.

Jean Viard, a renowned sociologist and academic who was a specialist on the National Front and helped work on the programme, said that 'Macron is offering something that starts with the same conclusion as the far-right: that the world is completely overwhelmed by the changes taking place.'

But his answer is that 'we are going to try to offer a positive response. We'll try another model,' he said.

Macron appeared to be partly inspired by a statement from the former French Socialist Prime Minister Laurent Fabius 30 years ago: that the far-right 'asks the right questions but gives the wrong responses.'

In January, in his most important pre-election speech on Europe (which he delivered in Berlin, speaking in English), Macron had pleaded for a deepening of the EU and the transfer of more national powers to headquarters in Brussels. 'Sovereignty is just how to protect your people, how to protect your interests and how to promote your interests in the rest of the world,' he said.[1] European citizens were best served by national governments pooling their resources in many areas rather than trying to act on their own.

This meant moving forward on a long-stalled common defence policy, which had been held back by reluctance among France, Germany and Britain to team up, and creating improved European intelligence and police teams. It meant reinforcing a common border protection force to check illegal immigration, with a system for dividing refugees up between member states once they arrived and expelling economic migrants. It meant collective efforts to fight climate change, including a Europe-wide functioning carbon market that raised the cost of pollution for emitters. It meant a more assertive trade policy to stop exports from Asia or America being dumped on the European market, such as Chinese steel. It meant the further harmonisation of social protections and business regulations. All these measures were designed to create jobs and offer greater protection.

But there was also a focus on equality, through an idea he had been pitching since his time touring European capitals as an economy minister: the eurozone needed its own budget and borrowing capacity to be able to transfer funds from rich members (particularly Germany with its large trade surplus and balanced budgets) to weaker states such as Italy, Greece or Spain to help them invest and modernise. The economic disaster in Greece had made plain how difficult it was for a member of the eurozone to regain competitiveness in a crisis. In the past, Greece could have devalued its currency – the drachma – to make its exports cheaper. Under the single currency, no such possibility existed. Fiscal transfers from wealthy to poor areas take place within all countries: the rich coastal US states finance the poorer 'flyover' ones, for example, while London and Paris provide a disproportionate amount of tax revenue which is then spent in depressed former industrial zones. Macron wanted to bring the same idea to the eurozone, but doing so would require a finance minister, and a new parliament to oversee the process.

It was a blueprint for a giant leap towards the United States of Europe. 'During the past decade, we failed altogether to progress, to have a new phase in European construction … I want to put an end to that,' Macron said in his Berlin speech, calling the ten years since voters in France and the Netherlands rejected an EU Constitution in referenda a 'lost decade'.

What had been intended as a keynote campaign speech went curiously unexplored in the French media, perhaps because it was delivered in English. Reaction the next day from the National Front focused on how Macron had neglected his mother tongue and how he had praised Merkel's open-door policy for refugees. 'Poor France!' tweeted Le Pen.

Macron's fervent belief in the EU as Europe's best defence in a globalised world explains his inability to understand Brexit and why Britain would prefer to stand alone rather than under the protective shield of the 28-member bloc. When negotiating trade deals, tackling the dominance of US internet giants Google or Facebook, confronting Russia, or speaking out about human rights or democracy in the world, France, in his view, was simply too small on its own.

This conclusion had been reached through reason – the rise of emerging markets meant that France had become relatively less important globally than before. He also felt a personal sense of attachment to the EU's civilising mission: the graveyards around Macron's hometown of Amiens were a daily reminder of France and Germany's ruinous past. And, being a man who came of age in the 1990s and 2000s, Europe was simply a way of life and a source of new opportunities.

Macron holds former Prime Minister David Cameron personally responsible for running a weak campaign for a 'Yes' vote in favour of the EU ahead of the British referendum, and for failing to make the case for membership with more conviction. Cameron campaigned as 'Yes but …', Macron said in February while in London, adding: 'If you are shy, you are dead.'[2] The latter words could be Macron's own motto in his journey from provincial student to president.

This criticism was mild compared to his views about the main architects of Brexit: the then mayor of London Boris Johnson, who was named UK foreign secretary after the referendum, and the then head of the UK Independence Party, Nigel Farage. 'The British are making a serious mistake over the long term. Boris Johnson enjoys giving flamboyant speeches but he has no strategic vision; the turmoil he created the day after Brexit proves it,' Macron told *Monocle* magazine.[3] 'Nigel Farage and Mr Johnson are responsible for this crime: they sailed the ship into battle and jumped overboard at the moment of crisis,' he said.

But even if Britain had voted to remain a member, Macron's plans for deeper European integration would find few takers among London politicians (or for that matter the wider British electorate) and would terrify the editors of Britain's influential right-wing Eurosceptic press. Cameron's re-negotiation had been specifically aimed at loosening Britain's ties to the EU and ensuring that the UK would not have to transfer more money via bail-outs for eurozone members. It reflected the long-held and majoritarian view that Britain should be an EU member with a foot both inside and outside the bloc. The country had far less of an emotional attachment to the project and its founding peace-spreading mission than its continental partners do, due to Britain's different experiences of Europe's 20th-century wars. Successive UK governments saw their primary role as being in acting as a bridge between America and the bloc.

Former British Prime Minister Tony Blair believes Macron still wants Britain to remain an EU member given the country's diplomatic and military clout. 'He knows Europe is going to be weaker without Britain,' Blair said. This might explain why he declared that the door was 'always open' if Britain changed its mind, when he met British Prime Minister Theresa May in June.

But London's departure could also be an opportunity for Macron: it removes a brake on his plans for EU reform and provides a potential source of fresh investment for France if multinationals abandon the UK, which has historically attracted foreign investment as a gateway for trade into the EU market.

In the post-Brexit world, Macron also wants the hordes of London-based French entrepreneurs and people with high-paying financial jobs – the inhabitants of 'Paris-on-Thames' – to return home. And he sees the French capital as being well placed to welcome the service sector jobs, including banking, that will cross the Channel. The pro-Paris lobby group Paris Europlace believes that 10,000 UK jobs will move to Paris, and the government presented plans to attract banks in July, offering tax cuts and new international schools for foreign staff. Evidence so far suggests Dublin, Frankfurt and Luxembourg remain more attractive than the French capital, however.[4]

As a former investment banker, economy minister and senior civil servant, Macron was set to be a formidable Brexit negotiator: both at ease with the intricate details of policy-making and aware of the needs of financial sector firms. Having not welcomed the result of Britain's referendum, he told *Monocle* in March: 'I'm a hard Brexiter.' If Brexit does go ahead, he will look for a clean break and to wring out of it every possible advantage for France.

'The intention isn't to sink the UK or humiliate it,' one of Macron's top advisors said during an interview on condition of anonymity. 'But there'll be consequences for every sector, including finance. It's obvious: Brexit will have a cost, otherwise belonging to the European Union wouldn't make sense for the other 27 members.'

When Macron spoke in front of several hundred journalists on 2 March to finally present his programme, he did not elaborate on his vision for European federalism or Brexit in such detail, but he did make clear his intentions: 'It is obviously Europe which is at the heart of our project,' he said. 'We can't succeed in the world as it is today without a real European strategy.'

He explained his support for a 'Buy European Act': new EU legislation that would oblige governments to order from companies that have factories located inside the bloc. Like his backing for tougher measures against trade dumping or more scrutiny for foreign investment in strategic sectors of the European economy, it was part of his vision of an EU that responded to voters' craving for greater protection from globalisation.

For his domestic programme, Macron's manifesto was also articulated around the three ideas of jobs, protection and equality. It was clearly inspired by the Scandinavian model of what is known as 'flexi-curity', which offers businesses freedom to hire-and-fire while also protecting individuals with a generous social security safety net. Macron saw encouraging entrepreneurship and boosting skills as not only the most obvious way to create wealth in France, but also as the means of preparing citizens for a future in which stable company jobs were increasingly rare. The 'Uberisation' of the economy and increasing levels of self-employment were durable trends that meant the state needed to be rolled back in areas where it smothered enterprise, while helping to protect risk-takers and the vulnerable.

'In this programme we are bringing together freedom and protection. It's the common thread that runs through it from the start,' he declared.

His headline economic reform was a plan to scrap France's rigid and centralised 3,300-page labour code to allow companies far greater freedom to negotiate working time, conditions and pay with their employees. This would undercut the power of trade unions to negotiate working conditions in collective agreements that covered a whole profession or sector of the economy. It was sacrilege for the French left, but it also satisfied a long-standing request from business groups backed by many economists and pro-enterprise think-tanks.

Macron also proposed slashing corporate tax from 33 per cent to 25 per cent which would make French companies more competitive and attract more foreign investment to France. He also wanted to reduce taxes on the wealthy to make the country more attractive for investors. These measures were part of his plan to shed France's unenviable role as a global champion in taxation: in 2016 it had the highest tax-to-GDP ratio in the eurozone at 45.5 per cent, far higher than Germany on 36.9 per cent. And it was the second-highest taxer among all leading industrialised nations, behind only Denmark, according to the Paris-based OECD research group. Public spending would also be cut by €60 billion over his term to bring down France's public deficit, while the public sector headcount would be reduced by 120,000. These spending-trimming measures would be counter-balanced by a state investment package of €50 billion focused on digital, energy and transport infrastructure. The broad trends of the economic programme – lower business taxes, lower public spending, more flexibility in the jobs market – mirrored the recommendations of the Commission to Liberate French Growth (where Macron had got his first break under his old mentor Jacques Attali) that were made back in 2008.

But there were new protections for the self-employed: small business owners would be able to claim unemployment benefits if they stopped working, offering them more security. On the other hand, the generous rights of regularly unemployed workers would be reduced: they could only turn down two job offers before losing their monthly benefits.

If there were no suitable jobs locally, jobseekers would be obliged to undergo adult re-training, which was to be expanded massively with a fund of €15 billion. This would help improve skills in areas of high unemployment and tackle the problem of jobs being destroyed by technological change.

'Work is going to change but we will help with this change, we will be there alongside it,' Macron said.

To tackle inequality, he proposed positive discrimination for deprived areas, not tax rises on the wealthy as proposed by Hollande in 2012. School class sizes would be halved for children aged five to seven in the lowest-achieving parts of the country to raise literacy standards, while the government would offer tax incentives for taking on employees who lived in high-unemployment areas. Schools in 'difficult' areas would be given autonomy to offer more attractive conditions to encourage better teachers. Positive discrimination and merit-based pay in the public sector struck at the heart of France's egalitarian one-size-fits-all state.

'We are not proposing to reform [France],' Macron explained further. 'We are proposing a complete and radical transformation. A change of software in many areas.'

And yet, despite these bold promises that would result in profound change if carried out, Macron would be accused of having a vague platform right to the end. Viard, the sociologist who had contributed to the programme, acknowledged as much. 'It's curious that people think he doesn't have a programme. It's been badly sold,' he said at the end of April.

Part of the problem was that it defied easy explanations. There was no political label that could be easily slapped on it. There were no soundbites for journalists or a single stand-out policy that summed up the whole programme. Even asking Macron's aides to define 'Macronism' elicited long and complicated answers.

The right-wing Fillon wanted an economic 'shock' of slashed public spending and labour market reform; Socialist Hamon was defined by his plans for universal income; far-right Le Pen was anti-immigration and anti-EU; while far-left Mélenchon wanted increased public spending and taxation on the rich. Macron seemed to want to modify so many things it was difficult to know what to focus on.

In the media and voters' minds, he was most strongly associated with his promise of political renewal: he embodied this personally as an outsider who had created a national political movement from scratch in less than twelve months. But he was also promising an overhaul just as significant of the national assembly. In parliamentary elections scheduled for June, En Marche would field candidates in all 577 constituencies, he said. Half of them would be women and half of them would never have held elected office before. One of their first responsibilities would be passing the new ethics law to clean up politics, which had been agreed during the election deal with the fellow centrist François Bayrou.

With the manifesto announced, En Marche began distributing 8 million printed copies which were sent to activists like Aurélie Perot and Pascale Fontenel in Le Mans who now had something to hand over to sceptical voters.

There was a new worry, however, outside of Macron's control. Fillon's situation had become so desperate that he was facing extreme pressure from inside the Republicans party to step aside in favour of Alain Juppé, the centre-right former prime minister he had defeated in the primary in November 2016.

On 1 March, Fillon had cancelled a scheduled trip to a farm show in Paris and called a press conference to announce that he had been summoned by magistrates investigating his wife's allegedly fake parliamentary job. He expected to be charged. There had also been new revelations about an undeclared loan from his billionaire friend Ladreit de Lacharrière.

But Fillon U-turned on his previous pledge to step aside if he was charged. The investigation was an attempt at a 'political assassination,' he said. 'It's not just me they are killing, but the French presidential election.' Dozens of aides and allies abandoned him, including the centre-right UDI party which was backing his candidacy. Horrified Republicans insiders marvelled at his obstinacy and some began to refer to Fillon's remaining team as 'sect-like' in its loyalty to the boss. Seventy per cent of French people polled thought he should call it quits.

For Macron, a switch to Juppé by the Republicans was potentially catastrophic. New polls which tested the impact of Juppé's late entrance into the race showed Macron slipping back into third place again and being eliminated in the first round.

The weekend of 4–5 March would be decisive. The Republicans party tried to patch up a deal between its three leaders, Fillon, Juppé and Sarkozy. Juppé was the most legitimate candidate to replace Fillon, but he would stand only if he was given complete freedom. Sarkozy would support Juppé but only if he could manoeuvre allies into key positions in his team. Bad blood between the three of them, exacerbated by the bitter primary campaign, made it hard to find an agreement.

After Fillon organised a defiant rally in central Paris of tens of thousands of supporters in Paris on the Sunday, Juppé called a press conference for the following morning, carried live on the rolling news networks which were being anxiously watched by the En Marche team gathered together in headquarters. Faced with the deadlock, Juppé threw the towel in, not without attacking Fillon's obstinacy and saying he had 'wasted' the presidential campaign.

On the same day, Fillon's ex-campaign director, who had quit over the scandal, went on the radio to give his own version of events. 'François Fillon is a victim of a system that has been in place for years in parliament by which MPs use the salaries of their assistants to top up their own income,' Patrick Stefanini told *Europe 1*.

The weekend left Fillon looking more isolated and damaged than ever. Just when it looked as if it couldn't get any worse, the Sunday paper *Journal du Dimanche* newspaper revealed that he had also accepted two suits worth €13,000 as a gift in February from a Franco-Lebanese lawyer known to be a middleman for African leaders and business figures. Two weeks later, he was officially charged over the fake job scandal.

'François Fillon, he's a bit like an advent calendar,' one Republicans MP with a dark sense of humour told *Le Parisien* newspaper in late March. 'Except each time you open a new window, instead of a chocolate you find a new scandal.'

Seeing Fillon's problems mount and the possibility of Juppé returning as a rival, many En Marche insiders began to worry about Macron's prospects. But at least in front of them, their leader remained unflappable. 'There were lots of people in the team who thought [Fillon] couldn't hang on, but he [Macron] kept saying "he'll stay the course",' Ndiaye said. 'It was a personal thing: he [Macron] believed that if Fillon gave up then he'd be left with nothing.' His political instincts and judgement of Fillon's character were correct. Fillon's dogged insistence on staying in the race dominated media coverage and squeezed out any serious debate about policy, which French voters were accustomed to, instead turning the election run-up into a spectacle of one man's defiance of all the odds. French comedian Nicolas Canteloup compared the Republicans candidate to the famed Dark Knight character from Monty Python who loses all of his limbs in a sword battle but vows to continue fighting.

And as well as Fillon's problems, Le Pen's legal woes were also mounting. The National Front leader was involved in at least six different cases which developed to varying degrees during the campaign. She invoked her legal immunity as a member of the European parliament to avoid hearings with French magistrates investigating alleged fraud in her use of her expenses. Le Pen was accused of misusing €340,000 of EU funds to pay assistants, including her chief of staff, for political work in France rather than at the parliament.

She was also being investigated for spreading violent imagery, having published images of Islamic State executions on her Twitter account, while the National Front faced a separate fraud investigation over the financing of its parliamentary campaign in 2012.

Socialist candidate Benoît Hamon's campaign team complained that the repeated scandals and legal cases had 'swallowed all the space', while Macron referred to a 'stolen campaign'. The sentiment was shared by most French voters, 81 per cent of whom said the campaign was 'unsatisfactory' in a poll in mid-April and 70 per cent of whom felt it failed to address 'the problems faced by French people'.[5] Macron now had a programme, but were people paying attention? It was briefly the centre of attention before being drowned out again in the cacophony of attacks and allegations launched daily by Fillon and Le Pen against the judiciary, the media and the government.

Le Monde warned in an editorial in late March that the French campaign featured 'the tone and some of the tactics that allowed Donald Trump to win the American election: reducing politics to scandal, allegations without proof, statements without fact, false claims and media hysteria: it's as if the full arsenal of Trumpism has been mobilised, in which the denial of reality and contempt for ideas wins.'

CHAPTER 16

Mightier than Le Pen?

AS THE CLOCK TICKED DOWN TO ELECTION DAY ON 23 April, an unprecedented series of televised debates offered the candidates their best chance to make an impression on voters. France had traditionally organised just one debate between the two rounds of the election, but in keeping with the longest, most intense presidential campaign the country had ever known, this time there would be two shows before the first round. The televised debates had been decisive in the primaries, helping the outsiders Fillon and Hamon to unforeseen victories. For Macron, they would be both a new experience and a risk: polls showed him as still the most likely winner of the election, but his support remained fragile, with a large proportion of voters still capable of changing their minds.

For Marine Le Pen, they confirmed her entry into mainstream French politics and her right to be treated as an equal. In 2002 when her father had made it through to the second round of the French elections, the then president Jacques Chirac had refused to debate with him. For decades, the French political class and media had tried to boycott and quarantine the National Front, treating it as an extremist fringe force. This strategy was no longer viable when a quarter of the country was preparing to vote for her. The sight of Le Pen on stage, smiling confidently beside her opponents, brought home once again the fact that far-right nationalism in France had been entirely normalised.

The first contest took place on 20 March and featured the top five contenders: Le Pen, Fillon, Macron, the Socialist Hamon and the far-left candidate Mélenchon. In total, eleven people had amassed the 500 signatures needed to run in the election, but the other six candidates included a former shepherd from the Pyrenees, a conspiracy theorist who wanted to colonise Mars and two Trotskyists. None of these was expected to win more than 5 per cent of votes.

Macron's performance in this first debate was solid but slightly subdued. At the beginning he seemed to betray rare nerves and at one point even lost his train of thought, for the first time that anyone could remember. He went out of his way to praise his rivals when he agreed with their policies, attempting to sound consensual and reasonable. The only real flashes of personality were when he took on Le Pen, who was as outspoken and provocative as ever: 'A few years ago we didn't see burkinis on our beaches. I know you're in favour Mr Macron,' she said, at one stage.

'No, excuse me,' Macron shot back. 'I'm not speaking on your behalf and I don't need a ventriloquist, I assure you, Madame Le Pen. When I've got something to say, I'll say it.'

'So what do you think of the burkini?', she asked.

'I think that the trap you are falling into with your provocations is that you're dividing society. It turns the 4 million Muslim people in our country, the vast majority of whom are not into communitarianism, into our enemies. And I say no to that,' he said.

This exchange made the all-important highlights reel for the millions of people who didn't sit through the three hours of often dense debate. But so did Le Pen's withering criticism of Macron at the end, when she managed to land a blow on his soft spot. Asked for his views on US president Donald Trump, Macron gave a waffly, meandering answer which referred to his 'diplomatic roadmap' for an independent, autonomous and strong France based on 'structured partnerships' that would provide the country with 'credibility and continuity'. Le Pen snorted, laughed and shook her head as he spoke.

'You know what Mr Macron? You have an incredible talent: you've just spoken for five minutes and I am utterly unable to sum up your thinking,' she said. 'You've said nothing, nothing! It's completely vacuous. Every time you talk you say you want a bit of this, a bit of that, but you never make up your mind.'

Macron's student friend Marc Ferracci admitted afterwards that 'it wasn't easy and he could have been better,' but he was confident that if Macron and Le Pen were in a two-way debate it would be different. 'That's a format that suits him. He might be a bit punchier in his responses to Le Pen,' he added. En Marche staffer Cédric O also wrote to a friend on email, saying Macron had been 'disappointing' in a message that was later leaked online.[1]

Fillon was reserved throughout the debate, accepting in his final presentation to voters that 'he had a few faults, but who doesn't?' The Socialist candidate Hamon struggled to make an impact, but he did attack Macron about the source of his campaign financing, raising the risk of 'chemical, pharmaceutical or banking lobbies' providing him with money and then expecting favours if he was elected.

The main winner from the evening appeared to be the far-left leader Mélenchon. The 65-year-old firebrand had limped along in fifth position for most of the campaign and his role had appeared to be confined to siphoning off votes from the Socialists. But in the debate, his clarity, humour and acid-tongued attacks on Le Pen in particular shone, in what was otherwise an often messy encounter.

Mélenchon uttered one of the lines of the evening when he accused the debate's moderators of having the 'modesty of a gazelle' for their reluctance to dare to question Fillon and Le Pen about their legal problems – a misguided attempt by the hosts to appear even-handed. In the aftermath, support for Mélenchon jumped by five points, taking him into fourth position, ahead of Hamon. He was also closing the gap on Fillon. 'It's like the spring, you don't see it then, boom! There are flowers,' he told a rally afterwards referring to the jump in his popularity.

Mélenchon's success was a sign of the times. Like Le Pen, he held globalisation responsible for France's problems, as well as the financial and political elite. In 2011, he'd penned a book called *Get Rid of Them All. Quick, a Citizen's Revolution*. His views on the European Union and the need for higher public spending and state intervention were also shared by Le Pen, though Mélenchon rejected the far-right leader's views on immigration and Islam. Having been born to white French parents in Morocco, he spoke admiringly of France's 'multi-coloured identity'. The former Trotskyist also favoured closer relations with the Russian President Putin and was an admirer of Latin American 'people's revolutions' led by the strongmen Hugo Chávez and Fidel Castro.

The second debate on 4 April featured all eleven candidates together for the first time in a demonstration of French *égalité* in action. Each candidate was given the same allotted time, allowing the smaller protest candidates their chance to air their views to a national audience of millions. They were for the most anticapitalist, anti-EU and anti-globalisation. The communist car mechanic Philippe Poutou refused to take part in a group photo at the start of the debate, and grew ruder and more confrontational as the night wore on.

'Aside from [fellow Communist and teacher] Nathalie Arthaud, I think I'm the only person standing at these lecterns to have a normal profession, a normal job,' he said in his opening remarks. He lambasted Fillon for 'stealing from public funds' and tackled Le Pen over her use of her parliamentary immunity to avoid prosecution. 'When we're called in by the police, there's no worker's immunity,' he said.

Poutou dared to say on prime-time television what many voters were saying in their living rooms and he briefly entered the hall of celebrated French leftist underdogs, which includes Olivier Besancenot, a charismatic part-time postman who ran for president in 2002 and 2007 with a pledge to abolish the stock market, or the anti-globalisation campaigner José Bové who became famous after trashing a McDonalds in 1999.

Macron tackled Le Pen on her pledge to withdraw France from the euro, which a majority of voters were against, according to polls. 'What you are proposing, Madame Le Pen, is a reduction in French people's purchasing power, because for savers and for workers, withdrawing from the euro will be a reduction in their spending power,' he said. He also compared her to her father: 'You're repeating the lies we've heard for 40 years, and that we heard from your father's mouth.'

But the main winner again seemed to be Mélenchon. In a poll taken immediately afterwards, he was judged to be the 'most convincing' candidate by 25 per cent of viewers, ahead of Macron on 21 per cent.

Mélenchon's rise began to ring alarm bells at En Marche. Although a career politician, he was also running as an outsider at the head of his France Unbowed movement. Among his proposals was a plan to scrap the executive presidency and return France to a parliamentary system. Macron's supporters spread an online video after the debate that highlighted Mélenchon's huge tax-and-spend plans. He proposed a €100 billion state spending plan that would be financed in part by taxing any income over €400,000 a year at 90 per cent (this proposed confiscatory measure would almost certainly be unconstitutional).

Macron also spoke out in an interview with *Le Monde* about how he felt he was being targeted by his opponents from the two mainstream parties instead of them uniting against their common enemy, Le Pen. 'There's major confusion in Hamon and Fillon's camps which have made me and En Marche the main target of their attacks. They've lost their bearings and we need to be clear-sighted.

'What strikes me in this campaign is that we've made Le Pen into something completely normal: the fact that she is expected to be in the second round. At the same time, we don't want to face up to the fact that she could win. That's the worst of all the risks.'[2]

On Monday 10 April, Macron called a meeting at headquarters at the start of the final fortnight of campaigning. He'd been annoyed by his discovery over the previous weekend that many of his exhausted helpers and members of the team had taken days off to recover. 'Kids, there are two weeks left and we can't miss a single second. We don't have a choice,' he began, sounding like a football manager giving a pep-talk to his tired and underperforming team at half-time, occasionally striking the table with his hand as Brigitte sat next to him. 'There's Le Pen, Fillon and now there's Mélenchon. We've been able to attack him, but we need to do more. People need to understand,' he said, referring to the risks of Mélenchon's radical programme.

The countdown to the vote was traditionally the most crucial time of the whole election period. 'Tell yourselves and tell everyone that there are people who will only start to tune in to the election in the next fortnight. Whoever wants it the most will win. In the final days, I'll do three rallies a day if I have to. No one will care what happens [at the rallies] but they'll see someone who wants to win ... we can lose it all in the next fortnight, we can lose it.'[3]

In reality, since the middle of March, the strain and fatigue of campaigning was starting to show, even on a man who had survived on four to five hours sleep a night since his student days. He and the team would all doze off whenever they got the opportunity, and only the adrenalin of being so close to a sensational victory drove them on. 'There were days when even the make-up couldn't hide the bags under his eyes,' communications chief Sibeth Ndiaye said.

The polls too were giving them sleepless nights as they showed a close four-way race developing between Macron, Le Pen, Fillon and Jean-Luc Mélenchon. And a third of voters had still not made up their minds who they were going to vote for.

'You could sense that voters were hesitating: they knew they wanted to get rid of the traditional parties in the Fifth Republic, but they weren't sure which path to take,' Ndiaye believes. 'For Macron, at that time, he saw it as a sign of the disarray in French democracy.'

The sense of anxiety among En Marche supporters was obvious at Macron's last major pre-election rally in Paris, when he packed out the 20,000-capacity Bercy stadium in Paris, a stone's throw from the economy ministry where he had first plotted his unlikely rise. The slick organisation this time also underlined how far the logistics chief Ludovic Chaker, who twelve months ago had never organised a political rally, had progressed since the movement's modest beginnings in the summer of 2016. Before it had been a matter of minimalist TED-style speeches with Macron alone on the stage. At Bercy, the warm-up speakers included the boss of Toulon rugby club, the Algerian-origin entrepreneur and comic book publisher Mourad Boudjellal. There were t-shirts and placards distributed by the thousands. Chants of 'we're going to win, we're going to win!' echoed around the auditorium before Macron took to the stage to En Marche's ear-splitting anthem, a specially composed track of piano-based electro with a throbbing bassline that had people on their feet dancing and cheering.

But in private many activists who had been out canvassing recently sounded less upbeat and betrayed their nerves. 'We're a bit worried by Mélenchon's breakthrough,' Dominique Dusart, a 57 year old who headed an En Marche committee in the Yonne area south of Paris, said as she queued at the VIP entrance. 'It's been a bit of a slap in the face because we weren't expecting it.'

Isabelle Nkounkou said she was 'crossing fingers' after her weekend's experience of handing out leaflets at markets in the

Parisian suburb of Cergy, north-west of the capital. 'Macron has given me an appetite for politics I never had before,' admitted the restaurant owner as she milled around waiting for Macron to appear. 'I've always voted but nothing more than that. We're working harder than ever on the ground but the last few days have been very tense.'

Macron bounded onto the stage looking energetic and as confident as ever. Brigitte and her daughters were sitting in his eyeline directly opposite him as he began his 90-minute speech. This included his pledge to 'rework Europe', promising to be the 'president who rekindles our European ambitions.' The goals were greeted with cheers.

François Heisbourg, the senior diplomat and national security advisor to Macron, was amazed. 'If someone had told me a year and a half ago that you'd have 20,000 people shrieking in a stadium every time Europe was mentioned, I'd have told them they were bonkers,' he said.

Macron also made his now-familiar promises of making France a better place to innovate, which would help solve the problem of mass unemployment and make sure the country benefited from the digital revolution.

But he also targeted his opponents in turn. Fillon had lost the 'moral authority' needed to be a head of state, Le Pen's programme was based on nostalgia for the past, while Mélenchon proposed turning France 'into Cuba without the sunshine' (the same phrase he had once used to describe President Hollande's plan for a 75 per cent tax on top earners).

He concluded by quoting one of his favourite French authors, Albert Camus, in a tribute to the generation that had remade France in the ruins of the Second World War: 'Each generation doubtless feels called upon to reform the world,' Camus had said as he accepted the Nobel Prize for Literature in 1957. 'Mine knows that it will not reform it, but its task is perhaps even greater. It consists in preventing the world from destroying itself.'

Macron told the crowd that the stakes in France's election were similar, as he set himself a task bigger than simply winning the presidency: the future of Western civilisation was in play too. 'Stopping the civilised world from destroying itself and enabling a future world to be built, that is our responsibility and our mission,' he said. 'For me, life, chance or perhaps destiny has provided me with the privilege of offering you this choice. I'm aware of the honour and the responsibility. I'm ready … I'm ready at your side, Brigitte,' he said. The crowd chanted Brigitte's name.

Le Pen for her part had also taken up this theme of a clash of civilisations, one in which, in her view, France risked losing its culture and identity for good in the face of mass immigration and unfettered globalisation. In the final straight, having started off the campaign looking to broaden support for her party, she reverted to far-right basics. The decision was driven by a perceptible softening in support, with polls showing her now falling behind Macron into second place. She had consistently topped forecasts for the first round with around 27–28 per cent since the end of January, but Macron had overtaken her in the final month before voting.

As well as the continued anxiety among voters about her policy of quitting the euro and her legal problems, she had suffered during the debates after the attacks by the car mechanic Poutou and Mélenchon. She also blundered on 10 April when she ignited a controversy about France's collaboration with the

Nazis during the Second World War. Her whole strategy since she had taken over the National Front in 2011 was based on trying to distance the party from its anti-Semitic past and her obnoxious Holocaust-denying father Jean-Marie who also consistently defended the war-time collaborationist leader Philippe Pétain. She had even reached out to French Jewish groups in an attempt to improve her party's image, calling them partners in the fight against Islamic extremism.

A documentary that was broadcast on French television in March, which showed a National Front official in the city of Nice selling Adolf Hitler memorabilia and also denying the extent of the Holocaust, had been a major setback. But this time it was Le Pen herself who scored the own goal, in the process undoing so much of her own marketing effort.

While being interview on the LCI news channel, she was asked if France was responsible for a notorious war-time roundup of 13,000 Jews in Paris. The victims, including women, the elderly and 4,000 children, were detained by French police acting on orders of German officers in Paris in 1942, and were packed into a cycling track called the *Vel' d'Hiv* near the Eiffel Tower in appalling conditions. They were then loaded into cattle wagons and deported to Nazi death camps.

In 1995, the newly elected French President Jacques Chirac was the first leader of the country to publicly acknowledge the role of France's collaborationist Vichy government in the atrocity: openly confronting the country's dark past, which had previously publicly been met with either denials or silence. 'Yes, the French and the French state seconded the occupying powers in their criminal madness,' he had said at a ceremony at the now-destroyed cycle track.

But in her interview with LCI 23 years later, Le Pen resurrected the self-serving argument of previous presidents: that the war-time collaborationist government was not 'France' and that the state then had been embodied by de Gaulle, during his time in exile in London. 'I don't think France is responsible for the *Vel' d'Hiv*,' she said, 'I think that, generally speaking, if there are people responsible, it's those who were in power at the time. It's not France.'

'France has been given a rough ride for years,' she continued. 'In reality, our children have been taught they had every reason to criticize it, to see only its darkest aspects. I want them to be proud to be French again.'

Macron called this statement 'a serious mistake' and didn't miss an opportunity to remind voters of her family history. 'Some had forgotten that Marine Le Pen is the daughter of Jean-Marie Le Pen,' he said. Israel also condemned her remarks, saying they reflected rising anti-Semitism that 'unfortunately, is once again raising its head.'

In one of her closing speeches in Marseille, Le Pen abandoned all pretences of how the new inclusive National Front was focused on the economy and regaining France's independence, delivering one of her darkest addresses that borrowed liberally from Donald Trump's playbook. As well as repeating her pledge to reduce net migration into France to 10,000 people a year, she proposed a moratorium on all immigration from her first day in office. She accused her rivals of wanting to transform France into a 'gigantic squat' filled with foreigners, which would 'relegate French people to being second-class citizens in their own countries'. Illegal immigrants would be refused treatment by the public health system, she promised. 'This is *our* country,' bellowed the crowd of 5,000 people in the spontaneous chant heard at all National Front rallies.

In keeping with an election campaign that had featured so many twists and turns, there was more drama to come right at the end, which would have unpredictable consequences for the outcome. On the evening of Thursday 20 April, as the leading candidates took part in a series of individual television interviews on France 2, a 39-year-old terrorist drove down the Champs-Élysées and opened fire with an automatic weapon on a police van posted outside a Turkish tourist office. A 37-year-old police officer, Xavier Jugelé, at the wheel of the stationary vehicle, was shot twice in the head and died instantly. A colleague was also injured. Jugelé, an activist for gay rights in the police force, had appeared once before in the French media when he was interviewed at the re-opening of the Bataclan hall the previous November, exactly one year after the massacre had taken place there. 'I'm here tonight as a witness, to defend our values. This concert is to celebrate life, to say no to terrorists,' he'd said.

His murderer was an introverted thug with a history of police violence and mental health problems, and little religious education. He'd been under investigation as a possible terror suspect since March, but was not on the state's official watch list of extremists. Other security forces on the Champs-Élysées reacted fast to the noise of his weapon, shooting him dead yards from the police van. A note claiming allegiance to the Islamic State group was found near his body.

Before news of the attack had broken, Le Pen had been interviewed on the France 2 show in which she'd accused the government of doing 'nothing' to protect the French people, deliberately ignoring their decision to send troops into the street after the Bataclan attacks, decree a state of emergency and pass a draconian new security law.

Another major terror attack on the eve of the election had the potential to sway voters. Remarkably, given the recent violence, voters had been telling pollsters since the end of 2016 that the economy and jobs were again their number one priority, rather than security. But analysts warned that any serious bloodshed on the scale of the Charlie Hebdo, Bataclan or Nice attacks would quickly reverse this trend, playing into Le Pen's hands. The attack on one of France's most famous boulevards might turn off more tourists from visiting France but it looked far from certain that it would influence an electorate that had become inured to isolated killings by extremists.

Things might have turned out very differently had a foiled plot which was thwarted in the final week of the campaign actually succeeded. Unbeknownst to voters, for a fortnight hundreds of police had been hunting two known Islamic extremists in their twenties who had eluded surveillance teams and were suspected of preparing an attack. The threat was deemed so serious that their pictures were distributed to the personal security teams of Le Pen, Macron and Fillon, who were deemed the most likely targets.

On the day before Marine Le Pen was going to address her rally in Marseille on 19 April, anti-terror police swooped on a rented student apartment in the city and arrested the pair, who had met in prison. They had amassed a cache of machine guns and pistols and were in possession of three kilograms of TATP, a highly volatile home-made explosive that had frequently been used in Islamic State terror attacks. The attack had been 'imminent', terror prosecutor François Molins told a press conference.

The mobile phones confiscated from the men included pictures of popular bars and busy streets in the southern port city, as well as the location of Le Pen's meeting. One of the two had sent a video of allegiance to Islamic State over the internet which had been intercepted and viewed by France's intelligence services. The potential attack marked a 'sliding doors' moment, a turning point when the fate of the election, and perhaps the destiny of the country, had been in the hands of France's overworked and highly stressed security forces.

Neither police nor prosecutors revealed the actual target of the two men, though it was assumed to be in Marseille because of the photos on their phones and the danger of transporting TATP over long distances. After the election, *Libération* newspaper said that Le Pen's rally was among their potential targets, leading her to claim that she had been deliberately left in the dark, presumably to stop her using the plot for political reasons. 'The ministry of justice should open an enquiry to probe the reasons for this serious concealment,' a statement from the National Front said in June. The trial of the two suspects may shed further light on the matter.

In the final polls, Macron and Le Pen still held a slight lead over Fillon and Mélenchon, but it was too close to call, and any combination of two of the four seemed conceivable as candidates for the second round. Mélenchon held all the momentum and the possibility of a second round of him versus Le Pen led to reports in the French media of investors pulling money out of the country to guard against the inevitable turbulence on financial markets that would be caused by a contest between the far-left and the far-right. Both candidates were Eurosceptics committed to massive increases in state spending. The imposition of capital controls to stop money from leaving the country in the event of this scenario was a very real possibility.

'There's enormous uncertainty about what is going to happen,' Dominique Reynié, the head of The Foundation for Political Innovation think-tank, told reporters. The experienced political expert and professor at Sciences Po said he had never taken so many calls from foreign investment groups looking for guidance on the likely result.

'If it's Mélenchon and Le Pen, it's a crisis which will result in problems for the country and major turbulence at the European level. I still can't understand how the French people, 58 per cent of whom own their own homes, are ready to vote for anti-system candidates who would endanger the value of their assets. But,' he added, 'all the outcomes are possible and lots of things can happen in the heads of voters in the final few days.'

CHAPTER 17

Election Day Nerves

MARCHING DOWN THE RUE CAMBRONNE IN THE SOUTH-west of Paris, Marie Mourait was in a hurry. At 79, she'd voted that morning in yet another election. She was old enough to remember the post-war years of the Fourth Republic, Charles de Gaulle in his pomp as president and Mitterrand's leftist breakthrough in 1981. She'd lived through France's bloody wars of decolonisation, student riots and mass strikes, not to mention the life-changing arrival of the internet and modern telecommunications. Though France had had its difficulties in adapting to changes in the past, she was alarmed by its current problems.

'The campaign has been terrible, the worst,' she said. The heels on her immaculate leather shoes clattered the pavement as she crossed roads and swerved round push-chairs and people with rare agility for someone her age. Her thoughts came as quickly as her footsteps.

'We've only talked about the secondary problems facing the country in this election. It's all been about scandals,' she said.

'We've got economic problems, security problems. We've got people roaming round the country shooting police officers now. We need a bit more strictness, a bit less of trying to understand the criminals. And it's unprecedented that France does so much worse than its neighbours.

'Our education system is a disaster. My husband rose to a senior job in a bank. He was a pure product of the state school system from a modest background. Schools gave everyone a chance to rise in life back then. It doesn't happen anymore.

'Then there's the problem of how we all get along together, immigration. I've got a Moroccan woman who helps me at home. She's a Muslim, she only eats Halal meat, but we see eye-to-eye on almost every subject. She talks about feeling stigmatised and the pressures from the Muslim community.'

Her harshest words, though, were reserved for outgoing President Hollande: 'The worst of the whole Fifth Republic, terrible,' she said.

She went through the large wooden door at her destination in a typical Parisian building, seven storeys of beige limestone and wrought-iron balconies. Inside at the back of the courtyard was a small Russian Orthodox church, known only to worshippers and local residents, where the Sunday service was about to begin. It was classic Paris: guarding its secrets from passers-by. Purple wisteria and other flowers in its garden were in bloom and the noise of the bustling street outside had faded to nothing.

The tranquil setting jarred with the brutal verdict she had just delivered on the country, but her views were typical of the grievances, insecurities and fears aired by so many voters at political rallies or during conversations at their workplaces or homes over months of campaigning. They confirmed that polls showing

France as one of the most depressed countries in the world, where nearly nine out of ten people thought it was on the wrong track, were no exaggeration.

On muddy farms in the countryside or sleepy old villages, people were worried about the loss of local communities or French identity and the decline of agriculture. Robert Velay, a local mayor who stopped to talk in the village of Puget-Théniers in southern France, was one among many who spoke out about their sense of nostalgia for a simpler, more gentle past. 'We were all alright here 30 years ago,' said the former butcher. His village, a stunning collection of stone cottages at the bottom of a steep valley mid-way between the Alps and the Mediterranean, was 'like all of rural France: we're doing badly,' he said. Local shops were progressively shutting, while several local youths had recently been roughed up when they ventured into the city of Nice, about an hour away by car. 'By North Africans,' he said pointedly.

In the simmering suburbs or hard-hit former industrial areas with high unemployment, the resentment over racism, immigration and inequality was on everyone's lips. In Aulnay-sous-Bois, a deprived north-eastern suburb of Paris, locals complained about being turned down for job interviews because of their address. 'There are people here who have got degrees who can't find work,' a 24-year-old local, a black internet technician called Babacar, explained. 'Everyone's scared of the housing estates. They think we're savages here.'

On the day of the election, Macron was at his holiday home in Le Touquet, where he and Brigitte cast their votes in front of the cameras in the morning. The couple went for a walk together through the sand dunes, holding hands as they contemplated their future in a place where they had shared so many moments since the start of their relationship more than twenty years ago.

It was the last opportunity to relax alone before the biggest night of their lives. Brigitte had once thought her husband would seek a career in the arts or literature, but instead she was now preparing herself for the possibility of taking on a public role at the age of 64. Her husband had promised to create an official 'First Lady' status for her (a plan he later shelved in the face of public resistance).

'It terrifies me, you can't imagine,' she'd told a friend in February as the polls showed Macron emerge as the frontrunner for the first time. 'If it happens, will I know what to do? Think of all the things I'll have to change and learn.'[1] As part of her preparations, she'd read a series of books about the wives of France's past leaders, concluding that 'not many of them were happy.'

In the twelve months since Macron had launched his movement in front of a few hundred people in Amiens, saying he wasn't sure if it would work, he'd raised nearly €15 million from tens of thousands of individual donors and seen 250,000 people sign up as members. Like the other candidates, his head was plastered on millions of posters all over the country, many of them defaced, and he'd endured innuendo about his sexuality, forensic examination of his finances and countless insults for being both an ex-banker and a media-fuelled sensation.

Macron and Brigitte returned to the house and chatted out on the deck with their closest political advisors – Ismaël Emelien, Benjamin Griveaux, Julien Denormandie, Ludovic Chaker, Sibeth Ndiaye and Sylvain Fort – with Macron serving them coffee from his €500 espresso machine. All of them were glued to their phones, checking the first results from France's overseas territories which had voted on Saturday. Shortly before lunchtime, they bundled into cars for the two-and-a-half hour drive back to Paris flanked by heavy security.

Turnout had been a major worry ahead of the vote which, along with the uncertainty about the accuracy of French polls, added to the sense that anything could happen. But long queues of people waiting in the sunshine outside polling stations were seen as being positive and the first official figures published in the morning were reassuring: turnout was in line with 2012 when around 80 per cent of registered voters had cast their ballots.

The moment of truth was scheduled for 8pm when national broadcasters would reveal a projection of the two winners based on early counting at a selection of polling stations. Macron took advice from his private pollster – who sounded positive – late in the day. The team huddled on the sixth floor of En Marche headquarters in front of a large flatscreen television. Macron and Brigitte sat hand-in-hand on a sofa, surrounded by advisors, friends and family including Macron's mother, as the final seconds ticked down.

'It's Emmanuel Macron who has topped the vote with 23.7 per cent. Marine Le Pen is in second place with 21.7 per cent,' announced presenter Laurent Delahousse on France 2. Brigitte jumped to her feet as Macron sat smiling broadly and surveying a scene of uncontained joy around him. His advisors jumped around, hugging each other and kissing like footballers at the end of a match. 'We did it, guys,' Denormandie said.

Thousands of En Marche supporters gathered at a results party at the Porte de Versailles exhibition centre in southern Paris exploded in joy, while a crowd of a few dozen well-wishers in the street outside the headquarters sang *The Marseillaise*. Macron went out on to the balcony to applaud them.

The reaction at Le Pen's victory gathering in the National Front stronghold in Hénin-Beaumont, a former mining village in north-east France, was more subdued. She'd qualified and won around a million more votes than in 2012 but she'd missed out on her target of finishing first. Her gain since 2012 was around three percentage points.

The results marked a profound change in the country's politics. For the first time in the history of the Fifth Republic, neither of France's two main parties – the centre-right Republicans and the left-wing Socialists – had qualified for the second round. 'I think it shows the deep malaise in our society among people who no longer felt represented by the traditional parties. It's a change in era,' Gérard Collomb, the mayor of Lyon and one of the earliest Socialist Party backers of Macron, said immediately afterwards.[2]

Macron spoke to French news agency AFP, announcing that 'we're clearly turning a page in French political history.' Then he headed to the victory party at the Porte de Versailles, where the movement had organised its first huge rally back in December 2016, when Macron had lost his composure in front of the crowd. When he stepped out of his car on election night, he raised both arms aloft in his by-now trademark style in front of cheering supporters. Once inside, he and Brigitte bounded onto the stage and then wandered around blowing kisses and waving to the mass of ecstatic fans, most of them activists in their twenties and thirties. Macron's speech was cheered to the rafters. 'In a year, we have changed the face of French politics,' he said.

This tone immediately jarred. Although he could be forgiven for his euphoria in private, Macron sounded triumphalist and a touch presumptuous, saying that En Marche had 'changed the course of the country'. He seemed to have lost sight of the fact that the far-right had made it through to the second round, something which had shocked the country in 2002. And if Macron lost to Le Pen – which still seemed like a possibility – En Marche would be a footnote in history.

Around midnight, he joined an after-party organised for a few friends and hundreds of volunteers and security staff at his favourite restaurant in southern Paris, *La Rotonde*, a Belle Epoque hangout that had been frequented by Picasso and other artists. The sight immediately recalled a notorious victory party by Nicolas Sarkozy in 2007 attended by top businessmen and celebrities at an extravagantly-priced bistro on the Champs-Élysées, *Fouquet's*. The party with the capital's rich and famous had set the tone for Sarkozy's flashy term in office, during which he earned himself the moniker 'The "Bling-Bling" President'.

Although *La Rotonde* was more modest than *Fouquet's*, its rich red velvet seating and atmospheric lighting looked similar in television pictures. And it was hardly a place to be seen for a man of the people: a steak and chips there costs €28. Some of Macron's advisors had warned him about the risk of Le Pen using the evening against him, *Le Canard enchaîné* later reported – warnings which Macron waved away.

After standing on a table and addressing the room, he enjoyed a plate of asparagus and ham with a glass of red wine. He left at around 1.30am to a barrage of hostile questions from reporters who asked him if this was 'his *Fouquet's* moment'. Cameras had filmed the scene inside, where a smattering of television personalities were gathered among the En Marche helpers. 'If you haven't understood that it was my pleasure tonight to treat my secretaries, my bodyguards, writers, people who've been with me from the start, then you've understood nothing about life,' he snapped.

The final results of the first round of voting showed Macron on 24.01 per cent of all ballots cast, Le Pen on 21.3 per cent, with Fillon at 20.1 per cent and Mélenchon at 19.58 per cent. Benoît Hamon, who had been abandoned by many of the Socialist Party heavyweights and who had been eclipsed by Mélenchon, scored a humiliating 6.36 per cent. Turnout was 76 per cent.

France's voters had fragmented into distinct blocks of almost equal size: the far-right of Le Pen, the conservative right of Fillon, and the hard-left represented by Mélenchon and Hamon. The so-called 'progressive centre' which Macron represented was a minority. The combined total of the anti-globalisation, anti-EU candidates on both the far-left and far-right fringes was around 50 per cent.

A breakdown of results by area and demography also revealed the deep geographic and social fractures in France. The country was divided roughly across a North–South line down the middle of the country. Le Pen finished top in the zone stretching across the South and Mediterranean coast, up the eastern flank of the country and into the former industrial areas of the north-east. Macron came first on the other side of the line all the way down the western side of France.

Macron won in the centre of big cities – Paris, Bordeaux and Lyon – while support for Le Pen was highest in semi-urban areas and villages. Areas of Le Pen's support tallied strongly with regions that experienced the most severe social difficulties as measured by unemployment, young people with no qualifications or single-parent families. Conversely, her voters were also concentrated in areas with the lowest level of immigrants.

These results broadly backed up the thesis that the election was a battle between those who saw the benefits of an open economy and globalisation in their own lives and those who felt that they were the victims of its excesses. Macron scored well among the better educated, wealthier classes, particularly among professionals and small entrepreneurs. The results also reflected the split between people living in rural areas who were anxious about the loss of their traditional way of life and French identity due to immigration and those who lived side-by-side with foreigners in their daily lives in cities.

'France torn apart' said a headline in Germany's *Frankfurter Allgemeine Zeitung* newspaper. 'Macron's victory is so narrow that in the two previous presidential elections, he wouldn't have won a place in the second round,' it noted correctly, warning against making any assumptions that he would win the run-off against Le Pen scheduled for 7 May. The *Guardian* also warned that 'the threat from the French extreme right is not over.'

From the Monday morning, Macron's team began poring over the data. A poll published immediately after the first round projected that he would win the run-off by 62 per cent to Le Pen's 38 per cent. 'We were a bit superstitious, which meant we hadn't really prepared anything beforehand,' said communications chief Ndiaye. 'We had some vague ideas, but we wanted to take the time to really understand the nature of the vote in the first round.'

While he bunkered down, Marine Le Pen was already out on the campaign trail, visiting a market in northern France early on Monday morning. Her colleagues in the National Front were making hay with the party Macron had held at *La Rotonde*. 'While all Macron's supporters recover from their showbiz evening at *La Rotonde*, Marine is at a market in Rouvroy,' campaign director David Rachline tweeted. Whatever the justifications for Macron's celebration, the optics of the event for a candidate who had done everything to avoid being seen as a bourgeois were terrible.

Macron didn't appear in public on Monday as criticism of his Sunday night celebrations mounted. 'We need to be humble. The election hasn't been won and we need to bring people together to win,' his ally Richard Ferrand, secretary general of En Marche, told the BFM channel.

But there was still no sign of him by Tuesday lunchtime. With a twenty-point lead in the polls, did he think victory was already in the bag? A cartoon in *Charlie Hebdo* that week showed him in the form of a hot-air balloon with his body being lifted off the floor by a giant inflated head. 'Macron! Come back!' shouted a crowd of people on the ground.

'I think the French people have understood that he thinks he has already won it,' Marine Le Pen said. 'It's disrespectful to our democracy and voters.'

Macron re-emerged on Tuesday evening for an interview on France 2 where he was challenged again over the dinner at *La Rotonde*. He replied that he had 'no regrets', adding: 'It was sincere and I take responsibility for it.' He had a full day of campaigning planned for the day after, Wednesday, when he intended to visit a factory in his home town of Amiens, owned by the US appliance manufacturer Whirlpool.

For months, workers there had been battling a decision by the multinational to shut the plant and shift production to Poland and had now gone on strike. This saga became the focus of attention throughout the campaign as the latest example of France's inability to compete with lower-cost countries in Eastern

Europe. The factory, which produced tumble dryers, was profit-able and employed 290 people, around a quarter of the number it had done fifteen years previously. It had made washing machines, too, before management outsourced their production to Slovakia.

Macron had deliberately avoided the site, knowing better than anyone how Hollande's visit to the under-threat Florange steel factory in 2012, also in the north-east, had damaged his credibility when the Mittal steel family shut the foundries after-wards. 'When you have a factory closure, politicians of all stripes head to the company and say "with me, this factory will not close",' Macron told a crowd in February. 'But what happens? We protect the jobs for a while because we're scared about failure … and then six months, eight months, a year later the factory fails, but much worse.

'We need to protect individuals, which is different. We shouldn't protect jobs,' he said as he defended the 'creative destruction' inherent in capitalism that sees some companies fail and others succeed – a break from the approach of successive French governments which have traditionally sought to protect politically-sensitive jobs by browbeating managers to keep facto-ries open or offering them inducements.

Having stayed away from Whirlpool until now, Macron reversed course and set up a meeting with trade union leaders at the local chamber of commerce building in the centre of Amiens. Again the optics were poor: Macron sat on one side of a large U-shaped table with his advisors, opposite the workers five metres away. It was an image of a line of suits against working-class men in high-visibility jackets and t-shirts.

Towards the end of the meeting, news came through that Marine Le Pen had arrived in Amiens and was visiting the site of the factory. Having been regularly frustrated by Macron shadowing her campaign stops ahead of the first round of the election, Le Pen turned the tables by arriving unannounced. It looked like a canny and effective ploy to upstage him. 'I've left everything in Paris to come here to greet you,' Le Pen told the strikers as she arrived. 'It's the expression of my complete support for you and your fight against these appalling economic and political policies. Everyone is watching you and you are the pride of the country,' she said. She was given a warm welcome and posed for selfies with strikers in the car park in front of the factory.

'Emmanuel Macron is with the oligarchs, with the employers,' Le Pen added. 'I am where I should be, with the employees of Whirlpool who are fighting this unfettered globalisation.'

After his hubristic speech on victory night and late start to campaigning, Macron risked being overshadowed on his first outing. 'Has she left?', he snapped at his team while still at the chamber of commerce, showing a flash of anger in front of the documentary team following him. 'Check. Please, let's be professional. Nothing has been professional for the last few days. The speech for tonight was dreadful, this meeting was badly organised. I felt it straight away.'

He said they'd made trouble for themselves by driving him into the meeting, and past the protesters outside, explaining: 'We've been bourgeois. I can't look like a banker.'

Macron's chief of staff Sophie Ferracci explained that he had been kept away from the crowd for security reasons. 'We can't listen to the security teams,' Macron replied. 'I'll never be completely safe. The country is like that. So we need to take the risk … we need to go. If you listen to security you end up like Hollande: maybe you're safe but actually you're dead [politically].'[3]

It was a crucial moment of his presidential campaign. The day perfectly encapsulated one of the biggest issues of the election and one of the most difficult challenges facing Western Europe and America: how to manage the process of companies shifting manufacturing jobs overseas whilst still offering new opportunities for the workers left behind at home. Le Pen and Macron had diametrically opposed solutions to the situation in Amiens. Le Pen had promised a tax of 35 per cent on products manufactured overseas by companies who had outsourced their manufacturing. She'd also raised the possibility of nationalising the site.

Speaking at the end of the election, Macron said he thought his campaign had hinged on the choices that he made at the chamber of commerce. 'If at that moment, I decide not to go to Whirlpool, I could lose the second round campaign and I could lose the election. I'm absolutely convinced about that,' he said.[4]

He set off in a convoy of cars for the Whirlpool parking lot. He was loudly jeered as he stepped out of his vehicle, with many strikers blowing whistles that had been distributed by National Front activists. The air was thick with choking black smoke from burning tyres on the picket line.

Macron attempted to plunge into the hostile crowd but was quickly surrounded by dozens of television cameras which, despite the efforts of his security team, made discussion impossible. Amid the chaos, his aides organised for the gate of the factory to be opened so that he and the workers could enter and speak more freely. The media were kept outside but the encounter was streamed live on Facebook by Sibeth Ndiaye, his communications chief.

'It needed Marine Le Pen to come and do her show here to make you turn up,' one of the Whirlpool workers told Macron.

'You probably think we're all illiterate,' shouted another to laughs, recalling his gaffe about the abattoir workers in his first week as economy minister. 'Mr Macron you're with the businessmen, the shareholders, you always agree with them,' said another.

Over 45 minutes, Macron stood in the centre of the workers, most of them in their forties or fifties, arguing his corner and passing a microphone around to take questions. Although there were regular jeers, the tension dropped. What could have resulted in a political lynching turned into a genuine, spontaneous and compelling confrontation between an angry crowd of people whose livelihoods were being lost because of outsourcing – enabled by the European Union – and a politician determined to argue the benefits of open trade and EU membership. Irrespective of the quality of his proposals and the pertinence of his analysis, it was both physically brave and from a political standpoint enormously risky. The equivalent for Le Pen would have been to head into a multi-ethnic suburb of Paris and start a discussion about French culture being swamped.

'The response to what is happening to you is not to stop globalisation nor to close our borders. Don't make this mistake. People who say that are lying,' Macron argued. 'After closing the borders what happens? Thousands of jobs that depend on them being open are lost.' He pointed to a Procter & Gamble consumer goods factory opposite the Whirlpool site which he said employed a thousand workers and exported 80 per cent of its production.

'I'm not going to promise to nationalise this site, ban the laying off of workers or save you with public money,' he added. 'I'm not going to make promises I can't keep.'

The correct response, he told the crowd, was cutting business taxes to help companies become more competitive – 'presents for the fat cats!' shouted a woman. He said that the government needed to invest in training for young people and adult education for laid-off workers who could then re-skill. 'Hollande's been talking about that for years. It's led to nothing!' said a man. 'We've never been trained!' said another.

The longer the exchange went on, the starker the contrast grew between Le Pen's lightning visit and the slogans she chanted, and Macron's engagement and willingness to fight his corner. What had looked like a communications disaster was turned into a possible victory.

That evening he gave one of his most direct and angry performances at a campaign rally in the nearby city of Arras, clearly fired up by the day's events. He attacked Le Pen for her 'demagogy' and criticised her 'fifteen minutes of selfies' in Amiens, adding: 'Don't offer your anger to the National Front: it doesn't deserve it. Don't give your hopes to the National Front: it'll betray you.' It was the sort of punchy and direct appeal to voters that had been lacking in so many of his often meandering and philosophical speeches.

Polls showed that Macron's lead was intact, while Le Pen insisted she needed to gain only 'ten little points' to overtake Macron. She announced a major breakthrough on 29 April, four days after the 'battle of Amiens', with major implications for future elections. Since the formation of the National Front and its first emergence as a force in European elections in 1984, France's mainstream parties had always worked together to try to block it. This so-called 'Republican front' operated most famously in 2002 when all the defeated candidates from across the political spectrum had called for voters to back the right-wing Jacques Chirac against Jean-Marie Le Pen. It had worked most recently in regional elections in 2015.

That front cracked and then shattered during the 2017 election. On the night of the first round results, the far-left candidate Jean-Luc Mélenchon refused to back Macron, or instruct his supporters to vote in his favour. His hundreds of thousands of followers were asked by him to vote online about how the France Unbowed movement should approach the second round. Two-thirds of them were in favour of abstaining or casting a spoiled ballot. Many characterised the choice between Le Pen and Macron as deciding between 'the plague and cholera'. Prime Minister Bernard Cazeneuve, who had taken over from Manuel Valls in December, warned that Mélenchon and his supporters risked being guilty of 'unforgiveable moral misjudgement'. The same criticism was levelled at *New York Times* commentator Ross Douthat who asked 'Is there a case for Le Pen?' in a column which came close to endorsing her.

Le Pen then announced her first ever alliance with the right-wing and virulently Eurosceptic candidate Nicolas Dupont-Aignan who had finished sixth in the first round with 4.7 per cent. Dupont-Aignan had previously identified as hard-right but in the mainstream Gaullist tradition. Le Pen clinched the deal by offering him the position of prime minister if she won.

She also began trying to modify her policy on the euro. She had promised to claw back France's ability to control its border, its budget and its currency, all of which would be 're-negotiated' with the EU within six months. The negotiation – impossible within that time frame – would destroy the EU in its current form and return the bloc to being a club of independent, trading nations.

But the prospect of returning to the franc was backed by only a minority of French people, not least because the franc would immediately drop against the euro, leading to a fall in the value of French savings, an increase in the price of imports and a sharp rise in the value of any debts held in euros by companies or private citizens.

Faced with this, Le Pen attempted to change her position on the currency. She said she no longer wanted a complete return to the franc but proposed that there would be two currencies: a franc that people would use 'to buy their baguette' and everyday purchases, and an 'ecu', based on the euro, which would be used for international trade. The negotiations with the EU might now take longer than six months, and maybe several years, her telegenic niece Marion Maréchal-Le Pen announced.

At her campaign rallies, Le Pen attacked Macron with a ferocity that suggested she had no intention of toning down her rhetoric to broaden her appeal after the first round. Her speech on 1 May in Paris opened with a half-hour diatribe against him that dripped with sarcasm and was filled with violent imagery. He was dangerous, backed by the oligarchy and as a former investment banker was used to destroying jobs. His aim was total economic war to the benefit of a few via trade deals that were aimed at destroying France. He planned to 'submerse' the country with immigrants, with this task organised by the 'migrant-loving German Chancellor Angela Merkel'. According to Le Pen, crime would spread across the country, while French people would have no choice but to learn to live with terror attacks. The system was trying to place its candidate in the presidency and avoid its legacy of 'the corpses of outsourced jobs and the ruins of closed factories.'

In the run up to the only debate between the two of them on 3 May, Macron sensed that she would continue to be inflammatory. 'I thought Marine Le Pen was going to be aggressive because she was [in her speech] on 1 May and the debate followed the same tone,' Macron said. The three-hour show on national television was watched by 16 million people and was Le Pen's last chance to try to close the gap.

French political debates had historically been a measured and generally cordial exchange of views which could often include dense passages of conversation about a line in the tax code or the inner workings of parliament. Compared to American debates, they could seem dull. The first-round French debates were already considered to have lowered the tone, but the Le Pen–Macron clash was something entirely new.

It was compared afterwards to a boxing match or mud-wrestling, but in truth it was more like a bullfight. Le Pen's tactic was to come charging out and hope to skewer Macron with a horn and leave him injured for the rest of the evening. Macron, anticipating her tactics, tried to play the matador.

She spoke first. Macron was the candidate for 'the "Uberisation" of the economy, of social brutality, for insecure jobs and a war of everyone against everyone ... The French people have been able to see the real Macron in this second round ... The forced smile has been transformed into a rictus grin. The mask has dropped from the candidate of the elite and the system ... you've used shameful arguments and they reveal the cold heart of the investment banker you've never stopped being.'

Macron grinned through the torrent of invective. 'You're not the candidate of finesse. You've just demonstrated it,' he said in reply. Over the course of the evening, he mentioned her surname, absent from her posters because of its poisonous associations, over and over again. He did so more than 160 times. He corrected her when she made false allegations and teased her when she looked up information in coloured files laid out in front of her. 'You are reading from a note that explains a different case to the one you just mentioned,' he said when she accused him of selling off a privately-owned French mobile phone company when he was economy minister. His team watching in a room backstage jumped to their feet, applauding and laughing. 'It's sad for you and it shows in front of our citizens that you are unprepared,' Macron added.

On eleven occasions he accused her of saying 'stupid things' and he constantly corrected her whenever she twisted or misrepresented his past actions or programme. 'What's extraordinary is that your strategy is simply to say a lot of lies and propose nothing to help the country,' he said. Towards the end of the evening, he risked lowering the tone himself, denouncing Le Pen as a 'parasite'.

With a more measured approach, Le Pen might have succeeded in putting Macron under pressure over some of the vulnerabilities in his programme, on immigration or even on deeper European integration, which many French people were queasy about. But the more she hammered away, sneering and calling him names, the more presidential he appeared in contrast.

Mid-way through, Macron pounced on her euro policy, asking her in a series of questions to explain exactly how consumers would use a new franc at the same time as big businesses and the central bank were carrying on using the euro or the 'ecu'. 'Are we leaving the euro or not?', he asked during his inquisition. 'Will our debt be paid in euros or francs?', he continued. Few French people, not to mention economists, had understood how Le Pen's dual currencies would work. She looked uncomfortable throughout. 'It's nonsense,' Macron said at the end of his cross-examination of Le Pen, herself a former lawyer. 'It's a deadly project, it's dangerous.'

In the immediate aftermath of the debate, posts on some far-right message boards showed that many supporters thought Le Pen had missed the target. Privately, many senior National Front figures were disappointed, and Le Pen's estranged father delivered his own withering verdict the day after. His daughter 'had not been up to it', he said.

Snap polls taken afterwards showed Macron as the clear winner and his team were overjoyed. 'Can someone pick her teeth up please?' joked his communications chief Sylvain Fort in front of the documentary team as he left the television set at the end. 'Brilliant', 'one of your best performances', 'even Brigitte thought it was good!' Macron's staffers told him as he returned to applause in his room backstage.

Le Pen later admitted she had got the tone and tactics completely wrong. 'Undeniably, it was a complete failure,' she said. 'I admit it. I made a choice: I wanted to demonstrate the genuine fears I had about Emmanuel Macron's programme, which I still have obviously. I did it with passion and spirit, perhaps with a bit too much passion, a bit too much spirit. I know some people weren't expecting that.'[5]

In fact, on the morning of the debate, staff had found her

exhausted and panicked at her home in Saint-Cloud in south-west Paris, a stone's throw from where she grew up in the ramshackle Le Pen family manor home which has panoramic views over Paris and is worth more than €3 million. 'Bruno! I can't see anything out of my left eye!' she told her advisor Bruno Bilde as he arrived at 10:30am.[6] She was diagnosed with an ocular migraine which causes temporary visual problems and usually leaves a thudding headache. Instead of preparing for the clash with Macron in the afternoon, she went to bed to sleep. Bilde even checked to see if it was possible to cancel or delay the debate, while campaign director David Rachline later conceded that Le Pen's diary had been overloaded with events and she was exhausted.

But even accounting for her physical difficulties on the night of the debate, Le Pen's second round campaign was deeply inept for someone who had spent six years trying to make the party more electable and less extreme. Perhaps she was unable to control her natural instincts as the moment of truth arrived. Or was she simply a bit too close to power, preferring to stay as a rabble-rouser in opposition rather than a leader responsible for implementing her radical programme? Like the top Brexit campaigners in Britain, perhaps she never intended to actually win. In any case, French voters missed an opportunity to understand what Macron actually had planned for them: he and his programme were never tested during the televised encounter.

Viewers listening in closely to Le Pen noticed, however, that she seemed to be insinuating that there could be surprises to come for Macron. When he accused the National Front of being the 'party of scandals', she replied cryptically: 'Oh really? I hope that we won't learn anything in the next few days or weeks.' She continued: 'No one understands your explanations about your finances ... I hope we won't learn you have an account in the Bahamas.'

Could the most unpredictable, rollercoaster election in recent history spring another surprise? US President Donald Trump had also raised uncertainty during an interview published on 2 April when he told the *Financial Times* that 'it's going to be a very interesting election. But you know some outside things have happened that maybe will change the course of that race.'

Despite Le Pen's debate failure, one group of people was still testing Macron's campaign: the hackers. After En Marche had gone public with their concerns that they were being targeted in February, IT staff had seen their networks continue to come under attack through repeated phishing attempts. In the final days of the election campaign, members of En Marche received another fake email purportedly from the movement's digital chief Mounir Mahjoubi asking them to download several files 'to protect yourself'. Anyone who did so had their computer compromised.

Russian hackers were being monitored by the National Security Agency, the US cyber-espionage unit. Testifying in front of US senators in May, NSA Director Michael S. Rogers said American intelligence agencies had watched the attacks unfold. Rogers informed his French counterparts and offered to help, saying: 'Look, we're watching the Russians. We're seeing them penetrate some of your infrastructure. Here's what we've seen.'

Macron was in the southern city of Albi on the penultimate day of campaigning when the team learned that their defences had been breached. Fund-raising and budget chief Cédric O and speechwriter Quentin Lafay had downloaded malware at some point which had enabled the hackers to access and copy their email inboxes. It was now a matter of time before this material emerged.

Late on the Friday night just before the end of official campaigning ahead of the vote on Sunday, an anonymous user called EMLEAKS posted a message on a document-sharing site called Pastebin that linked to 9GB of hacked data. Jack Posobiec, an American journalist with the far-right pro-Trump news website *The Rebel* with no obvious link to French politics, was the first to amplify the material with the hashtag #Macronleaks to his more than 100,000 followers on Twitter. Wikileaks quickly swung into action, posting the documents with secure links before the material could be blocked or taken down.

In a statement to the media late on Friday at around midnight, En Marche confirmed that its email system had been violated, saying it had been the 'victim of a massive and coordinated hack' while warning that fake information had been planted among the documents.

Unlike the breach of the US Democratic Party's emails, which occurred four months before voting, 'Macronleaks' struck only hours before the 'cooling off' period ahead of the election when media outlets, under French law, are prohibited from reporting any new material likely to sway voters. France's electoral authority, the CNCCEP, asked the media to avoid publishing any information from the leaked documents.

The timing of the leak, 24 hours before voting day, was baffling. Had the hackers not realised that French law would prevent media organisations reporting on the content of the messages? It looked like the dump was too late to sway the result. If the hackers had struck a week earlier, the National Front would have had a field day. Or was the release timed deliberately so that material would begin circulating online and Macron's team would be unable to rebut it in public? Far-right and pro-Russian Twitter accounts in France as well as the French-language website of the Russian state-funded news outlet Sputnik flouted the reporting ban. Le Pen's advisor Florian Philippot tweeted: 'Will we learn things through #Macronleaks that investigative journalists have deliberately killed? Terrifying! This shipwreck of democracy.' Fake emails and documents began being shared online, including one that purported to show a Macron staffer buying the stimulant mephedrone for their boss and having the drugs shipped to parliament.

But France's mainstream media ignored the material. Unlike the American cable networks and newspapers, which had feasted on the inbox of Clinton's campaign director John Podesta, in France there was a determination not to allow any efforts to destabilise the election succeed. There was also no French equivalent of aggressively right-wing US media organisations such as Fox News or Breitbart which had fanned the Clinton leaks. While news that the hack had taken place appeared on the main television stations and websites, no further detail was given.

Even if they failed to influence the presidential election, the hackers still risked destabilising Macron's attempts to govern if he was elected and could alter the outcome of the parliamentary elections scheduled in June when, whatever the result of the presidential elections, En Marche was hoping to win a majority.

Analysis by cybersecurity firms pointed the finger at Russian hackers, though no conclusive evidence has been presented. Finding irrefutable proof of state involvement in hacking remains extremely difficult. Many Western experts believe the attack was mounted in haste, with the hackers leaving behind tell-tale evidence such as the fact that some documents had passed through a Russian version of Word software. One person who modified a document was identified by researchers as a 32-year-old contractor with a Russian firm linked to the Russian military. Japanese cybersecurity firm Trend Micro said it believed the Macron campaign had been targeted by the same Russian hacking unit behind the Clinton hack, known under various names including Fancy Bears, Pawn Storm or APT 28.

But while US intelligence agencies have unanimously agreed that the Democratic Party hack was carried out by Russian hackers, French authorities have so far been reluctant to point the finger directly.

Journalists have since picked through the tens of thousands of emails and documents that were leaked, finding that they contained mostly humdrum exchanges about campaign organisation as well as some insights into the movement's fund-raising efforts. All of the most sensitive communication between En Marche staffers had been on the encrypted app Telegram since the beginning. When the messages were posted as a searchable database by Wikileaks in August, En Marche logistics chief Ludovic Chaker scrolled through some of them, recalling how he had told colleagues to treat email as an insecure form of communication. 'It made me realise how careful we'd been,' he said.

On the final election night on Sunday 7 May, the En Marche team gathered again in front of the television as the seconds ticked down, with Macron and Brigitte once more next to each other on a sofa awaiting the final results. Chaker said they were 'neither completely at ease nor overly worried' about the hack.

'I think if the fake documents had been of better quality, then it could have had a bigger effect,' he said.

Macron won with a far bigger margin than the polls had predicted, gaining 66.1 per cent of the vote versus 33.9 per cent for Le Pen. A large victory, but this time there were no wild celebrations in the room. The abstention rate was the highest since 1969, with one in four voters staying away from the polls. Le Pen had picked up 11 million votes, an increase of 3 million from the first round.

Possibly overcompensating for his triumphalism two weeks earlier, Macron appeared on stage for a brief and solemn address to the country from his headquarters shortly afterwards. 'Many difficulties have weakened us for too long. I don't underestimate any of them: neither the economic difficulties, nor the social fractures, nor the democratic blockages or the moral weakening of the country,' he said.

'France is turning a new page in its history tonight, I want it to be one of hope and of rediscovered confidence,' he added.

His victory party was organised to take place in front of the Louvre museum. It was an unusual choice, and one filled with symbolism. François Hollande had celebrated winning the presidency at the Place de la Bastille and Nicolas Sarkozy at the Place de la Concorde. The Louvre was geographically mid-way between the two of them: a good spot for a centrist. The former palace was also, more significantly, the ancient seat of royal power in Paris. This would be the first of several occasions in his first months in office when Macron would use the architecture of the former monarchy for his own prestige.

From the television pictures beamed live around the world, the setting looked stunning, with a stage placed in front of the bold glass pyramid that had been built in the vast courtyard of the palace in 1989. At around 10:30pm, Macron appeared in a doorway at the far eastern end of the courtyard to the sounds of Beethoven's *Ode to Joy*, which is the anthem of the European Union. In the dark, with bright spotlights casting sharp shadows behind him, he began a slow, solitary march to the stage. It took three and a half minutes to complete, so long that the music ended at one point and had to be restarted. The lighting, footsteps and the setting gave it an unmistakable look of film noir, like a scene from the 1949 classic *The Third Man*.

But the intended message of this political theatre was that Macron was accepting the inevitable solitude of power. It was also clearly influenced by the former Socialist President François Mitterrand who had walked alone into the Pantheon, the resting place for France's national heroes, on the day of his inauguration in 1981, also to the sounds of the *Ode to Joy*. But while Mitterrand had approached the Pantheon at the head of a cortège of thousands of supporters, Macron was entirely alone. It was the embodiment of de Gaulle's famous saying that the presidential election was 'the meeting of a man and the people.'

Backstage at the edge of the pyramid, the small circle of friends who had been involved in the first brainstorming sessions to launch En Marche an almost unbelievable eighteen months before, watched the scene unfold. They were all exhausted and were already busy preparing for government, but the sight of Macron walking towards them brought home what they had achieved. 'It was probably the moment when the penny dropped, when we realised he'd really become president. It was very emotional,' said Stanislas Guerini, one of the founding members of En Marche.

Macron climbed the steps onto the stage and was greeted with cheers from the large crowd of well-wishers. Some had climbed up the ornate cast-iron street lights for a better view. 'What we've done for so many months has neither a precedent, nor an equivalent,' Macron declared to wild cheers. 'Everyone said it was impossible. But they didn't know France!'

Television cameras captured the mass of tricolores, EU flags and an atmosphere that mixed ecstasy about Macron's achievement with a palpable sense of relief that France had turned its back on Marine Le Pen. Philippe Ambroisine, a cybersecurity expert, had brought his two young daughters along to witness 'this historic moment', saying: 'He's given us hope and a different message, that we shouldn't be scared about the changing world, that we can succeed in it.' There were echoes of the 'Providential man' theory: the idea that exceptional individuals have emerged suddenly and irresistibly at critical times throughout French history to lead the nation away from disaster.

But once Macron had finished speaking, the crowd quickly dispersed, perhaps because of the odd choice of entertainment afterwards. An unknown 'DJ and sculptor' with no discernible talent as a party host played dated house music accompanied by female dancers in stilettoes and red and silver leotards, sending many people fleeing for the exits.

A sizeable chunk of the crowd present that night was either agnostic or worried about Macron. 'I think he takes ages to say anything and when you listen to him it doesn't mean anything,' said the 21-year-old student Alicianne Turin, who had voted for Mélenchon in the first round.

Karim Ben Nas, a 36-year-old airport worker, had come to watch out of curiosity. 'It's people like us who are going to pay.

He's on the side of big business,' he said. Macron's support in the multi-ethnic suburbs was confined to young entrepreneurs or go-getters who were drawn by his enthusiasm for business, as well as his more inclusive view of French society and identity. Nas grudgingly admitted that Macron might help heal some of the divisions opened up by the campaign and give Frenchmen of North African origin like him a greater sense of belonging. 'We're still not considered to be French by some people, even though I've grown up here, I was born here,' he said.

Outside in the streets of Paris, a few car horns rang out and the occasional vehicle passed with people holding flags out of the window, but there were no scenes of mass celebration as there had been after Hollande's victory in 2012 when the party at the Bastille had continued until the early morning.

Perhaps it reflected the overall gloomy mood of the country and its scepticism after the disappointments of Hollande and Sarkozy. Or the fact that Le Pen's 11 million votes made celebrations seem misplaced. But where were the 250,000 members of En Marche? They were probably indoors, watching events on television or toasting Macron's success over wine at dinner parties. This was a middle-class takeover that had been built up the modern way, over the internet. People had come together behind a common cause – electing Macron – but the movement's roots were still shallow. It was an extraordinarily successful electoral vehicle, but En Marche had none of the history or sense of tribal belonging offered by membership of a traditional political party. There was also a detectable sense in the country that many voters were simply unsure what they had voted for after the most dirty, scandal-plagued campaign anyone could remember. 'It's still a bit vague in my head,' said David Stopper, a 22 year old from southern France as he left the Louvre that night. 'The country's fragmented, there's such a massive range of different opinions now. He's a good example for young people, being 39 and achieving what he has, but I'm waiting to see what happens. I wasn't totally convinced voting for him.'

Macron had achieved what almost no one besides him and his advisors – the 'kids' – thought achievable. He'd proved even many of his former mentors wrong. At 39, he was set to be the youngest leader of France since Napoleon and had won after standing in his first ever election at the head of a brand new political movement.

There was much to admire in En Marche: it had been created from nothing and had inspired thousands of people to take an interest in politics for the first time; his campaign had been endearingly amateur at times as his team of 30-somethings learned on the job, outwitting older and more experienced politicians in the process. En Marche volunteers were unfailingly polite and well-meaning at rallies around the country in an otherwise bad-tempered and ugly election campaign.

Guillaume Liegey, the partner in the Liegey Muller Pons consultancy that had helped En Marche to design its grassroots campaign, has been inundated with calls from politicians across Europe 'wanting to do a Macron' since the French elections.

Macron's success was the culmination of more than 20 years of climbing the rungs of Parisian society since arriving as a 16 year old in the capital as the love-struck son of two provincial doctors. He'd had a major leg up from his elite secondary school Henri IV, but he had then worked and networked furiously as he rose through the country's top universities, civil service, the Rothschild investment bank and the government. Always on the look out for new opportunities and quick to seize them when they presented themselves, he had chopped and changed his roles regularly in his pursuit of political power – so regularly that if he completes five years as president it will be the longest he has ever stayed in a single position.

The country had seen politicians emerge suddenly on the national stage before, like Georges Pompidou who was named prime minister in 1962. And voters had chosen a youthful president in the past – Valéry Giscard d'Estaing had been elected to the position aged 48. 'There have been precocious politicians before and others who have emerged suddenly, but never both at the same time,' noted the French historian Jean-François Sirinelli.[7] Pompidou was 58 when he was named premier and Giscard d'Estaing had been in politics for twenty years when he became president.

Macron had undoubtedly been favoured by good fortune. Looking back on the various stages of his success, the president's old advisor and friend Alain Minc said: 'If Juppé wins the primary, there's no Macron. If Hollande runs again, there's no Macron. If Valls wins the Socialist primary, there's no Macron, and if Fillon doesn't trip over his own shoe laces, there's no Macron.'

Minc is probably right that Juppé would have blocked Macron's path, but there are reasons to doubt whether Hollande or Valls as candidates would have been significant obstacles to his rise. And even without the fake job scandal that engulfed Fillon, Macron might still have succeeded. Fillon was exactly the sort of career politician French voters had tired of, and were keen to punish, and his ultra-conservative programme of budget cuts and his hard line on Muslims and French identity turned off large sections of the electorate. Even before the allegations about his wife's parliamentary job, his undeclared loan or the luxury suits he accepted from a shady lawyer, Fillon had lower approval ratings than Macron. And Macron was able to count on by far the largest and most energetic network of activists and donors in the presidential race. As Paul Ricœur, the philosopher who had greatly influenced Macron during their time working together, used to say: 'You never know what part is luck and what part is destiny.'

Whatever the role of luck, Macron showed remarkable skill in mounting a political start-up over a series of dinners in October 2015 and then sweeping into the presidency and parliament less than two years later. He foresaw and capitalised on the meta-trends that shaped the election: firstly voters' anger at traditional parties and politicians, common to all Western democracies but seen most obviously in the vote for Brexit and Donald Trump in 2016, as well as the support for Le Pen and Mélenchon in France. Secondly, he gambled that the primary system adopted by France's traditional parties of government would favour fringe candidates, leaving the centre-ground open.

His pitch to voters often echoed the anti-establishment, populist message – although he didn't express it in Trumpian terms, he too wanted to 'drain the swamp' by bringing fresh faces into French politics and he promised to 'make France great again' by restoring its self-respect and international prestige. Although he was pro-business and keen to cut enterprise-stifling regulations, he also said he understood that many French people wanted to enjoy greater protection from globalisation, which needed to be provided by the state.

In north-east Paris, as Macron celebrated at the Louvre and perhaps allowed himself to reflect on the reasons for his success, a few hundred anarchists and 'anti-capitalist' activists wasted little time beginning what was the first protest against his rule, an early taste of what looked likely to be huge resistance to his plans to change France. Tear gas was fired by police and around 140 people were arrested, including 29-year-old Adrien Gaillard. 'We originally wanted to go to the Louvre to boo him,' Gaillard said afterwards, adding that he believed that Macron's decision to celebrate at the Louvre in front of a pyramid – a Masonic form – was a sign he was a Freemason. The theory began circulating on social media from the evening of his victory. 'He's a spearhead from the Rothschild family and the banksters,' Gaillard added.

CHAPTER 18

President Macron

'MY TIME IN OFFICE WILL BE GUIDED BY TWO OBJECTIVES,' Macron declared in the inauguration speech he gave on 14 May in front of hundreds of dignitaries and political allies, as well as his family members, at the Élysée Palace. 'The first will be returning a sense of self-confidence to the French people which for too long has been weakened ... it is my job to convince them that our country, which today seems to be caught in headwinds blowing against the course of history, has all the necessary resources to be a leading nation.'

His second objective was restoring France to its place 'as a model for the world ... Because we will have given our people a taste for the future, and pride in who they are, the whole world will pay attention to the word of France.'

The European Union would be 'rebuilt [and] relaunched, because it protects us and enables us to carry our values into the world,' he said.

The VIP guests attending the ceremony had each walked up a vast and immaculate red carpet which had been rolled across the gravel courtyard of the palace. Both of Macron's parents and his siblings were among them, as were Brigitte's children. The founding members and key players in En Marche – Emelien, Denormandie, Griveaux, Cédric O and others – all strode up together and posed at the entrance of the palace, looking strikingly young and different, especially Macron's spokeswoman Sibeth Ndiaye who wore trainers.

When Macron arrived, he ambled alone up the carpet in front of the gathered media. Slowly. Very very slowly. It underlined what he had repeated so often to his team throughout the campaign: he was in charge of the tempo, and he alone planned to set the rhythm. The French people wanted authority – as he had theorised, they felt 'the absence of the king' – and now, it seemed, he planned to give it to them.

The end of every inauguration ceremony in France sees the incoming president wave off his predecessor in the courtyard. The sight of Macron bidding goodbye to Hollande was heavy with personal and political meaning. Macron had arrived at the Élysée in 2012 at Hollande's invitation as a young and unknown investment banker. Five years later, he'd helped force him out.

Hollande felt a burning sense of betrayal but had also come to the view that Macron's victory was partly his success and would guarantee a degree of continuity. He'd watched the results of the election on 7 May at an awkward and melancholic party he'd organised at the Elysée where his most loyal aides and ministers were convened. 'It was unfathomably sad,' said former health minister Marisol Touraine. 'Like one of those family parties where everyone puts on a good show but you shouldn't ask too many questions.'[1] Hollande clapped as the results came through on the television screen he and his guests were watching. Many attendees left at the first opportunity.

'Good luck,' Hollande mouthed as he got into his car and left the palace at the end of the televised inauguration ceremony. Macron waved from the entrance of his new home, with Brigitte, dressed in a pale blue Louis Vuitton skirt and jacket, at his side.

Perhaps the history books will be kinder to Hollande than the damning verdict of the overwhelming majority of French voters. He had helped usher in a new global agreement on climate change, held the country together through the worst wave of violence on French soil since the war and brought in same-sex marriage. He was right that he had played a role in Macron's emergence, but not just by promoting him. He had also created such widespread disaffection for France's traditional political class that Macron's rise as an anti-system outsider was possible – in the same way that the last chaotic years of the Fourth Republic in the 1950s had prepared the way for de Gaulle and the presidential system in 1958.

After the inauguration, Macron left the palace for his trip up the Champs-Élysées, taking the military command car to the top of boulevard, then finishing the last stretch to the Arc de Triomphe on foot, a brief rain shower splattering his suit as he approached the tomb of the unknown soldier. Just as on the evening of his election, there was no visible sign of public fervour. The crowds seeking a first glimpse of the president were noticeably thin, with spaces at the metal barriers erected along the Champs-Elysées for anyone who arrived at the last minute.

And although Macron had clinched the presidency, there were still two more rounds of voting ahead that would be crucial for his future. Stage two of his 'revolution' would take place in parliamentary elections scheduled for 11 and 18 June when he needed to win a majority to be able to implement his programme. The voting system was similar to the presidential one: unless one candidate scored more than 50 per cent in the first round, the top two, or sometimes top three candidates, advanced to a decisive second-round run-off.

En Marche needed to find and select candidates for each of the 577 constituencies. 'If you don't know the electoral map, then you have a liability,' François Heisbourg, a former senior French diplomat and national security advisor to Macron, said in an interview. 'This is going to be make-or-break for him because if he gets it wrong, he won't be able to govern.'

After their dramatic loss in the presidential election, the Republicans party was looking to make amends. 'I'm convinced that our ideas are in the majority in the country,' Laurent Wauquiez, who became head of the Republicans six months later, said after the presidential defeat. They and the Socialists now both aimed to win enough seats to produce at the least a hung parliament – which would force Macron's party to seek alliances. 'My idea is to offer him a deal in a coalition,' the Socialist chief Jean-Christophe Cambadélis said during an interview in his office in May.

En Marche, which was renamed La Republique En Marche (LREM, Republic on the Move) after the presidential election, had promised to field candidates in every constituency, half of whom would be women and half of whom would never have held public office before. This was a core part of Macron's appeal: overhauling parliament by bringing in complete novices from civil society. Anyone was free to apply online to seek to run for the party.

A nomination team headed by Jean-Paul Delevoye, a 70-year-old centre-right political insider, along with the young En Marche operatives Pierre Person, 28, and Stephane Séjourné, 31, had been working around the clock sifting through 19,000 applications. Delevoye was everything that Macron and his advisors were not: a vastly experienced politician, he had been a minister, MP, senator and mayor during his nearly 40 years in politics.

In the days after his inauguration, one of Macron's first tasks was to name a prime minister and government. He used the process as an opportunity to further fracture both of the traditional parties and siphon away their support. On 15 May, he named the 46-year-old centre-right Republicans MP and mayor Édouard Philippe as prime minister, making good on his promise to work across party lines. The bearded Philippe was a slightly older, taller, more austere version of Macron: he grew up in provincial northern France in a middle-class family (his parents were teachers, rather than medics like the Macrons) before going on to graduate from Sciences Po and ENA. He was a policy wonk, but loved literature and had written several political thrillers since 2007, one of which included a passage musing on the difficulties of being premier. He was also a fluent German speaker, another signal of goodwill sent by Macron to Berlin. Philippe was so fear-struck by the prospect of becoming prime minister that he admitted to losing six kilograms during the audition process.[2]

His political background and beliefs also illustrated Macron's theory when he started En Marche: that moderates on both the right and the left had more in common than they did with many people in their own parties. Philippe had been a long-time ally of the centre-right ex-premier Alain Juppé but had started out in politics as a follower of the centre-left former Socialist prime minister Michel Rocard, who had attended Macron's wedding.

Macron also lured the ambitious Republicans Bruno Le Maire and Gérald Darmanin for posts at the economy and finance ministry, whose appointments would underline for right-wing voters his intention to be both an economic reformer and fiscally responsible. The widely respected Socialist Jean-Yves Le Drian became foreign minister after having served as defence minister under Hollande, and there were senior jobs for Macron's most influential campaign backers: Collomb, the Socialist mayor of Lyon, became interior minister, his first central government job at the age of 70, while the centrist François Bayrou was given the justice portfolio with a mission to steer through a new law on ethics in public life.

Macron succeeded where Sarkozy and Hollande had failed in the past by convincing the popular celebrity environmentalist Nicolas Hulot to enter politics, a major coup which was intended to stress his commitment to sustainable development and fighting climate change, themes that had been lacking in his campaign. In 34-year-old women's rights activist Marlène Schiappa and former Olympic athlete Laura Flessel, who were named as ministers for women and sports, Macron made good on promises to provide opportunities to newcomers. He also named the Moroccan-origin En Marche IT supremo Mounir Mahjoubi as his digital industries minister. The cabinet was a melting pot of young and old, centre-left, centre-right and novices, with half of the jobs given to women.

Macron's own emphasis on promoting women, both in government and the candidates set to stand for LREM in the parliamentary elections, was also part of his pitch of modernity and political renewal. It had been a theme in French politics since at least 1995 when Alain Juppé appointed the most feminine government in history – a quarter of its members were women who became known paternalistically as the 'Jupettes' (a play on the word for skirt – *jupe*). Macron named a woman, Sylvie Goulard, as armed forces minister.

'I'm a belated convert to feminism,' Macron said on 21 March. 'But like all late converts, I'm determined. I really want to change things, to do things differently, better.'[3] The belatedness of his conversion can be judged by the number of women in the inner circle at the beginning of En Marche: there were none. Right to the end of the campaign, the only senior women were chief of staff Sophie Ferracci, the wife of Macron's best friend Marc Ferracci, and his much-photographed spokeswoman Sibeth Ndiaye. Besides his beloved grandmother, his mother and Brigitte, who are credited with offering emotional and creative succour, few women feature prominently in Macron's life story. All his closest friends and professional mentors have been men. The proof of his commitment to equality will be in his efforts to promote women for the duration of his term – unlike Juppé who dropped many of his 'Jupettes' once the positive political impact of their nominations had worn off.

In his first few weeks in office, Macron also launched himself almost immediately into a whirlwind of international diplomacy. The day after his inauguration, on 15 May, he made the by now traditional first visit to Berlin to meet Angela Merkel where a crowd of several hundred people stood outside the chancellery waving French and EU flags. 'In five years' time, I hope that when I come to visit the chancellor there will be an even bigger crowd because we will have produced results,' Macron said.

He wrangled an immediate public commitment out of Merkel that treaty change was now possible to deepen the bloc, something that had been out of the question ever since Brexit. 'From the German point of view, it's possible to change the treaties if it makes sense,' Merkel said. 'If we can say why, what for, what the point is, then Germany will be ready.'

While Macron's defeat of Marine Le Pen had been widely welcomed in Germany, the first signs of suspicion about the new French president's intentions were also beginning to show there, particularly regarding his vision for a eurozone budget, which would be partly financed by Germany. The front-page of the magazine *Der Spiegel* that week captioned him an 'Expensive Friend'.

Macron also sought to further bolster his commander-in-chief credentials (a priority since his military-themed inauguration day), by visiting French troops in Mali in operation against jihadists. In the process, he antagonised the media by trying to sideline the presidential press pack, handpicking journalists to accompany him. Journalists' groups quickly condemned what they saw as an attempt to interfere in their work.

His grand coming out on the international stage took place in Brussels for a NATO summit on 25 May. It was Macron's first meeting with US President Donald Trump who had endorsed Marine Le Pen as the 'strongest' candidate a few days before the first round of the presidential election and who had also been openly hostile to the EU during his own campaign in the US. If Le Pen's agenda was 'the polar opposite' of Macron's, so was the US president's. The meeting between Trump and the anti-Trump was keenly awaited.

The former philosopher's assistant and the populist television celebrity cum real estate heir had opposing views on everything from trade, globalisation, climate change and immigration. And it was hard to see what they might share in common: Macron had spent his entire adult lifetime with a woman 24 years older than him, while Trump was a boastful self-appointed playboy with a penchant for younger women who was now on his third marriage. While Trump has a famously short attention span and limited appetite for policy detail (National Security Council officials are reported to include the word 'Trump' in as many paragraphs of his briefing documents as possible to keep him reading), Macron had been publishing essays on government action in intellectual left-wing periodicals since his twenties. They both claimed to represent Western civilisation in some form, but their views of what it consisted of were as different as the glitzy golden interior of the Trump Tower penthouse and the Palace of Versailles.

That said, their first call together after Macron's victory had gone extremely well, according to Macron's old university friend and diplomatic advisor Aurélien Lechevallier. Trump had started by reading what sounded like pre-prepared talking points but gradually spoke more freely. 'I saw you at the Louvre, it was amazing,' he told Macron. Macron stressed their common background in business, his love of entrepreneurship and 'how we both want to take on the bureaucracy.' He had charmed his first billionaire in his mid-twenties (another property developer, Henry Hermand) – maybe Trump could be brought under his spell too.

They also bonded over their experience of defeating professional politicians. Trump 'seemed to like the fact that the President's victory had destroyed the traditional parties,' Lechevallier said. 'He also seemed to appreciate that the conversation was very courteous and polite, but also very direct.'

The meeting in Brussels two weeks after their first call was memorable for the appearance of the two presidents in front of the media, when Macron anticipated the famous Trump 'power' handshake and crunched the American's knuckles, leaving Trump struggling to free his fingers at the end. 'My handshake with him – it wasn't innocent,' Macron told the *Journal du Dimanche* newspaper afterwards. 'It's not the be-all-and-end-all of a policy, but it was a moment of truth.'

He added: 'Donald Trump, the Turkish president or the Russian president see relationships in terms of a balance of power. That doesn't bother me.' It was a statement of intent which echoed the promises he had made about restoring French pride in his inaugural address. Making the point publicly looked needlessly provocative vis-à-vis the thin-skinned leader of the world's superpower, but standing up to America has been a French tradition since de Gaulle and it played well domestically.

Macron travelled afterwards to the Italian village of Taormina on the island of Sicily to attend the G7. He, Merkel and the Canadian Prime Minister Justin Trudeau spent the meeting trying to convince Trump – in vain – to drop his opposition to the Paris climate change agreement, which had been reached after fraught negotiations in December 2015 and committed around 200 countries to emissions targets aimed at limiting global warming to well below 2 degrees Celsius.

On 1 June 2017, Trump announced his plan to withdraw the US from the Agreement, to the disappointment of America's allies. Macron seized on this opportunity, releasing a recorded message inviting American climate change scientists and entrepreneurs to come to France. 'Make our planet great again,' he said, recycling Trump's own slogan against him and capturing a memorable soundbite for the occasion (courtesy of Emelien). It was another bold move that won him instant plaudits at home, as well as 200,000 retweets, but it brought with it the risk of straining relations with Washington.

Macron took the same approach with Russian President Vladimir Putin, who had previously welcomed Marine Le Pen to Moscow in March. The two men had spoken by telephone after Macron's victory, during which Macron had complained about the hacking of his campaign and the attacks on him in Russian state media groups. 'Emmanuel Macron was very clear. He said everything that he thought in a very direct way, which is his style,' Aurélien Lechevallier explained. 'It helped clear the air.'

Macron invited Putin for a meeting in the splendour of the Palace of Versailles to visit an art exhibition on the Russian Tsar Peter the Great. After two hours of a 'direct and frank' exchange in private – diplomatic speak for a meeting in which the parties reach little agreement – Macron stood next to Putin at a press conference and continued to speak just as frankly and directly. He would be 'constantly vigilant' about gay rights in the Russian region of Chechnya following reports of the persecution and torture of gay men, he said. He also criticised the Kremlin-funded Russia Today network and the Sputnik news agency whose journalists Macron had banned from his campaign events due to their biased reporting. 'When media organs spread slanderous falsehoods, they are no longer journalists,' he said. Putin, normally as inscrutable as a lizard, squirmed slightly.

'The press conference was incredible,' said François Heisbourg, the national security advisor to Macron during the campaign and former diplomat. 'The toughness of the guy [Macron] is amazing. I've never seen anything like it.'

Diplomatic advisor Lechevallier said he believed that the diplomatic work 'helped create a form of pride in France, with the idea that "France is back". And obviously that has an impact domestically.' Macron had indeed made a supremely confident start as a statesman, drawing on his experience as deputy chief of staff at the Élysée under Hollande and his time as economy minister.

'He likes sending strong signals,' Lechevallier continued. 'He's shown that several times – the night at the Louvre, the command car on the Champs Élysées for the inauguration and also with Vladimir Putin. France is rediscovering its old grandeur, but with us, behind closed doors, he's still cracking jokes.'

Tony Blair, the former British prime minister, was one of many impressed onlookers. 'Macron has made France interesting and dynamic,' he said in an interview. 'For the first time in many years people are looking to France for inspiration and that is an extraordinary achievement.'

In the parliamentary elections in June, the Macron revolution was completed. The République en Marche party fielded candidates in around 450 out of 577 constituencies nationwide, while its centrist ally MoDem, the party of François Bayrou who had backed Macron at a critical time during the campaign in February, fielded another 75. They all stood as common candidates for the 'presidential majority': a coalition that backed Macron's policies. Around half of the LREM candidates had never held public office before and half were women, again as Macron had promised. Among them was a female bullfighter in the south of France, a former Rwandan orphan, a fireman and a star mathematician. Candidates from immigrant backgrounds were chosen for many suburban areas of Paris and other major cities, including the high-flying black corporate lawyer Laëtitia Avia. They stole the headlines, naturally, being the most obvious faces of political renewal that Macron had promised.

After the first round of voting on 11 June, some forecasts showed that LREM and MoDem would win as many as 490 out of 577 seats in the decisive second round the weekend afterwards in what would be a historic landslide. The results dashed all hopes among Republicans that they might bounce back from their presidential failure, and laid bare the depths of anti-Socialist feeling in the country. But the abstention rate was equally eye-catching: more than one in two voters stayed away from the polls, a historic high, and abstentionism was off the scale in some working-class areas. In the deprived northeastern Parisian suburb of Clichy-sous-Bois only one in four people cast a ballot.

'No Opposition for Macron: Record Abstention,' read a headline in Le Monde. 'It's not easy to explain to people that we're not electing an emperor,' the former right-wing prime minister Jean-Pierre Raffarin complained. The political analyst Christophe Barbier suggested that 'you could take a goat and give it Macron's endorsement and it would have a good chance of being elected.' Even Macron himself was said by Le Canard enchaîné to have been alarmed by the prospect of such a large parliamentary group.

Not even the first scandal for the government, which engulfed one of Macron's closest allies – the secretary general of En Marche, Richard Ferrand – seemed to make a difference. Le Canard enchaîné had revealed before the first round of voting that Ferrand benefited from an insider property deal while he was head of a health cooperative in his native Brittany region in 2011. The cooperative had paid for renovations on a building owned by Ferrand's partner, increasing its value significantly, and had taken out a long-term lease with her. Macron had named Ferrand to a large new ministry of 'territorial cohesion' comprising housing, urban planning and local services. Ferrand denied any wrongdoing and toughed out the media pressure until after the parliamentary elections, when he stepped down to take the job as head of the LREM parliamentary group.

In the second round on 18 June, fears about the parliament being a rubber-stamping chamber for Macron's proposals led some voters to come out in support of opposition candidates, but the dynamic of the first round remained intact: most of those who cast their ballots were driven by the desire to 'give Macron a chance'.

'The desire for change is really strong, which means that people have less concern about voting for someone they don't know,' said Romain Perron, a 33-year-old who worked in finance, after casting his vote in Paris. Sandrine, a 48-year-old civil servant, explained that 'we are in a system that offers a majority to the president once he's elected. It should give him the chance to reform, and our country needs reforms.'

LREM won 308 out of the 577 seats in the end, lower than the polls had projected, but still a majority on its own, meaning that Macron could govern if needed without Bayrou's MoDem party which had won a record 42. Though the woman bullfighter failed to make the cut, the results transformed France's lower house of parliament, the National Assembly, making it younger, more ethnically diverse and far less experienced.

The Republicans won just 112 seats, down from 199 in the last election in 2012, becoming the largest opposition force in parliament, while Le Pen and Mélenchon faced grave disappointment. While they both won their individual battles and were able, personally, to enter parliament, their parties finished with just eight and seventeen MPs respectively.

The most humiliating result was suffered by the outgoing Socialists, the party Macron had briefly joined in 2006 and had unsuccessfully attempted to stand for. They lost more than 250 seats in total to finish with just 30 MPs. 'Voters wanted to give the president his chance, they gave none to his opponents,' the party boss Cambadélis told reporters bitterly. The Socialists faced political and financial oblivion, forcing them to sell their headquarters in central Paris.

Many of the Socialist MPs who managed to survive did so because they were judged to be 'compatible' with Macron: meaning that LREM had not put up a rival candidate in their constituencies. LREM cut similar deals with some moderate Republicans who were then elected, meaning Macron could count on support beyond even his own huge majority. This strategy, overseen by Macron, Richard Ferrand and nominations chief Jean-Paul Delevoye, had also put pressure on rival politicians to climb aboard the Macron bandwagon before the vote.

Those who were invited but refused paid the consequences, as did others who had crossed the president at some point in his many careers or were deemed to be threats to his vision.

Benoît Hamon, the Socialist presidential candidate who had helped to block Macron's first law in parliament in 2015, was defeated by a LREM candidate. So was the bright young hope for the future of the Socialists and long-time Macron critic, Najat Vallaud-Belkacem. The socialist chief Cambadélis, who had tussled with Macron repeatedly when he was economy minister, crashed out in the first round. Nathalie Kosciusko-Morizet, a senior Republicans figure and another young hope for the future, found herself facing a strong LREM candidate in her Paris constituency, the articulate former journalist and business consultant Gilles Le Gendre. Kosciusko-Morizet had toyed with the idea of joining Macron before opting out. She lost her seat and is one of many now seeking a new role outside of politics.

Macron also made his old government rival Manuel Valls beg to stand as an LREM candidate. Valls, who had been prime minister only six months before, was told dismissively to apply online like the other 19,000 candidates and was then refused a berth with the party. As a compromise, LREM decided not to field a candidate against him.

'They played around right to the end, they humiliated, isolated [me] and all of it to end up with a compromise,' Valls said afterwards. 'I've no illusions about Macron and his team. Hollande is nasty but within limits. Macron is nasty, but there are no rules so there are no limits.' Having made his feelings known, Valls nonetheless vowed to support the government once elected.

'He treated Valls with extraordinary contempt,' said the former Socialist budget minister Christian Eckert, who worked with both men in government. 'Ideologically I don't think there's much which separates them. I found it very inelegant.'

Aquilino Morelle, Macron's old colleague at the Elysée and a former Socialist speechwriter, also said he thought it was 'cruel the way they handled Valls and Kosciusko-Morizet,' adding: 'He handed out punishments. But that's part of his character too.'

The president even got his revenge on the Republicans MP Nicolas Dhuicq, who had been quoted by the Russian news agency Sputnik referring to Macron as an agent for US banks with a 'gay lobby' behind him. He lost his seat too.

By the middle of June 2017, Macron had shown himself to be a masterful political strategist in plotting his stunning route to power in the presidential election, and he followed that up by engineering a landslide parliamentary victory through the deft composition of his first government and a ruthless and clever nomination process.

Many observers were surprised at how Macron, at just 39 years of age, seemed to slip so seamlessly into the presidential role at home and abroad. But he had spent much of his adult life surrounded by business and political leaders and his spare time was spent pondering the dynamics of power and government. He had announced in advance to those who were careful enough to take him at his word exactly what sort of a president he intended to be – one from the quasi-monarchical mould of Charles de Gaulle – and he has not wavered from this in office. His own reference was the ancient Roman supreme god Jupiter, the deity of the skies who was believed to send rain and lightning and was worshipped on the summits of hills throughout Italy.

'He will be Jupiterian, very authoritarian, very manipulative, very ungrateful, very cynical – all the qualities you need for this job,' Alain Minc said.

CHAPTER 19

The Regicidal Monarchists

OVER THE SUMMER OF 2017, WITH THE PARLIAMENTARY elections won, his first moves on the international stage widely praised and his domestic political rivals in disarray, Macron was able to begin implementing his programme from a position of overwhelming strength. He could count on an already-favourable and improving economic environment and huge reserves of good-will around Europe.

The French central bank began to lift its forecasts for eco-nomic growth, which ended up being 2.0 per cent over the year – a six-year high, and far higher than the 1.1 per cent posted in 2016. Investor confidence also picked up almost immediately. In addition, surveys showed that the French as a whole were slightly less miserable, with 69 per cent saying they thought the country was in decline compared with 85 per cent at the start of the year.

Also in Macron's favour was the widespread feeling that the country must move forward somehow, that the resistance to change that was seen and heard so often in protests on the streets of France over the years must in some way be overcome.

Theories that France was somehow a 'blocked society' go back decades, outlined in the 1970s in an influential book by the same name by the sociologist Michel Crozier. 'My feeling is that the French people have been voting for change for quite a long time, but it's not quite worked out,' the former British Prime Minister Tony Blair commented just after the election. 'At this point in time, Macron has an enormous opportunity.'

Macron had also won with a clear and coherent programme, which was validated in both the presidential and the parliamentary elections. Jean Pisani-Ferry, the economist and Macron ally who had been in charge of assembling his manifesto, said that the president was determined to avoid the mistakes of Jacques Chirac, Sarkozy and particularly Hollande in 'being elected on one platform and then governing with another'.

'No-one can be surprised when he says: "I want to reform labour law or pensions". No-one can say it's a trick,' Pisani-Ferry explained.

But, aware of the vagaries of public opinion and the uniquely unstable state of Western democracies, Macron himself was taking nothing for granted. His immediate predecessors had made strong starts in their presidencies, only to fritter away their political capital. 'The French people are regicidal monarchists, and I say that with full awareness,' Macron had said in May. 'They like choosing a king in order to quickly get rid of him.'[1] This old French reflex would soon reappear.

By August, just three months into his rule, one poll showed that only 36 per cent of voters held a favourable view of Macron. His approval ratings had fallen faster than even those of Sarkozy and Hollande. Part of the explanation was down to the inevitable difficulties faced by both a government and political party that were new and inexperienced, colliding with the realities of running an impatient and deeply divided country.

But much of the damage was self-inflicted. Though Macron had correctly diagnosed France as wanting for authority after its failed experiment with a 'normal' president under François Hollande, his own transition to being a Jupiter-like leader immediately after he took office appeared brutal and contrived at times. Much of his appeal as a candidate had been his youth, freshness and approachability. In his desire to give himself stature as president, by cloaking himself in the imagery of France's royal past and its Republican grandeur, he instead drew attention to other less appealing sides of his character: a tendency to be self-regarding and big-headed. News that he spent €26,000 on make-up services in his first three months in office were a blow to his scrupulous public image management.

He gave his critics early ammunition with another condescending turn of phrase when using a metaphor about a railway station in front of a group of internet entrepreneurs in late June 2017: 'A railway station is a place where you cross people who have succeeded and people who are nothing,' he said. The point he had been trying to make about inequality was entirely lost in the outcry resulting from his choice of words.

Faced with almost no political opposition, he needlessly picked a fight with the French media. Inspired by Obama, he made clear that he wanted to keep reporters at a distance, and also end what he saw as the overly cosy relationship between politicians and journalists in France (conveniently forgetting how he himself had courted the press enthusiastically while still a minister). He declared that he intended to move an office used by the French presidential media out of the Élysée Palace, ending a tradition started under Mitterrand which had been intended to show the French government's commitment to transparency.

While the media were held at bay, Macron's communications team were regularly distributing pictures and videos over social media of him playing tennis, boxing and being lowered from a helicopter onto a nuclear submarine. The latter images of him in a jumpsuit recalled President Putin, whose posed action-man pictures, including a trip on a submarine in 2015, form a regular, and key part of his PR effort.

When asked why Macron refused interviews, an aide said that his thinking was 'too complex' to explain in a question-and-answer format. When Macron was faced with a reporter who tried to ask him about domestic politics during a G20 meeting in Germany in July, he replied haughtily: 'We are here discussing essential issues which deserve better than comments about everyday news ... You are bringing up the events of daily life and it's not my role to comment on them.'

As so often in his first year in power, Macron seemed to be using Hollande as the anti-model: the previous president had been too close to reporters, so Macron must push them back. But creating an antagonistic relationship with the media so early in his term was a mistake. Perhaps as a consequence, many delighted in reporting the teething problems in his new government. Coverage of parliament, which might have focused on the inspiring stories of how new MPs from civil society were taking their place in the assembly, was instead dominated by their apparent lack of preparedness and amateurism. 'Maybe we weren't ready for the job immediately, but that was normal,' said Pierre Person, the 29-year-old MP and a former campaign aide, in an interview in his office. 'We needed to learn.' Beginners' mistakes would

continue throughout the first year, including in January 2018
when only a handful of ruling party MPs turned up for an address
by the German parliamentary speaker, former finance minister
Wolfgang Schäuble, in what was an unintentional but embar-
rassing snub.

Macron's high-handed approach reflected his own desire to
assert himself as president. Despite his outwardly flawless self-
assurance, he was privately conscious of his age and inexperience
as he took office, and was determined to show that he would brook
no challenge to his authority. This explained his clumsy treatment
of the army chief, General Pierre de Villiers, only a few months
after taking power which led to another damaging episode.

One of the first tasks of the new government had been to
finalise an interim budget for the rest of 2017, which was trick-
ier than anticipated because the outgoing Socialists had saddled
Macron with spending commitments that were around €8 billion higher than expected. Cost savings had to be found across
the government, and an €850-million cut was pencilled in for
the military.

During a closed-doors parliamentary committee hearing,
General de Villiers pointed out that the highly stretched armed
forces were active in West Africa, the Middle East and on the
streets of France under the country's state of emergency – which
had been in place since 2015. In leaked comments which provoked fury in the Élysée, de Villiers told lawmakers that he
wouldn't allow the army to be 'screwed'.

On 13 July, on the eve of the Bastille Day military parade,
Macron used an annual summer military garden party as an occasion to reply bluntly and publicly to the top brass: 'I've made
commitments, I'm your boss,' he told the audience. 'I intend to

maintain the commitments I made in front of our citizens and in front of our army. And I have no need for any pressure or commentary in this regard.'

The next day, de Villiers's humiliation was completed at the ceremonial start of the Bastille Day parade when the army chief took his place next to Macron in an open-top jeep. Five days later, he resigned.

Macron was right to stand his ground over the difficult choices that were made in the budget, particularly when faced with a clearly political general (de Villiers had threatened to resign under the previous government in 2014 over funding for the military). But the decorated soldier was also defending the rank and file at a time when public sympathy for the forces was high, given their public role in patrolling the streets. Humiliating de Villiers in front of other generals under his command at a military event looked authoritarian as well as tin-eared.

On top of this, Macron's first government began to be scandal-struck within a very short space of time, with problems surfacing less than a month into his office. The former secretary general of En Marche (and social affairs minister) Richard Ferrand had been the first to step down because of his past insider property dealings while he was head of a public health cooperative in Brittany.

In the week after the parliamentary elections, four ministers from the centrist party MoDem quit – including the justice minister and party chief François Bayrou as well as the army minister Sylvie Goulard – over an inquiry into the misuse of funds at the European parliament. All denied wrongdoing.

The departure of the MoDem ministers had the advantage of making the multi-party government more cohesive – and the exit of the abrasive Bayrou was certainly not lamented in the Élysée – but it was an early blow to the government's image. Macron reshuffled and filled the vacant posts with loyalists, naming the little-known and unelected Florence Parly – a former executive from Air France and the state railways – as armed forces minister, despite her lack of military experience.

Having been showered with praise as a student, banker and civil servant, and having become accustomed to ever-climbing approval ratings, Macron entered the biggest test of his first year in a power in September in a highly unfamiliar position: he was unpopular, and the knives were out. Was it possible that the regicidal monarchists he had theorised about were already preparing the guillotine for him?

As France came back to work after the traditional month-long break in August, Macron steeled himself for his first showdown with the trade unions and protesters. Given the lack of parliamentary opposition, a view had formed in the country that only fearsome French street protests – the great crusher of presidential ambitions – could serve as a counter-force to the audacious young leader.

At stake now was his labour market reform, the centrepiece of his economic programme and a change he insisted was essential if France were to signal to its European partners and investors that it was finally serious about improving its business environment. The reform would be pushed through using presidential executive orders, a rarely used constitutional power which would avoid a long parliamentary debate. Its aims were clear: ripping up the rigid central labour code and restricting the unions in their powers to set pay and working conditions in many sectors of the economy via collective bargaining. Instead, small companies in particular would be offered new opportunities to negotiate directly with their staff. The reform would also regulate the labour courts, setting upper limits on compensation for workers who were dismissed from their jobs. If he succeeded, Macron would be taken seriously; failure, though, would embolden his opponents and undermine the rest of his term.

'I've told him from the beginning that he needs to show a bit more humility. He only got 23 per cent of voters in the first round [of the presidential election],' the head of the hard-left CGT union, Philippe Martinez, said in an interview in his office over the summer. The former car worker led the public resistance, calling for the first strike on 12 September.

Macron had further succeeded in stirring up his opponents during a trip to Athens the week before, by deriding them as 'slackers, cynics and extremists'. Bruno Cautrès, an analyst at the Cevipof political research institute at Sciences Po, said that this choice of words had 'thrown oil on the fire'. Undeterred, Macron followed up in early October with another broadside at a group of protesting workers who were worried about a factory closure in central France. In comments caught on camera he told them they should 'stop causing such a bloody racket' and find jobs instead.

'Our political elites have grown used to not really saying anything, by using sterile language,' Macron added, as he defended himself in his first formal interview with a French television channel in October, five months after his election.

The first day of the strikes called against the reform saw many protesters carry banners saying: 'Slackers of the world unite' and 'Proud to be slackers'. The interior ministry calculated turnout to be around 220,000 people, while the CGT put the numbers at 400,000 in 180 demonstrations held nationwide – large by the standards of most countries but smaller than the height of the resistance to Hollande's less ambitious reforms the previous year. Public services were barely affected. 'It's a first one and it looks like it's a success,' the CGT supremo Martinez told reporters, putting on a brave face.

A second round of strikes was called for the following week on 21 September, while the far-left leader Jean-Luc Mélenchon urged followers of his France Unbowed movement to join separate rallies two days after that. 'The political rallies might be bigger than the trade union ones,' commented Jérôme Sainte-Marie from the polling group PollingVox.

In the end, the resistance movement never got going. Turnout for the CGT protests halved on the second day of action and Mélenchon's meeting drew only 30,000, according to police. It was notable chiefly for a clumsy remark from Mélenchon that appeared to equate the current government with the German occupation during the Second World War. 'It's the street [protests] that toppled France's kings, it's the street that drove out the Nazis,' he roared.

Far from toppling Macron, the street showed itself to be divided, and weak. The president rammed through the planned changes, saying that they constituted 'an unprecedented transformation of our social model [and] the economic functioning of our country'.

Protests continued but the number of demonstrators fell to 40,000 in October and the movement had fizzled out by the end of November. Demoralised, Mélenchon conceded that Macron had 'won the first point'.

'We were the last country in the whole of Europe that still had a social resistance mechanism, which meant that the harshest bits of the liberal reform agenda that swept through Britain, Germany, Spain, even Portugal and Italy, had not hit France,' he told an interviewer mournfully. 'It's obvious that if young people decide to mobilise, then we're on the way, we're in the game, but it's not the case,' he added.[2]

The sequence was illuminating for what it showed about the inability of either the CGT or Mélenchon to fire up opposition. It was the first skirmish in what will surely be a long fight, but it illustrated several important dynamics for Macron's term: firstly, the strength of his mandate thanks to his clear and coherent programme; secondly, how the power of the unions had declined, more than twenty years since they had last brought the country to a standstill in 1995; and thirdly, how Macron intended to operate in his negotiations with the trade unions.

Both he and the government had spent three months discussing the changes with union leaders, inviting them to the Élysée individually to express their views: whereupon Macron had deployed his powers of flattery and persuasion in person. This contrasted with Hollande's 2016 labour law changes, which some unions only learned about from the newspapers.

Macron was intent on showing that he was open to dialogue, and that he was prepared to listen. Both the more moderate CFDT, the biggest union in the private sector, as well as the usually hard-line FO, declined to join the protests in September as a result of Macron's persuasion, leaving the CGT isolated.

But the wording of the executive orders was kept a secret until the last minute. When they were unveiled, some felt they went too far in favouring company bosses, including the head of the CFDT, Laurent Berger, whose support Macron will need further down the line. 'We feel like we were listened to, but not heard,' Berger said afterwards. For future rounds of reforms, union leaders said they would be wise to these tactics.

'We consulted the unions, we didn't negotiate,' Macron's closest advisor Ismaël Emelien said in an interview in his office in February 2018. There would be none of the back-pedalling performed by previous French presidents who were ready to accept compromises to buy the peace, he said. 'We explained what we wanted to do and we were very firm on the objectives. In our method if someone can persuade us that there's a more efficient, quicker or less costly way of getting to the same place, we're ready to adapt.'

Macron used the 2018 budget, passed by parliament in December 2017 after months of negotiations, to send another business-friendly signal to investors and entrepreneurs. It cut corporate taxes on many businesses from 33 per cent to 28 per cent, beginning the process of lowering the rate for all companies to 25 per cent by 2022. Most controversially, it scrapped France's wealth tax on the highest earners that had brought in about €4 billion in revenue each year. In its place came a flat tax at 30 per cent on the earnings of financial investments such as dividends and capital gains, that eliminated progressive taxation (which could reach 55 per cent). The stated aim was to increase funding for French businesses and make the country more attractive to investors. The left-wing economist Thomas Piketty, who remained close to the Socialist Party, called the move a 'heavy moral, economic, and historical mistake'.

Coupled with the first reductions in public spending and reports that luxury items such as yachts and jewellery would escape higher levels of taxation, Macron's opponents on the left labelled him the 'president of the rich' – a damaging nickname that had been used for Sarkozy, who had never shaken it off. *Libération* ran a front-page article calling Macron Sarkozy's 'long-lost son'. After a parliamentary amendment, higher taxes were ultimately imposed on yachts and other luxury items.

The respected French Economic Observatory at Sciences Po concluded that the overall impact of the cuts would mostly benefit the top 10 per cent of households measured by income, and warned that 'financing them by cutting public spending would significantly deepen the inequality produced by these measures.' There were also serious reasons to doubt that the multi-billion-euro tax cut for the wealthy would be re-invested in the French economy, as many top earners could opt instead to invest overseas or in unproductive assets.

Macron sees income inequality as the price to pay for reducing the joblessness that affects a quarter of French young people. 'The main source of inequality in France is unemployment,' explained his chief of staff Alexis Kohler. 'The main source of poverty in France is unemployment.' The tax cuts and the labour reform signalled to foreign investors and business owners that they could count on a supportive government in Paris that, crucially, could deliver on its promises. And if France could stop its wealthy from fleeing the country whilst also attracting new companies, then eliminating the wealth tax would be a success, Prime Minister Philippe argued. 'The Brexit discussion is underway. There is a major opportunity that France can attract companies and investors currently based in the United Kingdom,' he added.[3]

As well as investor roadshows and regular trips to London by French officials, the government launched a charm offensive at the chief executives of banks headquartered in the British capital.

'Struck by the positive energy here in Paris,' the head of Goldman Sachs, Lloyd Blankfein cooed on Twitter in November. 'And the food's good too!'

The greater Paris region set up a hotline staffed with English speakers for companies looking to relocate from Britain after Brexit, while posters at Heathrow airport in London and the Eurostar terminal sprung up asking: 'Tired of the fog? Try the Frogs!' In their eagerness to lure expats, the government promised new international schools and opt-outs from having to pay into the state pension scheme.

In a memo leaked to *The Mail on Sunday* newspaper in June, the City of London's envoy to the EU, Jeremy Browne, warned that the French were in favour of the 'hardest Brexit. They are crystal clear about their underlying objective: the weakening of Britain, the ongoing degradation of the City of London.'

'For sure we want to attract maximum [banking] activity. Why? Because this decision has an impact for a lot of players, a lot of players will decide to be part of the EU and Eurozone and they have to choose between different countries,' Macron told the BBC journalist Andrew Marr in January 2018.

Domestically, over the first year of his term in power, Macron stayed remarkably true to his election programme. 'I'm doing what I said I would. That might surprise people perhaps,' he explained in December 2017.[4] At Christmas, En Marche had taken to sending out emails to members with the title message: 'We said it, we did it' that listed its legislative achievements. These included the promised law that raised ethical standards in parliament, banning the employment of spouses and family members by lawmakers (which had famously torpedoed Macron's right-wing rival François Fillon's presidential bid).

There was also a new security law to replace the state of emergency that had been introduced by Hollande. This latter legislation made many of the emergency provisions permanent – such as powers to place suspected radicals under house arrest or to close religious sites – and was denounced by human rights groups. As part of his social agenda, school class sizes were also halved for pupils aged five to six in specially-designated priority areas of high poverty and low achievement, again as promised in the manifesto. This measure was the flagship social policy announcement of Macron's first year, aimed at improving the lives of France's most impoverished. The change attacked inequalities at their source – underachieving children tend to grow up to be underachieving adults. It was a key marker of his approach to inequality that was different from the traditional French left, which focused on taxation and redistribution. The man who had promoted low-cost bus services to allow the 'poor' to travel more also wanted to improve schools in deprived areas in order to provide the tickets that would lead them out of those areas and into prosperity.

From December, something almost unprecedented happened. Macron's ratings and those of his Prime Minister Édouard Philippe began rising again. Part of this was down to a change in strategy in how Macron communicated. Out went the Jupiterian president of the first months, the distant monarch-like figure who would limit himself to speeches and stay above the fray of everyday politics, and in came a more hands-on leader who would make the case for the actions of his government in person. His prominence on the international stage, in stark contrast to Hollande, also appealed to the deep-rooted attachment in France to the idea of the country as a 'great power' that was once again relevant. 'Before they [presidents] used to fall and then never come back, but he's rebounding,' Pascal Perrineau, a veteran political science professor at Sciences Po, said.

In Europe, Macron's blueprint for the future of the EU immediately set the agenda at the Council meetings in Brussels that are attended by the bloc's leaders. After a decade of crisis-management at these summits, from the economic turmoil of the sovereign debt crisis in Greece, Spain and Ireland to Brexit, Macron had immediate success in creating a sense of forward momentum. It was a remarkable feat. No-one could say if Macron would succeed, less still if European voters actually wanted his proposals, but the change in dynamic was extraordinary for a project that many observers saw as being at risk of unravelling after Britain's decision to leave.

In the short-term, Macron focused on pushing his so-called 'protective Europe' agenda, that aimed to offer greater safe-guards for Europeans worried about the effects of unfair trade, mass migration, or other undesirable consequences of globalisation. This included an overhaul of an arcane piece of legislation called 'The Posted Workers Act' that allowed European companies to send their employees to other EU states without paying social charges there. It was a source of particular resentment in France, where lower-cost Eastern Europeans were able to undercut their French rivals domestically, particularly in the building sector.

The European Commission, meanwhile, put forward proposals to create new powers to screen foreign investments coming into strategic sectors of the bloc's economy, as proposed by Macron. This, and new anti-dumping measures to block the sale of overly cheap imports on the European market, were seen as targeting state-backed Chinese firms in particular, which Macron had accused in the past of destroying EU jobs – and raising opposition to trade and globalisation in the process. Macron had railed against the slow and ineffective EU response to cheap Chinese steel imports back in his time as economy minister. Other French ideas – like a 'Buy European Act' to oblige governments to buy more from EU-based companies – were quietly shelved in the face of resistance from some northern European countries, worried that Macron's agenda was a cover for old-fashioned French protectionism.

'The "protective Europe" agenda has been well established,' commented Macron's top Europe advisor Clément Beaune in an interview over a breakfast of fresh fruit and croissants at the Élysée. 'I'm not saying that everyone agrees with it, but there's a recognition that Europe needs to act as a bloc in some areas.

'The president understood that if we want to defend the European project, if we want to defend openness – to trade, to migration, for example – you need to provide a framework and a level of protection at the European level,' he added.

His bigger vision for a new wave of federalism through institutional change and the further pooling of sovereignty was put on the backburner until the end of September, when Germany held its general election. In the run up, Macron spent months wooing Angela Merkel, making Berlin his first trip after his election victory and doing his best in subsequent meetings to show deference to the naturally cautious chancellor, while also prodding her to take action on EU reform. His style didn't always go down well with German diplomats. One top official in the foreign ministry accused him of acting like a 'Sun King' with a 'God-given right to rule'.

But the 'Merkron' power couple flourished, both leaders sharing an interest in policy detail that would often see them being the only ones who were personally making written notes during summit discussions at the G7 or in Brussels. They regularly coordinated their public statements and had detailed technical discussions on EU policy during their frequent phone calls.

Macron bet everything on her emerging from the vote in a position of strength to put in place an ambitious shared agenda in what was expected to be her final, and fourth, term in office. 'What I really value in her is that she has never tried to tap the brakes on my élan, my enthusiasm,' Macron said with characteristic immodesty.[5]

In the end, however, Merkel was unexpectedly left weakened by a vote that saw the German far-right party, the AfD, come third with a historic 13 per cent of the vote, driven mostly by its opposition to her immigration policy. Merkel's conservative Christian Democrat (CDU) party had come top, but with its worst result since 1945. She attempted first to stitch together a coalition government with the Green Party and the pro-business liberals the Free Democrats (FDP). The latter was led by Christian Lindner, who had previously spoken out against Macron's Europe plans and drawn up 'red lines' ruling out the French plan for a new eurozone budget that was designed to help economically weaker members of the common currency area.

Two days after the German vote, Macron scheduled a major speech on Europe at the Sorbonne University in central Paris, to lay out his Europe vision once again. If his ideas were not included in the detailed coalition agreement that was now under discussion in Berlin, there was no chance of them coming to fruition. It was an undisguised intervention in German politics.

The speech, titled 'The Initiative for Europe', was brimming with proposals – some new, others well-worn – and almost all were familiar to anyone who had paid attention to his EU campaign speech in Berlin in January. It was a passionate call, which he made over more than 90 minutes, for European nations to raise their ambitions and go further in linking their economies, governments and armies. 'The Europe that we know is too weak, too slow, too inefficient,' he said.

He again argued for an EU-wide agency to handle asylum requests, a beefed-up common border force and an EU prosecutors' office for terrorism and organised crime, which were all projects either underway in Brussels or in existence already. He reprised an old French idea for an EU-wide financial transaction tax and also called for a carbon tax on imports from companies that manufacture and pollute outside the EU. Other suggestions included new efforts to harmonise corporation tax across the bloc and a system for raising levies on American internet and technology giants.

He wanted a new European innovation agency to invest in the technologies of the future, as well as common emergency response teams. In the defence sector, he called for the first stage in creating a European army – a rapid reaction force – as well as a common defence budget and a shared military doctrine 'by the start of the next decade'. 'We need big new projects,' he pleaded.

At an institutional level, the biggest project of all was the creation of a new budget for the eurozone which he had said in an interview with *Le Point* magazine in August should be the equivalent of 'several points of GDP' – which would amount to hundreds of billions of euros in total. It would be overseen by a new eurozone finance minister and parliament. 'I don't have red lines, I only have horizons,' he said, referring to Lindner's obstruction, while leaving the size of the budget deliberately vague so as to avoid complicating Merkel's coalition building.

The overall message was summarised by a senior member of his team during an interview as 'a Europe that is based on the open sharing of sovereignty in the full knowledge that this means pooling more of our resources, including on issues that affect our national sovereignty.'

Reaction was cautious in Germany, where Merkel praised his 'passion' but was non-committal on his proposals, saying that 'it always depends on the actual arrangements.' There was hostility among nationalist parties across the continent, particularly in many Eastern European countries. In the Czech Republic, Prime Minister Andrej Babiš urged him to 'concentrate on France' instead. 'All these proposals that we'll have a minister of the eurozone and all of this further integration – [European Commission chief Jean-Claude] Juncker and Macron should think of why Brexit happened,' Babiš added.

In Britain, commentators focused on Macron's suggestion that 'in a few years, if it wants, the United Kingdom could find its place' in a restructured European Union. Macron's vision for the future is a multi-speed Europe – or a series of 'concentric circles', as the French put it – with the Franco-German duo in the middle followed by the eurozone as the most integrated area, politically and economically. In the outer circles would be other countries who are less willing to pool their sovereignty. 'There will be various levels of participation, of implication,' Beaune said. 'It's hard to imagine that the United Kingdom could not, or would not want to, come back into this reformed European Union.' This would imply another referendum in the future, assuming that the Brexit process is completed in spite of the extraordinary difficulties and costs to Britain.

Merkel's talks with Lindner broke down on 19 November and she turned instead to the centre-left SPD as a potential partner, in a bid to renew an unloved right–left governing partnership of the previous four years. This bent Macron's calendar out of shape – he had been hoping to start work on his EU agenda in early 2018 – but it did spark hopes of a German government that would be far more compatible with his ideas. The SPD leader Martin Schultz, a long-time Macron ally and former head of the EU Parliament, called for the creation of a 'United States of Europe' by 2025 in a speech in December.

Further afield, Macron continued his efforts to project himself as a global statesman with a series of meetings with foreign leaders in Paris and trips abroad. His relentless travel left staffers and journalists often struggling to keep up. But what was striking was his willingness (and his early successes) in building relationships with some of the world's prickly nationalist strongmen. 'He's built relationships based on dialogue and being candid,' Macron's diplomatic advisor and university friend Aurélien Lechevallier said in an interview in March 2018. 'They talk to each other, but to really say things, to put all the problems out on the table. All of them respect that.'

Macron bonded over football with the Turkish President Tayyip Erdoğan, brought a French horse as a present for the Chinese President Xi Jinping as he arrived in Beijing for talks, and jetted to Riyadh in November 2017 to meet the impulsive but powerful 32-year-old Crown Prince Mohammed bin Salman. Other potentially tricky visitors to Paris included India's Hindu nationalist leader Narendra Modi, with whom Macron struck up immediately warm ties, as well as Israeli Prime Minister Benjamin Netanyahu. The latter was welcomed to Paris twice in the first six months of Macron's presidency. 'The lunch in the Élysée is superb, the conversation is superb too,' Netanyahu said after his second visit at a joint press conference.

Despite his self-professed commitment to straight-talking, Macron failed to raise human rights publicly during his trip to China in January, and similarly dodged the subject at a press conference with Egyptian autocrat Abdel Fattah el-Sisi in Paris in October. 'As I don't accept being lectured on how to govern my country, I don't lecture others,' Macron said at a joint press conference.

He also failed to follow up on the serious allegations made by him and members of his team about Russian interference in the French election. The playbook of hacking and disinformation looked unmistakably similar to the one deployed to influence the US presidential vote. Russian links to the far-right National Front are a matter of public record. Yet by failing to order any sort of public investigation, Macron deprived French voters of the right to know whether the sanctity of their democratic system had come under attack. American voters have been better served by their justice system, lawmakers and the heads of their intelligence services. 'There have been internal investigations which were carried out. They did not lead to public trials,' Lechevallier said.

Buying peace with Putin looks like a tactical decision. But the approach smacks of short-sightedness. If there were attempts to influence the election, the methods need to be exposed for the sake of other democracies and to send a warning to Moscow about future attempts. If there is no evidence, then the climate of suspicion towards the Kremlin can be lifted. 'The response has been political by clearly opposing these sorts of attacks or intentions,' Lechevallier continued. 'There's been no attempt to brush this issue under the carpet. It's a major issue for Europe because we will have the European election campaign and campaigns in other European countries where we will be extremely vigilant.'

After making a favourable early impression on Donald Trump, Macron followed up with an invitation for the US president to visit Paris for the national celebrations on Bastille Day on 14 July 2017, which again showcased his ability to spot an opportunity and size up a political adversary. Having seen that he was prepared to stand up to Trump with his muscular knuckle-crushing grip at their first meeting, the French public largely accepted his argument that France needed to build ties with the leader of the world's superpower.

In contrast, the British Prime Minister Theresa May dashed to Washington after Trump's election to be his first foreign visitor, but was criticised in the media for appearing too keen to please and was photographed holding his hand awkwardly at the White House in an image that defined the visit. In Trump's binary view of people as either 'winners' or 'losers', Macron was worthy of respect; May, as subsequent events have shown, was not.

Macron personally showed Trump around Napoleon's tomb in Paris and then wowed him with a dinner up the Eiffel Tower. The two men seemed to be constantly patting each other on the back or touching each other at the elbow. 'The friendship between our two nations and ourselves is unbreakable,' Trump said warmly at a joint press conference.

The US leader seemed to purr as he sat on stage as guest of honour during the annual military parade down the Champs-Élysées, looking more engaged and animated than many

US reporters had seen him in months. US and French fighter jets swooped overhead and troops marched past in a ceremony that marked 100 years since the entry of the United States into the First World War.

Macron grinned like a man whose diplomatic masterclass had been executed to near perfection. Along the way, he'd had to endure some crass and tasteless remarks from the one-time owner of the Miss Universe beauty pageant, who had appraised his wife Brigitte like a contestant as they met for the first time: 'You're in such great shape,' Trump told her before he turned to Macron: 'She's in such good physical shape. Beautiful.'

But Macron had correctly noticed how isolated Trump was internationally and how vulnerable he would be to personal flattery and the charms of Paris. 'My aim with Donald Trump is to anchor him in the Franco–American alliance,' Macron explained afterwards in an interview with the *Journal du Dimanche*. Britain has long prided itself on its 'special relationship' with the United States, but it was Macron, not Prime Minister May in London, who was able to establish the stronger bond.

'Macron is very intelligent and he speaks perfect English and he worked Trump out,' a French diplomat said, asking not to be named. 'He knows how to talk to him. Our British friends rubbed him up the wrong way at the beginning,' he chuckled.

The American leader's two-day visit to Paris ended with a nearly 30-second handshake with Macron which resembled a friendly arm-wrestle at one point. 'He's a great guy – smart, strong, loves holding my hand,' Trump said of his new friend afterwards in an interview with *The New York Times*.

Since then, the US leader has taken up the curious habit of sending Macron press clippings, sometimes annotated with his own writing, a French official revealed on the condition of anonymity. One *New York Times* article commenting on their relationship, which Trump sent Macron at the end of August 2017, was covered in florescent highlighter pen and included a message scrawled in the margin: 'Yes, Emmanuel, it's true. I love you!'

Such are the difficulties faced by US officials in explaining policy to Trump that American diplomats have been known to ask for Macron to place a call to the Oval Office to relay a message, sometimes even suggesting what language to use. Among other occasions, this occurred in October 2017 when Trump was considering walking away from the 2015 Iran nuclear deal, against the advice of his foreign and defence secretaries.

'We are not going to change Donald Trump's convictions or the programme on which he was democratically elected,' Macron's diplomatic advisor Lechevallier said. 'But there is a possibility to try to work with him to modify his decisions so that he tones them down. Or to work collectively with others to help overcome the consequences, on the climate change issue for example.'

CHAPTER 20

Into Big Open Spaces

THROUGHOUT THE FRENETIC DOMESTIC REFORMS, THE
European statesmanship and the globe-trotting in his first year
in office, the question of Macron's political identity continued
to baffle French intellectuals and political analysts, who reached
vainly into the past for comparisons that might illuminate.
His speeches had echoes of the visionary ambition of Charles
de Gaulle; his youth and reformist zeal recalled Valéry Giscard
d'Estaing in the 1970s; his desire for Europe-building and his rich
literary culture had a likeness with François Mitterrand, while
the feverish energy was redolent of Nicolas Sarkozy. But in each
case he was sufficiently different from each of them to render the
parallels almost meaningless.

The Fifth Republic has had no equivalent. The centre-left political current known as the deuxième gauche, from which he hails,
has produced no national leaders and, even then, Macron is much
too statist to be given this label easily. Glimpses of an authoritarian streak saw some observers reach back to the last time France
had a precocious leader of his age, more than 200 years ago. The

philosopher Pierre-André Taguieff ended a vitriolic book about the president warning that he was a smiling despot-in-the-making and 'a little avatar of [Napoleon] Bonaparte.'

Alain Duhamel, the veteran political journalist who has reported on every president since de Gaulle, called him a political 'kaleidoscope' who could not be pigeonholed. The writer and intellectual Marc Lambron put forward a novel theory that Macron was an amalgam of four distinct groups of people who have left their imprint on France over the last century: the professorial and intellectual political elite of the Third Republic in the 1920s and 30s; the technocratic generation of ENA graduates who drove France's post-war economic revival in the 1950s and 60s; the ostentatious moneymen and first global capitalists of the 1980s; and the new disruptive internet generation which came of age in the early 2000s. The leftist thinker Régis Debray described Macron as the arrival of 'globalised Neo-Protestantism' in his 2017 book *The New Power*.

Internationally, Macron was most frequently compared to Tony Blair, Bill Clinton or Gerhard Schröder and he has borrowed policies and tactics from each of them. But all were from a different era. He was a teenager when Clinton was first elected and still shy of his 20th birthday when Blair came to power. Like them, Macron is a pro-enterprise liberal, albeit with French characteristics, but his agenda is designed to meet the global challenges of the 21st century: open trade, dizzying technological progress, cross-border terrorism, mass migration and climate change. In each of those areas, he sees the need for strong state action. 'For decades, it was very fashionable to say "it's the end of the state, there are only private actors",' Macron told an audience in Davos in January 2018 where he was given star billing. 'To respond to these challenges, we need states and global cooperation.'

Having promised to be 'neither of the left, nor the right', Macron has been true to his word in power. His post-ideological buzzwords are 'efficiency', 'pragmatism' and 'mobility', and his catchphrase remains 'at the same time'. 'The "at the same time" is not at all a form of centrism, it's not a sort of "in the middle",' said his chief of staff Alexis Kohler. 'On the contrary, there's a form of radicalism in the reforms. We believe in efficiency and justice, and efficiency and justice are not right-wing or left-wing.'

Assessing the start of his efforts, and the prospects for his term in office, is best done on three distinct levels: the French, the European and the international one.

In France, he has made an impressive start in his bid to move the economy and social system towards the so-called 'Nordic' or 'Scandinavian' model which seeks to provide flexibility for companies along with a strong social safety net for individuals. Tax cuts have brought France more in line with its European peers, while Macron's labour market reform will enable businesses to adapt their workforces more easily to market needs. His rhetoric and understanding of the needs of entrepreneurs has inspired a dramatic change in the way France is viewed at home and abroad. 'He has given France a pro-start-up, pro-entrepreneur image abroad that we did not really have before,' Xavier Niel, his billionaire friend, told foreign reporters.

Ahead of the Davos gathering of the world's elite in the Swiss Alps in January, Macron illustrated his pulling power by luring 140 foreign CEOs to an event at the Versailles Palace. But after sweet-talking them there, he gave those same CEOs, titans of free-market capitalism, a lecture on tax avoidance when two days later he rose to speak at the Davos networking event. 'I'll tell you very frankly, if you believe everything you've heard or the things that seem important in Davos ... then you can't do tax optimisation in the way it is done today,' Macron said.

He has led efforts in Europe to impose a new tax on the American internet giants Google, Amazon, Facebook and Apple (referred to as GAFA in France). Their billionaire owners, ever eager to publicise their personal philanthropic efforts, happily take advantage of European tax legislation to pay derisory sums to governments for the public services they depend on. Macron's willingness to stand up to them, and other powerful business lobbies, is the best way to demonstrate how he is not in thrall to the corporate bosses and financiers who smoothed his path to the top. If he is serious about taking on vested interests he must tackle monopolistic and rent-seeking corporations and other private sector abuses with the same vigour he has shown in cracking down on French trade union or public sector lobbies.

Overall in France, only a fool would see his first achievements as being anything more than the laying of foundation stones. Much of his early work, as his advisors concede, has been making changes that France has dodged or delayed in previous decades.

The country's history has been marked by spasms of sudden change in the past, rather than gradual adjustment. As Paul Ricœur, Macron's philosophical mentor, once said: 'The French Revolution only happened because France hadn't been able to reform in time.' The country is now on the cusp of an important period of modernisation brought about through intelligent policy-making. Macron's rhetoric of a 'revolution' or a 'transformation' is typically overblown.

But voters and observers are right to have high expectations. There is an undeniable sense of movement and activity that optimists see as revitalising a long-lost sense of national pride. As ever with Macron, luck and good timing have played a part in reinforcing this more positive image of France: the opening of the glittering new Louvre museum in Abu Dhabi in November gave him a chance to stress the influence of French soft power overseas, while the country won the right to host the 2023 rugby World Cup and the 2024 Olympics in late 2017, the fruit of years of intensive lobbying. 'French people are starting to love France again,' said Perrineau, the political science professor from Sciences Po, in December.

But results domestically will depend on implementation. 'It's a bit early to be giving the Nobel Prize for reforms,' quipped Henri Poupart-Lafarge, the head of the French industrial giant Alstom, in January.

The next phase of Macronism will see changes made to the unemployment benefits system that will force claimants into jobs or training, while opening up the safety net to the self-employed who were previously unable to fall back on generous jobseeker' allowances if their businesses failed.

Another fundamental building block will be an effective and properly-funded adult training programme that can be used to re-skill workers who lose their jobs due to downsizing by companies or job cuts forced by technological change. A total of €15 billion has been earmarked for this idea – the one that was met with such scepticism by the late-career assembly line workers whom Macron encountered in Amiens at the Whirlpool factory in the final weeks of his election campaign. To work successfully it requires a complete revamp of existing training schemes and the re-skilling of the civil servants involved in guiding and assisting jobseekers.

Conversations with Macron's closest aides reveal an almost obsessive focus on speed, as they seek to implement the main contours of the programme within 18–24 months. 'Our only concern is to do everything quickly because we know that it takes time to produce results and we want results as quickly as possible, even if that means it's more difficult to explain our actions as much as we'd like. That's the price of doing what we want to do,' Macron's advisor Emelien explained.

Alexis Kohler implies that there is an awareness that the window of opportunity for Macron – with his political opponents floored, the unions confused, and the parliamentary party still ultra-loyal – might slam shut. 'At some point, you can keep refining [a reform] and it's all well and good to aim for perfection, but if you arrive too late, then it's not worth anything,' he said.

The Élysée staff has been reorganised to make it more nimble and reactive by removing upper levels of management, Kohler added. 'Generally speaking, the state suffers from having too much senior management, rather like big companies,' he explained. The result is a highly centralised structure with Kohler, Emelien and Macron at its apex.

An overhaul of the *baccalaureate*, the main high school exam introduced under Napoleon, and controversial changes to introduce selective entrance criteria for public universities are intended to better prepare young people for the jobs of tomorrow, and reverse France's slide down the international education rankings. Under the current system, France's mainstream public universities – i.e. not the highly selective elite institutions attended by Macron – are obliged to offer spaces for all applicants. Anyone who has passed the *baccalaureate* can apply for any course they like, regardless of their ability, and tuition fees are low. Unsurprisingly, drop-out rates are more than 50 per cent for first-year students.

Further down the line, an overhaul of the French pensions system threatens to spark a major confrontation with the public sector trade unions, whose members stand to see their retirement rights diluted. Macron's idea is to harmonise pension rights across different sectors of the economy in a bid to create a level playing field. Under the current system, France has 37 different special pension regimes for workers in various sectors of the economy, meaning that rights vary between, say, an electrician at state energy giant EDF, a train driver for the SNCF, or a dancer at the Paris Opera, all of whom have individual privileges. In the future, in theory, everyone across the public and private sector will have the same rights. It will create winners and noisy, angry losers, such as civil servants or train drivers. 'During the campaign, at best people might have heard about the idea of the reform, but no one understood the consequences,' said Gilles Finchelstein from the Jean-Jaurès Foundation.

In other areas, Macron's progress has been less impressive. Despite his stated intention to balance the books by the end of his term, the 2018 budget forecast little reduction in France's chronic overspending, though higher-than-expected economic growth should help reduce the imbalance in the medium-term. The budget deficit was forecast by the European Commission to be 2.9 per cent in 2018 in its first assessment, just under the EU limit of 3.0 per cent. Debt is at 96.9 per cent of GDP, far above the limit of 60 per cent.

Having pledged to reduce the public sector headcount by 120,000 over his term, the government announced cuts of just 1,600 for its first full year in office. But it has signalled it intends to take on a reform of the French civil service, one of the biggest taboos in French politics. Ideas include heresies such as introducing more merit-based pay, performance evaluations for staff and appraisals by the public of the services they use. On top of these ideas – which will be fiercely resisted – the government is proposing voluntary redundancies and the greater use of private contractors for some services.

Showing a remarkable appetite for conflict, Macron also tackled reform of the state SNCF railways, whose high-speed TGV trains are the envy of the world but whose annual losses and debt of more than €50 billion are an ever-growing burden. Its highly unionised workforce will not submit without a fight.

Is it possible for Macron to push through so many changes in so many areas without facing the wrath of protesters and major falls in his approval rating? Certainly not. His popularity will remain volatile, reflecting his lack of a clear and stable political base, but also the nature of his grumpy and impatient electorate. He won the first fight in his battle with 'the street' in September and October 2017, but other confrontations loom in 2018 and beyond. 'He knows very well that he won't always be popular. His only obsession is results,' his friend and advisor Grangeon said.

He is right to go fast at the start of his term, but he also risks provoking several different groups of people simultaneously. By kicking over so many bee nests, he runs the risks of being swarmed by his opponents – students, civil servants, teachers, train drivers, Mélenchon's supporters – who could coalesce into a large, united force. Kohler acknowledged the possibility, but said: 'The biggest risk for France would be to do nothing.'.

Macron has also slapped down autonomy-seeking nationalists on the Mediterranean island of Corsica, cancelled a planned airport in western France against the wishes of local lawmakers, and antagonised motorists by lowering the speed limit on medium-sized roads. No reasonable critic could accuse him of lacking political courage. 'We're taking on all of the difficult subjects,' said Emelien.

Although he was perceived as a centrist at the time of the election, voters watching the flurry of announcements perceived him as moving to the right while in power, according to a survey by Ifop[1] – not surprising, given that the initial focus of his agenda was on traditionally right-wing issues of tax cuts, public sector efficiency measures, and law and order. Some advisors and members of the parliamentary majority have urged him to put forward more of a social agenda, which Pierre Person, the campaign aide and MP, believes will come later in the term.

Macron paid little specific attention to the subject of the still-toxic French suburbs and the scourges of high crime, unemployment, Islamism and drugs which blight the lives of the majority of law-abiding citizens who live there. The suburbs remain a tinderbox of seething resentment that led to mass riots in 2005 and near-rebellion again during the election campaign. 'He has a philosophical approach which seeks to create examples of people who succeed and move on,' his friend and advisor Philippe Grangeon explained in an interview. 'And if the economy is doing better, then they [people in the suburbs] should be the first to feel the effects.' The problem is that the modern technology-led economy that Macron foresees will create few of the unskilled blue-collar jobs on which working-class areas have historically depended.

In his first year in power, Macron spent more time defending the right of the rich to be respected and admired than he did discussing ways to improve the plight of the poor or the marginalised. 'In order for our society to do better, we need people who succeed,' he told TF1.[2] 'We shouldn't be jealous of them, we should say "it's fantastic".' Using a rock climbing metaphor, he added: 'If we start by throwing stones at the person at the head of the rope, then it's the whole team which falls.'

To meet the coming challenges, Macron's Republic on the Move (LREM) party and his government will be crucial in making the case for change, but both remain works-in-progress. At the grassroots level, the formidable election-winning political movement he built, which went from nothing to 250,000 members in twelve months, is at a virtual standstill. Many local committees, once populated with enthusiastic door-knockers, have emptied. 'It's a ghost party,' one senior campaigner said in November 2017.

Béatrice Faillès, an LREM organiser in Paris who stood for parliament, said that some left-leaning party activists had taken a backseat, either concerned about Macron's initial overwhelming focus on the economy or waiting for a stronger social agenda to emerge. 'Only time will tell, but the singularity, the balance, represented by LREM, must be defended at all costs because it provides the only way for France and for Europe to avoid populism,' she said.

Other complaints target the new appointees running the party, who in Faillès' view are 'not totally representative socially' of the movement as a whole, lacking working-class figures, as well as small business owners and artisans who were once the backbone of the organisation at the local level. The party's new leader, smooth-talking MP and minister Christophe Castaner, was elected unopposed on the president's instructions after a vote open only to national party bigwigs in November 2017. Participatory democracy it was not.

As well as juggling his multiple jobs, the biggest challenge for Castaner will be in keeping grassroots members engaged amid a pervasive sense that the organisation has morphed from what felt like a fresh and exciting citizen's movement into a top-down party which risks being tainted by the compromises and back-room dealing with allies that are part of politics. Faillès believes that feedback from local committees needs to be taken into account much more by the leadership, 'otherwise the *Marcheurs* will feel less and less involved as members, and only as voters.'

Elections for the Senate in September were an early disappointment for the party, while two calamitous byelection results in February 2018 – both won by the right-wing Republicans – were an early warning sign. Elections for the European parliament in 2019 and mid-term municipal polls slated for 2020 will be a crucial test of Macron's popularity. His dreams of a second mandate will depend on the ability of La Republique En Marche! to structure itself nationally. The fractured and demoralised opposition will not remain becalmed indefinitely. The last two French presidents served only one term.

Pierre Person, the MP, as well as other senior party figures, want to turn LREM into a hybrid of both a political party and a service provider, which would, for example, offer training opportunities to members, or organise community events. 'It's easy to imagine that in theory, the implementation is more difficult,' he admits. One disgruntled party member dismissed the idea of members becoming community organisers offering computer training to the elderly, jewellery-making sessions, or recycling seminars. 'We didn't join a political party to become scouts,' he said.

Emelien, the main behind-the-scenes architect of En Marche along with Julien Denormandie, believes LREM will be ready to compete in the elections come 2019 and 2020. 'It's a laboratory for what a political movement should be in the 21st century. We're trying lots of different things ... There are thousands of citizen's projects underway and it's taking off,' he insisted.

In the government, after a nervy early start, Édouard Philippe has settled into his role as prime minister and has become an effective foil to the president. But he was said in November to rate only five (out of 22) of his cabinet colleagues highly, reflecting the shortcomings of what was a callow team. Macron appointed specialists, not politicians, in many ministries, including health, education and justice. But while the ministers have credibility as reformers who know their sectors, they have struggled to make the case for the collective ambitions and vision of the president.

The last major and crucial focus of Macron's domestic agenda is the politically explosive topic of immigration, reliably among the top concerns identified by voters in elections across the Western world in recent years and a key driver of both the Brexit vote and Donald Trump's election. Inspired by his famous 'en même temps' (at the same time) catchphrase, Macron and the government have put forward a three-point immigration policy that he describes as mixing both 'humanity' and 'efficiency'. For refugees fleeing war or persecution, he has promised to speed up the processing of their demands and improve reception conditions and housing. For those migrants whose demands for asylum have been rejected, he has promised to be 'uncompromising'. And thirdly he has pledged to work on economic development and education in Africa along with the EU, while strengthening borders along the routes that migrants take to Europe.

He is right to conclude that voters cannot be expected to welcome (and pay for, in the short-term) genuine refugees if they have no faith that the asylum system correctly sifts out the people in need of help from those simply seeking a better life in France (however understandable their impulse might be). 'France cannot take in all of the world's misery,' he said, reprising a controversial soundbite from his old mentor Michel Rocard, the centre-left prime minister.

This hard line on economic migrants – an 'unprecedented harshness' according to an article in *Le Monde* from December 2017– will require unpleasant and unpalatable administrative and security work, including identity checks, detention centres and a major increase in deportations. The expulsion of a fifteen-year-old Kosovan schoolgirl called Leonarda in 2013 provides a cautionary tale. After being dragged off a school bus by border agents, the French-speaking student was expelled, sparking major protests from students, who blockaded schools, and accusations that the then-ruling Socialist Party risked 'losing its soul' in the words of parliamentary speaker Claude Bartolone. Many lawmakers within Macron's new parliamentary party feel the same, providing the first signs of an ideological split in LREM.

A total of 15,000 people were expelled from France in 2017, according to Ministry of the Interior data, but that figure will rise sharply under Macron's plans, particularly if a stronger economy makes France an ever-more attractive destination. 'Those who don't get asylum or are not granted a residence permit have no business staying here,' Emelien said in a sign of the uncompromising attitude in the Élysée. 'It's not a harsher policy, it's about execution, which is one of the characteristics of President Macron's style. One of our guiding principles is maintaining the credibility of our commitments.'

France received a record 100,000 asylum requests in 2017; Albanians formed the largest group of these asylum seekers that year, although most of them had no hope of being granted the right to stay.

Pisani-Ferry, a long-time ally since at least 2011 who played a leading role in En Marche, broke publicly with Macron on the issue of immigration in January, as did the head of the centre-left Terra Nova think-tank, Thierry Pech. They penned a highly critical column in *Le Monde* that stung Macron personally, according to aides. One friend of Macron's, again speaking on condition of anonymity, said he had stopped discussing immigration with the president because they had fallen out over the issue.

But the alternative to his plan is an immigration system that continues to be seen as ineffective, nourishing the dark forces of racism, intolerance and cynicism that has fuelled the far right in Europe and in France particularly. In typical fashion, Macron calls these forces the 'sad passions' – as described by the 17th century Dutch Enlightenment philosopher Spinoza. The inability of centre-left political parties across Europe to offer a coherent policy response on immigration explains in large part their dismal recent election results.

French public opinion was overwhelmingly behind Macron's stance, and it also took the sting out of the rhetoric of the far-right on the issue that has fuelled their rise more than any other over the last 40 years. But there were two major problems: firstly, the government will face the same difficulties as its predecessors – the countries of origin, whether they be in Africa or South Asia, have little interest or incentive to take back their citizens. 'We're going to put maximum pressure on them. There's no messing about,' one advisor in the Élysée said (although many previous governments have tried and failed).

Secondly, France has no control over the external border of the European Union, in Italy or Greece for example. Once inside Europe's passport-free area, new arrivals can travel over national borders easily, despite recent efforts to beef up security. Macron is pushing for a collective European solution of increased joint border controls and a refugee-sharing system between members. The bloc's response, years after the crisis burst into the open in 2015, has so far been woeful.

Europe advisor Beaune says 'the most effective' action has been efforts to close down people-smuggling routes through Africa which led to a dramatic fall in new arrivals at the end of 2017 and early 2018. This has seen the EU apply political pressure, coupled with increased funding and aid, for border controls in impoverished nations with poor human rights records, such as Niger or Chad. It has also led to persistent rumours and accusations from some rights groups that the EU is working with warlords in lawless Libya, the main departure point for the EU, to prevent dangerously overloaded boats, packed with migrants, making the short crossing from the north African shore to southern Italy.

Barring an unexpected crisis, Macron's French agenda should overall be helped by the powerful pick-up in economic growth underway globally, which will give him the leeway to introduce his economic reforms and improve the public finances at the same time. Breaking France out of its cycle of low growth and rising debt would be a huge achievement in itself.

The unemployment rate dropped sharply in his first year, falling to its lowest level since 2009 in the final quarter of the year, to 8.9 per cent. It was the biggest drop over a single quarter in more than two decades.[3] It must come down further if Macron is to demonstrate that the medicine of increased flexibility in the labour market and measures to encourage entrepreneurship is working. 'If at the end of 2018, the illness is still there, it'll be extremely serious,' said Macron's friend and advisor Grangeon in an interview at his home. 'Economic growth isn't enough. The growth needs to produce jobs.'

The 2017 French election was notable for the fact that a major political party picked a candidate, the Socialist Benoît Hamon, who proposed measures for a 'post-work' society in which robots and computers would increasingly take the place of humans, particularly in the services sector. The pace of job-killing technological change is an unknown variable in the years ahead. But having stood as the 'candidate for work', Macron must now produce it.

And if not? 'The conclusion that I have reached is that the National Front will be a formidable force in five years' time, having done their introspection, if we have not governed well,' he said in May 2017, during an interview. A failed Macron presidency would raise the very real spectre of a far-right or far-left candidate winning power. The country only narrowly escaped a choice between Le Pen or Mélenchon in the second round of the 2017 election.

A failed mandate would be felt most acutely by the professional and middle classes who mobilised so strongly to bring Macron to power in the first place: people like 57-year-old Laurence David-Moalic, the civil servant who headed En Marche in Macron's hometown of Amiens. 'I can't imagine this man lying to us,' she said. But if he did? 'We'd be like spurned lovers. We'd smash everything up. We've put a lot of faith in him,' she explained.

In Europe, he has raised the stakes to a similar level. While Macron sees the National Front winning in 2022 as the potential cost of his failure in France, he also sees the immediate fate of the EU as lying in his hands. 'I have no other choice but to make Europe work,' he told *Paris Match* in May 2017. 'The failure of Europe will be mine. It's the responsibility I took during the election.'

His strategy is to lead an avant-garde group of countries, the members of the nineteen-member eurozone, into a much deeper and closer structure that will harmonise economic, defence and migration policies to a far greater extent. This new multi-speed Europe will run into resistance from other countries who are left on the sidelines – notably the nationalist members Hungary and Poland who Macron has regularly criticised since taking power. It is also a different vision to the one held by the European Commission President Jean-Claude Juncker, who has called for all EU members to advance at the same speed. The avant-garde of the avant-garde will be France and Germany, and unless a common roadmap can be hammered out first by the core partners at the heart of the European Union then little will be achieved.

Macron has been helped by recent developments in the EU's immediate neighbourhood and beyond. The bloc had been thought by some to be heading towards disintegration after the

Brexit vote, but the confusion in Britain and the complexity of negotiating its divorce have served as an argument in favour of the project. European solidarity has been boosted further by Trump's aggressive nationalism, while the assertiveness of authoritarian Russia and Turkey on the EU's eastern and southern borders have given the club a long-absent sense of cohesion and purpose.

But Euro-scepticism remains a virulent force, and it is easy to forget, as Macron positions France at the vanguard of European federalists, that the first round of the presidential election saw around half of French voters opt for candidates bent on ripping up much of the post-war project. Italy's election in March also saw roughly the same proportion of people vote for Euro-sceptic parties. 'It is a warning that our societies are split, it's almost 50–50: between those people who suffered from the economic crisis and who don't have confidence in the European project, or reject it completely, and who are also opposed to trade or immigration – and the rest,' said his Europe advisor Clément Beaune. 'It validates and underlines the need for the "protective Europe" agenda that we've put forward.'

Macron has placed great emphasis on the symbols and shared history of Europe in his bid to foster a much stronger sense of shared identity, which is essential for developing his policy ideas that depend on solidarity: such as northern European taxpayers coughing up more money for weaker southern European nations. The EU has seeped into the identities of many citizens across the continent, but it remains diffuse and peripheral compared to the more visceral pull of nationalism. A series of public consultations to discuss the role of the EU in every country, bar Britain and Hungary, are set to take place in 2018, again at Macron's instigation.

With the new German government in Berlin, rapid progress is possible in areas such as harmonising corporate tax rates, setting up a new European fund to finance cutting-edge technologies, and further joint European defence cooperation. Fully harmonising regulation for the banking sector across the eurozone, long-stalled due to resistance from Germany and other northern European nations, is now within reach and should result in common deposit insurance for savers across the area. There is also broad agreement on increasing the powers and lending capacity of the bailout fund known as the European Stability Mechanism, which will become a lender-of-last-resort for member states in financial crisis, replacing the need for the IMF in Europe.

These advances will depend on Germany (and German voters) accepting greater liabilities in the event of future crises. Many in Merkel's party and the country at large still have bitter memories of the repeated multi-billion-euro bailouts needed by Greece, and want better budget management and healthier banking practices in southern Europe first.

The new Macron-backed budget is an even more difficult proposition because it involves giving, not lending, more money to weaker states. Part of the budget would be for funding infrastructure upgrades on a permanent basis in weaker members (so-called 'investment funds'), while a second function would be to provide emergency budget financing ('stabilisation funds') in the event of a major economic crisis. Macron's call for an annual budget worth 2 per cent of GDP looks highly unrealistic. Beaune says anything below 1 per cent would be pointless. 'What is the most attainable in a short space of time is the investment fund. There's an awareness in Germany and Europe that we need more investment in the eurozone,' he said.

Negotiating in Europe is a slow and difficult process, involving endless compromises, coalition building and last-minute fudges – the opposite of how Macron operates in France.

It also remains unclear how the coming wave of changes in the EU will be handled at the legal level. Most of it can be done through simple treaties signed by each of the governments, but there may be pressure, or a legal necessity at some point, to change the EU's founding treaties. This would trigger a series of highly risky referenda and parliamentary votes around the bloc. Macron, the ever-confident gambler, has openly welcomed this, while Merkel has agreed in principle. The risk with every attempt to deepen the EU's federal structure, via steps that create new inter-dependencies, is that voters have a tendency to shoot down the grand plans of their leaders when given the opportunity, as referenda in France, the Netherlands, Britain, Denmark and Ireland have shown over the last three decades.

Internationally, Macron's diplomacy has been stylish. When he repeats his mantra that 'France is back', foreign listeners take him seriously. He took centre stage in resolving a potentially destabilising crisis in Lebanon in November when the Lebanese Prime Minister Saad Hariri was held by Saudi authorities under duress during a visit to Riyadh. And he has led efforts, with mixed results, to expand a counter-terror force in West Africa known as the G5 Sahel. Both territories are traditional areas of French influence. Macron has made repeated trips to West Africa, attempting to use his age (as the first French president born after the end of French colonial rule on the continent) as a means to reset ties. Various foreign policy priorities intersect in the area: limiting migration to Europe, preventing the spread of Islamist groups across the region and promoting French business interests.

But the biggest question for Macron's diplomatic efforts outside Europe is: how will he leverage the relationships he has been nurturing with leaders around the world and leave a foreign policy legacy? As his advisors stress, the aim in the first phase of his presidency was establishing himself as a leader, and opening up dialogue with as many partners as possible – which, on both counts, he has succeeded with. 'The question is whether this approach will lead to results,' said Lechevallier. 'The problem we have is in transforming these good relationships into something substantial,' admitted another senior French diplomat. At some point, his eagerness to keep talking to everyone risks being interpreted as weakness.

The cynical view is that France remains a medium-sized power, good at organising international conferences and keen to show leadership under Macron, but still lacking the economic and military clout to really influence world events. He is only a bit-part player in the talks over the future of post-war Syria, and his early efforts to find a solution in war-wracked Libya have made little impact. He is courting both Israeli and Palestinian leaders, but past French peace efforts have come to nought. Trump, though outwardly friendly, shows little sign that he listens to the advice of his plucky Gallic friend. Macron continues to lobby him intensively to reverse his decision to withdraw from the Paris climate change accord. Trump hinted he might change course while in Paris in July. 'But then he goes back to Washington and nothing, I mean *nothing*, happens,' a French official said on condition of anonymity.

But whatever the limits of French power, Macron was the only Western leader in 2018 able to persuasively articulate the case for multilateralism and global institutions, openness, the fight against climate change, trade and cooperation. In a world of advancing authoritarianism and illiberal democracies, such a voice is essential. Trump has committed to 'America-first' isolationism; Britain will remain suffocated by Brexit for years; while Merkel has neither the temperament, nor the ability, due to Germany's history, to step into the role of leader of the free world. As he has shown throughout his life, Macron is an insatiable climber, always eyeing the next platform, the next rung on the ladder, and leader of the free world is a title he will happily accept. 'He's completely at ease with that idea,' one advisor said.

Macron's international efforts might end up being measured by the bad things that he helps prevent through his mediation and argumentation. When asked if the French president should be seen as a sort of international fireman, Lechevallier acknowledged and expanded the metaphor: 'There are indeed comments and decisions taken by the major international powers today that have the capacity to start fires. We need to be able to soothe those tensions,' he said from his office.

The dangerous and unstable wider world is capable of springing a major crisis that could sap Macron's energies and divert his attention from the core French and European agenda. There are plenty of potential threats to choose from: America's stand-off with North Korea; a major new conflict in the Middle East between Saudi Arabia and Iran; dangerous new tensions between the Trump administration and China; a military escalation in Syria. Already, Macron's international responsibilities are time-consuming. 'He is personally involved; he's constantly calling people,' Lechevallier added. 'You need to go beyond the image of the simple fireman because he's also reactive, he's proposing things.'

Trans-Atlantic tensions over trade sparked by US protection-ism remain a major concern. Trump remains implacably opposed to the European Union, which he sees as restricting US companies and challenging US hegemony, and he is determined to tackle the German trade surplus with America. 'He's said to Macron sev-eral times: "I want tariffs", this exact phrase,' an alarmed French diplomat said in February. 'There's a risk that sooner or later it'll happen.' In March, Trump threatened duties of 25 per cent on imported steel and 10 per cent on aluminium, which EU export-ers only narrowly avoided. He also raised the spectre of levies on European car imports in a move that would affect German manufacturers such as Mercedes, BMW and Volkswagen hardest.

Macron has also taken a leading role in tackling the exis-tential environmental threat to the world, organising the One Planet Summit in Paris in December 2017, where he warned 'we are losing the battle.' But for his intentions to be credible, France will need to up its game. The world needs good examples, not more speeches and conferences. The country missed its own carbon emissions target in 2016, the year after the Paris climate change accord had been toasted with champagne. Macron and his celebrity Environment Minister Nicolas Hulot pushed through a law banning new fossil fuel extraction projects. But France has little domestic oil and gas production anyway. Bolder leadership is needed at home.

Surveying the dangers in France, Europe and the world, Macron was not exaggerating when he repeated the words 'our task is immense' on five occasions as he spoke at the Louvre before thousands of supporters at his victory party on the night of his election. How will he personally cope with the pressure?

Aides and friends say the risk of failure is ever-present in his mind, yet he continues to crack jokes and lighten the atmosphere when out of sight of the media. An exchange with his bodyguards, caught by cameras in January, saw him tease them for not knowing how to write. One of them jokingly called him an 'asshole' in return. But he drives his presidential team and government colleagues hard, explaining that the long hours and short deadlines are what is demanded by the electorate.

His habit of making condescending and counter-productive remarks continues, reinforcing perceptions of him as insensitive, aloof or arrogant. He courted problems in Burkino Faso during a trip in November with a risqué joke in front of hundreds of students that his host, President Roch Marc Christian Kaboré, had gone to fix the air-conditioning when he left the stiflingly hot room to relieve himself in the toilet. His characterisation of his opponents as 'slackers', or his decision to celebrate his 40th birthday in December 2017 in grand style at a château, were further own goals.

On a personal level, keeping his ego in check will remain a challenge, the more so since he has already cut his ties with some of the people who accompanied him on his rise through the civil service, presidential staff and economy ministry. Many past leaders have found the Élysée Palace, with its hundreds of high-ceiled rooms and manicured gardens, to be a gilded cage. 'We feel cut off at our level,' one staffer admitted. 'So at his, it's a thousand times worse.' A political advisor who has known him for ten years commented that 'the risk is that he thinks he's still connected, although he isn't.'

Aides insist that he receives hundreds of text messages and emails each day which he reads when he can. And he makes regular two-day trips to all corners of provincial France where time is always scheduled for him to meet, greet and chat with the general public. 'He loves convincing people. He needs to meet people who don't agree with him,' Emelien said.

Finchelstein, the head of the Jean-Jaurès Foundation who once had regular dinners with him, says 'one of the questions is whether he can keep channels open to the outside, including to people who can tell him unpleasant things. His wife can, which is good, but it's not enough.'

Brigitte is a discreet but popular presence at her husband's side in public and remains a vital conduit for many people with messages to pass on behind the scenes. She is still the ultimate sounding board for his ideas and plans. Sometimes hidden behind sunglasses and a hat, she's known to leave the Élysée for intelligence-gathering missions on foot around Paris.

The couple have redecorated to make the palace more modern, buying contemporary artworks and sculptures and moving out old furniture. His office features a large painting of French hero Marianne and the national motto '*liberté, égalité, fraternité*', painted by the American artist Shepard Fairey who created the emblematic 'Hope' poster of Barack Obama in 2008. 'I don't think he loves living there, but he sees it as part of his responsibilities,' one aide said on condition of anonymity. The garden occasionally echoes with the sounds of their grandchildren playing, or the barks of their new pet, an ill-disciplined black Labrador–Griffon mix called Nemo.

The couple still take time out at their seaside retreat in Le Touquet, and they use the La Lanterne presidential holiday home outside Paris with its swimming pool and tennis court. One night each week is normally reserved just for them. Staff sometimes book seats at a cinema, theatre or concert hall for them and they slip in under the cover of darkness and leave without being noticed, an aide said. They also insist on being able to take regular walks together around Paris. It is in these rare moments that Macron disconnects from the job. 'I don't allow myself much time off,' he told reporters in February.

He will need all of his energy, skill, charisma and the Midas touch that was evident throughout his extraordinary rise as he bounds ahead into the future, brimming with ideas, shaking hands, winking and ever eager to seduce. The boy from Amiens who grew up reading the novels of Stendhal with his grandmother used to fantasise about romantic fictional heroes like Julien Sorel, whose lives led them 'into the unknown, into danger and big open spaces', he once said. He is now the lead character in his own uncertain adventure, with far-reaching consequences for France, Europe and the world.

Notes

Chapter 1

1. Confidence survey by CEVIPOF, Sciences Po, January 2017.
2. *Les Hommes Providentiels: Histoire d'une Fascination Française* by Jean Garrigues, published by Seuil, 2012.
3. *Un Personnage de roman* by Philippe Besson, page 79, published by Julliard, 2017.
4. Interview with *Le 1*, 8 July 2015.

Chapter 2

1. *Emmanuel Macron, un Jeune Homme si Parfait* by Anne Fulda, published by Plon, 2017.
2. *Révolution* by Emmanuel Macron, page 17, published by XO, 2016.
3. Interview with *Le 1*, 3 February 2017.
4. Interview with *Le 1*, February 2017.
5. Interview with *Le 1*, February 2017.
6. *Révolution*, page 17.
7. Interview with French author Emmanuel Carrère, *Guardian*, 20 October 2017.
8. 'Les secrets d'enfance d'Emmanuel Macron et Najat Valaud-Belkacem', *Vanity Fair*, February 2017.
9. *Emmanuel Macron, un jeune homme si parfait*, page 21.
10. *Les politiques aussi ont une mère* by Bernard Pascuito and Olivier Biscaye, published by Albin Michel, 2017.
11. Interview with *Journal du Dimanche*, 12 February 2017.

12. 'Brigitte, l'autre Macron', *L'Express*, 28 October 2015.

13. *Les Macron,* by Caroline Derrien and Candice Nedelec, published by Fayard, 2017.

14. Documentary: *Emmanuel Macron, la Stratégie du Météore*, France 3, 21 November 2016.

15. 'Les secrets d'enfance d'Emmanuel Macron et Najat Valaud-Belkacem'.

16. Documentary: *Emmanuel Macron, la Stratégie du Météore*.

17. Documentary: *Emmanuel Macron, la Stratégie du Météore*.

18. *Révolution*, page 18.

19. *Les Macron*, page 27.

20. Appearance on *Au tableau!*, C8 channel, March 2017.

21. Interview with *Paris Match*, 13 April 2016.

Chapter 3

1. *Révolution*, page 19.

2. *Le Parisien*, 23 January 2015.

3. 'Avec Macron, L'Elysée décroche le poupon', *Libération*, 17 September 2012.

4. Documentary: *Emmanuel Macron, la Stratégie du Météore*.

5. Documentary: *Ainsi soit Macron*, France 3, 8 May 2017.

6. *Paris Match*, 13 April 2016.

7. *Emmanuel Macron, un jeune homme si parfait*, page 62.

8. *Révolution*, page 19.

9. Interview with *L'Obs*, February 2016.

10. Interview published by the Sciences Po magazine *Rue Saint-Guillaume*, April 2010.

11. Sciences Po website, May 2017.

12. Paul Ricœur archives.

13. *Le Monde*, 1 September 2016.

14. Interview with France Culture radio, 9 March 2017.

Chapter 4

1. Interview published by the Sciences Po magazine *Rue Saint-Guillaume*, April 2010.

2. Interview with *Agence France-Presse*, 7 October 2015.

3. Interview broadcast on Radio France Bleu, 26 February 2016.

4. Interview broadcast on Radio France Bleu, 26 February 2016.

5. *Le Figaro*, 18 September 2016.

6. *Emmanuel Macron, un jeune homme si parfait*, page 125.

7. Declaration to the HATVP public watchdog when Macron was named economy minister in 2014.

8. Interview with *Paris Match*, 12 May 2017.

9. Comments made by Macron in Clermont-Ferrand.

10. Interview published by the Sciences Po magazine *Rue Saint-Guillaume*, April 2010.

Chapter 5

1. *Emmanuel Macron, un jeune homme si parfait*, page 46.

2. *Emmanuel Macron, un jeune homme si parfait*, page 46.

3. *Révolution*, page 31.

4. *Paris Match*, 13 April 2016.

5. *Emmanuel Macron, un jeune homme si parfait*, page 63.

6. Interview with *BFM TV*, April 2016.

7. Documentary: *Emmanuel Macron, la Stratégie du Météore*.

8. *Révolution*, page 31.

9. *L'ambigu Monsieur Macron* by Marc Endeweld, page 98, published by Flammarion, 2015.

10. *L'ambigu Monsieur Macron*, page 103.

Chapter 6

1. Interview with the Sciences Po magazine *Rue Saint-Guillaume*, April 2010.

2. Interview with *Society*, April 2016.

3. Documentary: *Rothschild, le pouvoir d'un nom*, France 2, 2 December 2016.

4. Documentary: *Emmanuel Macron, la Stratégie du Météore*.

5. Interview with the *Financial Times*, 27 March 2017.

6. Interview with *Le Point*, 29 September 2017.

7. Interview with the *Wall Street Journal*, 9 March 2015.
8. *Wall Street Journal*, 28 April 2017.
9. Data from Reuters, *Fusions & Acquisitions* magazine, 17 March 2010.
10. *L'ambigu Monsieur Macron*, page 123.
11. Interview with *Le Figaro*, 8 September 2011.
12. *L'ambigu Monsieur Macron*, page 141.

Chapter 7

1. Pre-tax income declared to the Haute Autorité pour la Transparence de la Vie Publique, August 2014.
2. Documentary: *Danse avec le FN*, Canal+, 20 April 2015.
3. Interview, *Les Echos*, 28 August 2013.
4. *Hollande mise sur 'la persévérance' pour surmonter 'une crise exceptionnelle'*, AFP, 22 April 2013.
5. *Emmanuel Macron, un jeune homme si parfait*, page 187.
6. Interview with *Libération*, 26 August 2014.
7. Poll by CSA-Les Echos-Radio Classique, published 5 June 2014.

Chapter 8

1. *Emmanuel Macron: Les coulisses d'une victoire* by François-Xavier Bourmaud, page 29, published by Éditions l'Archipel, 2017.
2. Documentary: *À l'Élysée, un temps de président*, France 3, 28 September 2015.
3. Interview with *Libération*, 6 June 2016.
4. Interview with *Mediapart*, 2 November 2016.
5. 'L'épisode du «49.3» fragilise le réformisme de Valls et électrise le groupe PS', Agence France-Presse, 20 February 2015.
6. *Emmanuel Macron, un jeune homme si parfait*, page 27.

Chapter 9

1. Poll by Ifop for *Paris Match*, 24 February 2015.
2. Figures published in *Le Figaro*, 6 October 2016.
3. Interview with *Mediapart*, 2 November 2016.
4. Rich list compiled by *Challenges* magazine, 2017.

5. 'Elysée: pot de départ en grande pompe pour Emmanuel Macron', *L'Express*, 27 July 2014.

6. Interview at the Crif lobby group, 22 March 2017.

7. Interview with *Il Sole 24*, 5 September 2015.

8. ONS Population by Country of Birth and Nationality, 2015.

Chapter 10

1. *Un Président ne devrait pas dire ça…* by Gérard Davet et Fabrice Lhomme, page 458, published by Stock, 2016.

2. Interview with *Mediapart*, 2 November 2016.

3. Address to the nation, 1 December 2016.

4. *Un Président ne devrait pas dire ça…*, page 462.

Chapter 11

1. *Un Président ne devrait pas dire ça…*, page 456.

2. 'Bérézina politique pour le président français, qui y croit toujours', Agence France-Presse, 13 May 2016.

3. Interview with *Mediapart*, November 2016.

4. Interview with *Mediapart*, November 2016.

5. Interview with *Le 1*, September 2016.

6. *Un Président ne devrait pas dire ça…*, page 465.

Chapter 12

1. Internal accounting document, *Mediapart*.

2. Poll by the Elabe group, AFP, 22 September 2016.

3. Interview in 1998 with the Canal Plus journalist Karl Zéro.

4. Documentary: *Emmanuel Macron: Les coulisses d'une victoire*, TF1, 8 May 2017.

5. Documentary: *En Marche vers L'Elysée*, France 2, 11 May 2017.

6. Interview, *Le Parisien*, 24 October 2017.

Chapter 13

1. Documentary: *En Marche vers l'Elysée*.

2. Rosie Pinhas-Delpuech writing in *Libération*, 9 February 2017.

3. Interview with *Ambition Intime*, M6 channel, 6 November 2016.

4. Kantar Sofres, published 29 January 2017.

5. Quoted by Agence France-Presse, 9 February 2017.

Chapter 14

1. *Un Personnage de roman*, page 122.

2. Interview with *Le Parisien*, 12 April 2017.

3. OpinionWay, Elabe survey for Les Echos-Radio Classique, 21 February 2017.

4. Documentary: *En Marche vers l'Elysée*.

5. Documentary: *Emmanuel Macron: Les coulisses d'une victoire*.

Chapter 15

1. Speech at Humboldt University, 10 January 2017.

2. Quoted by the *New Statesman*, 23 February 2017.

3. Interview with *Monocle*, March 2017.

4. Research by the EY accountancy group analysing public statements by 222 financial firms, July 2017.

5. Poll by Harris Interactive, *Le Figaro*, 14 April 2017.

Chapter 16

1. Email sent 21 March and found in archive released by Wikileaks, 2017.

2. Interview with *Le Monde*, 4 April 2017.

3. Documentary: *Emmanuel Macron: Les coulisses d'une victoire*.

Chapter 17

1. *Un personnage de roman*, pages 143–4.

2. Interview on France 2, 23 April 2017.

3. Documentary: *Emmanuel Macron: Les coulisses d'une victoire*.

4. Documentary: *En Marche vers l'Elysée*.

5. Interview on TF1, 19 May 2017.

6. 'Retour sur les coulisses du naufrage de Marine Le Pen', *Le Monde*, 14 July 2017.

7. Interview with *Les Echos*, 5 May 2017.

Chapter 18

1. Interview with *Le Monde*, 4 August 2017.
2. Interview with *Live* Magazine, 27 November 2017.
3. Interview with *Vanity Fair*, May 2017.

Chapter 19

1. Interview with *Paris Match*, 5 May 2017.
2. Interview, *Franceinfo* radio, 29 October 2017.
3. Interview with *Libération*, 3 October 2017.
4. Interview, *France 2*, 17 December 2017.
5. Interview with *Der Spiegel*, 13 November 2017.

Chapter 20

1. Survey published 28 November, 2017.
2. Interview with *TF1*, 15 October 2017.
3. Figures from Bloomberg financial news agency, 15 February 2018.

Acknowledgements

My first thanks go to the people who agreed to speak to me to make this book possible, including the scores of ordinary French voters who stopped to chat during my travels around the country for the election campaign. Dozens of friends, former colleagues and advisors of Emmanuel Macron, as well as politicians both friendly and critical, also placed their trust in me by agreeing to meet or talk on the phone. I am grateful to all of them.

The reporting, research and writing has been an all-consuming task. My partner Natacha has lived through every moment of frustration and elation and has been a constant source of encouragement. My children Arlette and Marlow have been patient while I spent weeks away from them and evenings in front of my computer. My parents Ali and Derek as well as my sisters Claire and Abi have willed me on throughout.

Jitendra Joshi, Michael Thurston, Mary Gilliver, Will Thomas and Marc Burleigh kindly lent me their homes at various times where I found the quiet needed to write, while my friend Helen Conford played a vital role in helping guide me through the publishing world. My assistant Valerie Dekimpe deserves a special mention for the hours she spent diligently working on interviews. During my day job, AFP colleagues Guy Jackson and Richard Carter went out of their way to assist me, while Frederic Dumoulin generously opened up his contacts book. Alan Brooke, a professional coach who I consulted during the writing process, helped me immensely.

Thank you to my agent Susanna Lea who placed her faith in me and took on a book with a very uncertain future when we first discussed it. And last but by no means least, thank you to my superb editor Tom Webber at Icon Books whose sharp mind and exacting standards improved my manuscript at every step.

Index

ABOUT THE AUTHOR

Adam Plowright is a British journalist and writer. Over his fifteen-year career, he's reported from London, Brussels, Paris and New Delhi and has travelled widely on assignment in Europe and Asia. He has lived on-and-off in Paris since 2002 and currently works there as a correspondent for *Agence France-Presse*.